POLITICS AND HUMAN RIGHTS

Edited by David Beetham

BLACKWELL
Publishers

ISBN 0 631 19666 8

First published 1995

Blackwell Publishers
108 Cowley Road, Oxford, OX4 IJF, U.K.

and

238 Main Street,
Cambridge, MA 02142, USA.

British Library Cataloguing in Publication Data
Applied for

Library of Congress Cataloguing in Publication Data
Applied for

Printed and bound in Great Britain by
Athenaeum Press Ltd, Gateshead, Tyne & Wear.

This book is printed on acid-free paper

CONTENTS

Introduction: Human Rights in the Study of Politics

David Beetham

The idea of human rights, together with the institutions and practices that give it expression, constitute one of the pervasive features of our political world. Yet the subject is one that has to date occupied only a marginal position within the discipline of political science.[1] Although a few scholars have devoted their research to it, and although the conceptual analysis of 'rights' has been an important theme within political theory, the study of *human* rights can hardly be said to belong to the mainstream of the discipline. Symptomatic of this marginal position is the paucity of politics courses devoted to it, whether in whole or in part. An international survey of human rights courses undertaken in 1989 underlined the very limited contribution of political scientists to the subject.[2] And an analysis made in 1991 of the place of human rights within US textbooks on international relations concluded that, despite the increasing impact of human rights considerations on foreign policy, most American political scientists 'do not think human rights is an important part of international relations'.[3]

The reasons for this marginal position are not hard to find. Most obvious is a persistent scepticism about the status of human rights within all the main branches of the discipline: political theory, comparative politics and international relations alike. Where political theorists remain uncomfortable with the philosophical presuppositions of human rights, and students of comparative politics may question the appropriateness of Western derived rights-concepts and standards to societies with different political traditions and levels of economic development, the study of international relations emphasizes the practical limitation of any human rights project in a world in which national and ethnic loyalties remain pervasive, and individual states still control the means of effective law enforcement.

Of these different sources of scepticism about human rights, that of political theory has the longest history, dating from a variety of critical responses to the declaration of the rights of man in the French revolution. Conservatives from Burke onwards have argued that meaningful rights can only be protected in the context of the distinctive national traditions and legal orders within which they

---

[1] I use the term 'science' here in the widest sense.

[2] K. Pritchard, 'Political science and the teaching of human rights', *Human Rights Quarterly*, 11 (1989), 459–75.

[3] D. P. Forsythe, *The Internationalization of Human Rights* (Lexington MA, Lexington Books, 1991), p. 174.

have evolved, and from which they derive their appropriateness.[4] Utilitarians from Bentham onwards have insisted that only positive legal rights can count as 'rights', and that these derive their justification from the principle of utility, not from some vague and illusory rights of man.[5] Feminists from Wollstone-craft onwards have denounced the exclusion of women from the rights of *man*, either because they have not been considered fully 'human', or, more recently, because the distinctive ways in which womens' rights are violated by men have not been included in a male-determined, state-oriented definition of human rights.[6] Marxists for their part have insisted that the egotism of rights-claims belongs to a lower, bourgeois stage of historical evolution, which awaits to be transcended by the social cooperation and rounded development of human capacities made possible in a communist society.[7] Added to all these different historical strands of scepticism is a pervasive temper of contemporary political philosophy, which rejects any 'foundationalism' – the attempt to ground rights in a universal human nature or human rationality – and insists on the context-dependency of our most fundamental conceptions. From this perspective it is the negotiation of difference, not the assertion of similarity, that becomes the most pressing political imperative.[8]

Such a conclusion can be reinforced from the practice of comparative political analysis, or at least that tendency which sees the purpose of comparison, not so much to discover uniformities or general laws, or to chart a single development path that all countries are fated to follow, albeit at differing paces and from different starting points; but rather the better to identify the distinctiveness or singularity of national and regional political traditions. From this standpoint the supposedly 'universal' human rights can be seen to bear all the hallmarks of their local, Western origin: the elevation of individual freedom above the collective good; of rights above duties; of self-interest above social responsibility; of civil and political liberties above economic and social protection. The assertion of these priorities as universal values may at best be inappropriate to societies with different social and political traditions; at worst it smacks of neo-imperialism, for example when progress in human rights is made a condition of economic aid and cooperation.[9]

A final source of scepticism about human rights is to be found in some longstanding features of international relations, both in theory and practice. Certainly, the study of international relations has long since progressed from a

---

[4] E. Burke, *Reflections on the Revolution in France* (London, Dent, 1964). The critiques of the rights of man by, respectively, Burke, Bentham and Marx are reproduced, with a commentary, in J. Waldron (ed.), *Nonsense upon Stilts* (London, Methuen, 1987).

[5] J. Bentham, 'A critical examination of the Declaration of Rights' in B. Parekh (ed.), *Bentham's Political Thought* (London, Croom Helm, 1973), pp. 257–90.

[6] M. Wollstonecraft, *A Vindication of the Rights of Women* (London, Dent, 1970). For a contemporary critique see C. MacKinnon, 'Crimes of war, crimes of peace' in S. Shute and S. Hurley (eds), *On Human Rights* (New York, Basic, 1993), pp. 83–110.

[7] K. Marx, 'On the Jewish question', in Waldron, *Nonsense upon Stilts*, pp. 137–50. See also S. Lukes, 'Can a Marxist believe in human rights?', *Praxis International*, 1.4 (1982), 334–45.

[8] See Susan Mendus 'Human rights in political theory' in this volume.

[9] Such arguments are advanced particularly forcefully from within non-Western regions themselves. See Fred Halliday 'Relativism and universalism in human rights: the case of the Islamic Middle East', Sidgi Kaballo, 'Human rights and democratization in Africa', and Kenneth Christie, 'Regime security and human rights in Southeast Asia' in this volume.

simplistic 'realist' paradigm, according to which sovereign states constitute the only significant actors on the international scene. Yet a more complex understanding of the international arena as multi-layered or multi-dimensional does not *of itself* encourage optimism about the possibility of effective international cooperation such as the human rights project requires. Such cooperation continues to be persistently hostage to some recalcitrant facts about states and nations respectively. States remain the only legitimate controllers of physical coercion, on which effective law enforcement depends. And nations and ethnic groups remain the most potent sources of political identity and political loyalty alike. These factors not only lie at the root of many of the most serious human rights abuses; they also make governments exceedingly wary of sacrificing their own troops to protect the nationals of other states against such abuses, whether through independent action or under the auspices of the United Nations. The universalist assumptions of human rights, in other words, as of the UN itself, seem repeatedly vulnerable to the particularisms of both nation and state.[10]

If, then, the universalism required by the human rights project is deemed philosophically insecure, morally problematic and politically impractical by mainstream tendencies within the discipline, then it is hardly surprising that political science as a whole should have preferred to keep the subject at arms length. Its marginal status has been further reinforced by an academic division of labour, which has assigned the study of human rights to the discipline of law rather than politics.[11] The formulation of international treaties as legal documents, the process of monitoring their compliance by committees established under these treaties, the accumulation of case-law through the judgements of international courts – all these are eminently suited to analysis from a legal perspective. The fact that, from the standpoint of enforceability, such law may be categorized as 'soft' law, in contrast to the 'hard' law of enforceable domestic jurisdiction, makes it no less amenable to legal modes of analysis.

What is involved here, however, is more than a simple academic division of labour. In the Anglo-Saxon world, at least, despite the evident fact that the enactment, interpretation and enforcement of societally binding rules provides the chief focus for political activity, the disciplines of law and political science are divided by a seemingly unbridgeable gulf. No doubt this has something to do with the fact that academic law is intimately involved with both professional training and legal practice, and as a consequence subjects that might offer potential links with political science, such as jurisprudence or administrative law, occupy only a peripheral status – a condition that is reciprocated from the other side. Whatever the reason for the divide, however, once human rights became characterized as a subject of legal study, it has proved difficult to recover it as a legitimate subject of study for political science.

In the light of all these considerations, the aim of this volume is to do more than bring together a collection of interesting papers on the politics of human

[10] For a discussion and assessment of such objections see R. J. Vincent, *Human Rights and International Relations* (Cambridge, Cambridge University Press, 1986); Forsythe, *The Internationalization of Human Rights*, ch. 7.

[11] The evidence of Pritchard's survey is conclusive on this point; see Pritchard, 'Political science and the teaching of human rights', p. 465.

rights, which will advance the subject for specialists (though it is certainly hoped to do that). It also has a more programmatic aim: to show why the subject deserves a more substantial place within the discipline of political science. One way of showing this is to address the sources of scepticism outlined above, and explain why they might not be as well founded as they appear at first sight. All our contributors engage with this issue at one point or another. A second way is to show how the subject of human rights increasingly provides a point of convergence between law and politics, while also identifying what are the distinctive perspectives that political analysis can bring to bear upon it. A third way is to show how the study of human rights might be incorporated into the politics curriculum, in view of the way it impinges on central issues that are currently matters of debate within the different areas of the discipline. The remainder of the introduction is devoted to a consideration of this threefold agenda, drawing upon the contributions that follow in the rest of the volume.

Addressing the Sources of Scepticism

The simplest response to scepticism about human rights is to look at what has changed in the world since 1945. Not only have we witnessed the dissolution of empires in face of the principle of national self-determination. The sovereignty of the nation state has itself become circumscribed, not only in the sense that it has lost the *power* to control much of what matters for the welfare and security of its citizens, but that it has surrendered exclusive *jurisdiction* also (and the one could be argued to follow from the other). There has been a mushrooming growth of international treaties and regulatory regimes to which states have voluntarily signed up, but from which it is in most instances inconceivable that they should withdraw, even when they discover that some of the consequences of what they have signed are not to their liking.[12] In the case of human rights, these treaties set limits to domestic law, and involve bodies external to the state in monitoring their compliance. It is now generally accepted that it is no longer just an internal matter for states how they treat their citizens, nor even what kind of constitutional arrangements they subscribe to.

As both Forsythe and Rosas point out, we inhabit two worlds, or two paradigms, simultaneously. One is what Forsythe calls the 'anarchical society' of individual states, the other the 'global governance' of international standard setting; as he shows, foreign policy is conducted within both these worlds. Rosas writes of the transition from the Westfalian system of state sovereignty to a multi-layered system regulated by universal principles of law. Although this second world, to which human rights belong, is still embryonic, its development has been cumulative. Whereas the failures to avert human rights abuses are often highly visible and shocking, they tend to obscure the gradual and unspectacular development in both the range and robustness of human rights standard setting, whose cumulative impact is only fully apparent, as Storey demonstrates in the European context, by comparison with 30 or 40 years ago. With the increasing interdependence of states, it becomes more and

---

[12] See Allan Rosas, 'State sovereignty and human rights: towards a global constitutional project' and Hugo Storey, 'Human rights and the new Europe: experience and experiment' in this volume.

more difficult for them to ignore the pressure of international opinion on human rights issues; this very interdependence could over time provide as effective a backing to regulation as outright force.

The contributions on non-European regions of the world in this issue cast doubt on whether human rights can be treated merely as 'Western'. As Halliday points out, exposing the origin of ideas does not determine the question of their validity, nor the extent of their current acceptance. Nor does the fact that Western countries may be selective or guilty of double standards in their application of human rights principles invalidate the principles themselves. Developing countries have in any case themselves contributed to the modification and extension of human rights concepts and standards, and continue to do so, as Boyle's account of the World Conference on Human Rights in Vienna makes clear. Claims to cultural distinctiveness for their part need to be treated with some caution when they are advanced by political élites to justify their rejection of human rights claims. As the articles on different regions by Halliday, Kaballo and Christie suggest, such arguments readily serve to legitimate the suppression of internal dissent, or to resist the increasing differentiation of the societies concerned, and the pluralization of their own values.

The existence of cultural differences, in any case, does not rule out the possibility of a philosophical grounding for human rights, though there are different ways in which this can be attempted. Mendus, taking her starting point from the observation that cultures are not monolithic nor identities fixed, locates the justification for human rights in an exploration of the necessary conditions for dialogue and for respecting difference between diverse peoples, in a world in which they also face common threats to the realization of any conception of the good life. This is a version of political philosophy, not as the search for first principles, but as the systematic reflection on the implications of existing practice. In his contribution, Freeman offers a more detailed analysis of the implications for human rights of the fact that we are members of cultural groups, with distinctive ways of life worth protecting; and he shows how some *collective* rights can be defended on the grounds of fundamental human interests, and in a way that complements individual rights without infringing them. Like Freeman, Beetham locates a defence of human rights both in a conception of human nature and in contingent facts about the world: in particular the common threat to human well-being posed by the unfettered market economy and the unfettered power of the contemporary state or its surrogates.

Taken together, the arguments of the contributors do not remove all scepticism about the project of human rights in the contemporary world. What they suggest is that the case for it is better grounded than sceptics would allow. Any adequate assessment of the condition of human rights, in other words, has to acknowledge the pressures contributing towards, as well as the constraints upon, their realization.

Human Rights in Law and Political Science

The evidence of this volume, to which both lawyers and political scientists have contributed, suggests that the subject of human rights will prove to be an increasingly fruitful source of cooperation between the two disciplines. Not the least compelling reason for dialogue between these different cultural communities is that their subjects of study have been brought closer together by changes taking place in the world. The development of international law, already referred to, constitutes a significant regulatory regime in international relations. Its evolution coincides with an increasing interest among political scientists with the wider processes of 'governance', as distinct from government.

In addition, since 1989 there has developed a widespread recognition of the intimate connection between human rights and the process of democratization. As Kaballo observes, this is based on a mutual interdependency: without the guarantee of civil and political liberties, there can be no effective democracy; at the same time a regime dependent on free and fair elections and based on popular consent is the best guarantor of human rights. Governments acknowledge this connection when they make progress in democracy and human rights a condition of economic aid, or, as with the European Union, set high standards in both as a condition of membership. Oppressed peoples recognize it when they couch their struggle for democracy in the language of human rights, as Panizza demonstrates from the example of Latin America.

If we can point to a convergence, then, between the fields of study in law and political science, we can also identify distinctive disciplinary perspectives each brings to bear upon the common subject of human rights. For law the central focus is upon *justiciability*: the formulation of principles or norms in terms that make them amenable to adjudication in a court of law, and the processes whereby such adjudication is rendered possible and carried forward. For lawyers the challenge of human rights is to render them justiciable.[13] From this perspective, the texts of declarations and treaties of human rights constitute only one moment, as it were, albeit a significant one, in an ongoing process which embraces the *travaux préparatoires* or preliminary negotiations on the text, as well as its subsequent interpretations in the case law of courts and the decisions of authoritative international committees. Anyone familiar with the ridicule heaped by Bentham on the French declaration of the rights of man will know the fun that can be made of human rights texts by scrupulous philosophical minds.[14] However, these texts take on a different light when they are seen as part of a continuing *process* of defining and consolidating legal norms. In this light, the judgements of the European Court of Human Rights have a considerable importance for human rights more globally; and civil and political rights offer a model for how economic and social rights might be made justiciable.

For political science, on the other hand, the central focus of the discipline is upon *the struggle to influence and control the exercise of public power*. From this standpoint, a number of distinct perspectives on human rights emerge, which recur throughout this collection. One is the way in which the language of human rights is appealed to and becomes a subject of contestation in the process of political struggle, whether between states or within them. This can be seen in the ongoing conflicts between East and West, or North and South, and in the disagreements about the place and definition of human rights in Asian and Islamic cultures. It can be seen in the struggles to influence foreign

---

[13] I am indebted to Hugo Storey for discussions on this point.
[14] Bentham, 'A critical examination of the Declaration of Rights'.

policy, of which the USA is a prime example, with its conflicts between liberal elements in public opinion and powerful economic interests, or between Congress and the Presidency. Above all it can be seen in the struggles of oppressed and marginal groups and social classes everywhere to protect or advance their interests in the political arena. The language of human rights now constitutes an authoritative international discourse, which can be appealed to by the underprivileged and vulnerable to justify, and extend support for, their struggles.

In the struggle to influence policy, human rights NGOs now play an increasingly important role. Political science has always given a central place to the study of interest and pressure groups, and more recently to new social and political movements. Human rights NGOs constitute an impressive example of both, not least in their international membership and focus, and in their contribution to an emergent international public opinion and 'civil society'. In her wide-ranging analysis of NGOs at the UN, Brett attempts an assessment of their impact in monitoring and publicizing human rights abuses, in lobbying governments, in providing expertise to UN committees, and in influencing the content of human rights treaties and conventions. Boyle's account of the World Conference on Human Rights in Vienna emphasizes the significant presence of NGOs and the impact made, especially by women's organizations, on the content of the final declaration.

These accounts of human rights campaigning show that the concern of political scientists with organized struggle and of lawyers with justiciability are complementary. Any body of established law can be seen as the crystallization of political struggles and compromises in justiciable form: a kind of sedimentation of past struggles as well as the site for new ones. In the case of human rights law, campaigning groups exercise an influence not only over the content of law, but also over its implementation. However important the work of lawyers and judges in this regard may be, it often requires the work of human rights groups, in providing support for individual cases and documenting evidence, sometimes at considerable risk to themselves, for the rule of law to be upheld. Here we see law itself as an irreducibly *political* phenomenon.

This intersection of law and politics exposes the perennial problem of the conflict between power and justice, whether power is defined in terms of military force or economic ownership, of 'state interests' or the limits of tolerance of key popular constituencies. Nowhere is this conflict more acute than in the dilemma confronting newly established democracies over whether, or how far, to prosecute the personnel of the old regime for human rights violations. Should justice for the families of the dead be pursued at the risk of alienating still powerful groups, especially the military, whose support may be necessary to the stability, or even the operation, of the new government? Or should these groups be humoured, at the risk of compromising the moral authority of the democratic order? There is no easy answer. As Panizza concludes from his study of the transitions to democracy in Latin America, the outcome depends upon the manner in which the transition itself occurred, as well as upon the political skill and determination of the new authorities. As he shows, the issue is one of reaching not only a compromise between power and justice, but a reconciliation between the needs of past and future: of finding a way to 'turn the page without closing the book'.

In the end, we might reasonably conclude, disciplinary distinctions between law and politics become secondary to the requirements of the subject of human rights itself, which demands attention to considerations of both power and justice, of political struggle and justiciability, if the subject is to be adequately understood. It is perhaps symptomatic of this conjunction that it is not always easy to tell which disciplinary base our individual authors come from, except perhaps from a careful perusal of their footnotes, or from their biographical details at the end of the volume.

Human Rights in the Politics Curriculum

If the argument presented so far carries any force, then one conclusion that follows is that the subject of human rights merits a more secure place in the politics curriculum than it has so far enjoyed. This might be achieved in one of two different ways. The first is for human rights to take their place as one topic among others in mainstream courses in different branches of the discipline. The case for this lies not only in its intrinsic importance, but also in the way it impinges upon so many central questions of debate in these different sub-disciplines, such as: the conceptualization of the contemporary international system, and the nature of state sovereignty within it; the intersection between global and regional identities, and the tension between universalism and cultural specificity; the meaning of democracy, and the problems of democratic transition and consolidation; the characterization of different traditions of political theorizing, and the nature of political theory itself.

A second approach would be through the introduction of the subject of human rights as a self-standing course or half-course in its own right. This could be taught with its centre of gravity in any area of the discipline, though with the potential to reach beyond it; indeed, it is a subject that lends itself to collaborative teaching by colleagues from different specialisms. One advantage, dare I say it, of the increasing modularization of courses in UK universities, is that the process facilitates the exploration of particular themes within a shorter compass than previously. Human rights could be one such. In this context the present volume offers not so much a text book as an indication of some of the ways in which human rights might be treated from the standpoint of the politics curriculum, and references to some of the reading relevant to it.

One common objection to the introduction of a new subject into the curriculum – the lack of suitable student reading – is not here a problem. There is now a considerable choice of books, both single- and multi-authored, covering every aspect of the subject, from introductory texts and collections of readings and documents, to the consideration of human rights in more specialized aspects: in international relations and international law, in foreign policy, in the politics of developing countries or particular regions, in political theory, both past and present, or in relation to democracy, to women's rights, to social and economic rights, and so on. The main human rights journal from a multi-disciplinary social science perspective, the *Human Rights Quarterly*, has over the years published some notable contributions to the central issues of debate in the field. In addition there are the occasional contributions on the subject to mainstream journals in political science and political philosophy. The subject of human rights, in other words, is already a well-developed one; it is also one to which, in my experience, students respond with enthusiasm.

In the final analysis, the justification for human rights as a theme in the curriculum lies in its ability to engage our critical intelligence and our moral sensitivity together; and to develop a clearer understanding, not only of how the world is, but of what kind of world we might come to inhabit. In doing so, it offers a challenge to both idealism and scepticism alike. The subject exemplifies, that is to say, a recurrent feature of the political condition: not only the struggle for power and influence between competing interests, but the collective striving for human betterment in an imperfect world. Something of this complexity is illustrated in the pages that follow.

Human Rights in Political Theory

Susan Mendus*

'The principle that human rights must be defended has become one of the
commonplaces of our age ... virtually no one actually rejects the principle
of defending human rights.'[1]
'There are no [human] rights and belief in them is one with belief in
unicorns and witches.'[2]

The two quotations draw attention to a considerable, and interesting,
conundrum inherent in any attempt to discuss the status of human rights in
political theory. This is that, in recent years, as political commitment to human
rights has grown, philosophical commitment has waned. Since 1945, political
commitment has been expressed in numerous Charters and Declarations of
which the 1948 Universal Declaration of Human Rights and the European
Convention for the Protection of Human Rights are only the most familiar.
Simultaneously, membership of organizations such as Amnesty International
has burgeoned, and human rights legislation has increased at both national and
international level. Even though, as Lukes points out, human rights are
violated virtually everywhere, the principle that they should be defended is
asserted virtually everywhere. 'Virtually no one actually rejects the principle of
defending human rights.'

No one, that is, except political philosophers. For in the same post-war
period, the philosophical credentials of human rights have been subjected to
considerable scrutiny, and have regularly been found wanting. There is, of
course, nothing new in philosophical scepticism about human rights: every
undergraduate student is familiar with Bentham's assertion that '*Natural rights*
is simple nonsense: natural and imprescriptible rights, rhetorical nonsense –
nonsense upon stilts'.[3] And with Karl Marx's allegation that 'none of the so-
called rights of man goes beyond egoistic man, man as he is in civil society,
namely an individual withdrawn behind his private interests and whims and
separated from the community'.[4] But what is troubling is that these
philosophical reservations have increased rather than diminished against a

---

* I am grateful to David Beetham, both for the initial invitation to contribute to this volume, and
for his very helpful comments on an earlier draft of the paper. My thanks also go to John Horton,
Peter Jones, and Peter Nicholson for their constructive written comments, and to the members of
the Political Theory Workshop at the University of York where the first draft of the paper was
discussed.

[1] S. Lukes, 'Five fables about human rights', in S. Shute and S. Hurley (eds), *On Human Rights:
The Oxford Amnesty Lectures, 1993* (New York, Basic, 1993), p. 20.
[2] A. MacIntyre, *After Virtue* (London, Duckworth, 1981), p. 67.
[3] J. Bentham, *Anarchical Fallacies* as printed in Jeremy Waldron (ed.), *Nonsense upon Stilts:
Bentham, Burke and Marx on the Rights of Man* (London, Methuen, 1987), p. 53.
[4] K. Marx, *On the Jewish Question* as printed in Waldron, *Nonsense upon Stilts*, p. 147.

political background almost wholly hospitable to the defence of human rights. Influential strands within political theory thus run directly counter to influential strands within political practice and generate not only a question about the status of human rights in political theory, but also a question about the status of political theory itself. For something, surely, has gone wrong if political theory persists in rejecting as indefensible precisely those concepts which political practice endorses as indispensable?

My aim in this paper is to suggest a possible *rapprochment* between theory and practice: if it is true, as MacIntyre claims, that belief in human rights is a mere superstition, akin to belief in unicorns and witches, then that has worrying implications for practical policies which invoke human rights. If, on the other hand, appeal to human rights is indispensable in practical politics, then that has alarming implications for the direction and self-understanding of a great deal of contemporary political theory. What is needed, therefore, is a clearer understanding of what rights claims actually imply in practice, together with a clearer understanding of the proper role of political theory in informing political practice.

Theories of Rights

The quotations from Bentham and Marx, cited earlier, draw attention to two familiar theoretical problems associated with human rights. Bentham, like MacIntyre after him, is concerned about the ontological status of rights: the invocation of human rights in political argument may appear no more than an appeal to unjustified intuition unless and until evidence is provided for the existence of the rights invoked. And MacIntyre and Bentham are at one in thinking that no such evidence is available. Thus MacIntyre scathingly concludes:

> the best reason for asserting so bluntly that there are no such rights is indeed of precisely the same type as the best reason we possess for asserting that there are no witches, and the best reason which we possess for asserting that there are no unicorns: every attempt to give good reasons for believing that there are such rights has failed.[5]

MacIntyre's language is, perhaps, unhelpfully provocative: for one thing, claims about what does or does not count as a 'good reason' for the existence of human rights will be every bit as controversial as claims about whether there are such rights. Unlike unicorns and witches, human rights are not thought of as spatio-temporal objects and, for that reason alone, claims about their existence are not controverted by physical and biological science. In this context, therefore, what counts as a 'good reason' will itself be disputable. Nevertheless, MacIntyre's criticism does indicate a genuine difficulty inherent in appeal to human rights. This is that such appeal is naturally interpreted as foundationalist either in the sense that it invokes rights as a basic category, or in the sense that it implies a background which is essentially theological. But appeal to intuition is unduly optimistic and, in the modern world at any rate, theological premisses are of limited persuasive power. Either way, theories of

---

[5] MacIntyre, *After Virtue*, p. 67.

human rights purport to provide a foundation for moral and political thinking, but the foundation is elusive and precarious.

Moreover, it is important to note that these concerns about human rights spring, in part, from a particular conception of what philosophy in general, and political philosophy in particular, can do. MacIntyre's attack on human rights is in fact an attack on a much more general understanding (or, as he sees it, misunderstanding) of the nature and purpose of philosophy – a conception which arose in the Enlightenment period and which, in MacIntyre's view, has infected philosophy ever since. The aim is to provide foundations for political beliefs and practices and to base those foundations in reason itself. Philosophy aims to justify, and it can justify by showing how the political and moral practices in which we engage are ones which spring from and are sanctioned by reason. But MacIntyre contends that there is no such thing as human reason *tout court* and consequently no distinctively *human* rights. All rationality must be embedded in a tradition and therefore foundationalist accounts must hope to find their foundations, not in reason itself, but in the specific conceptions of reason which spring from within specific traditions. But, of course, an understanding of human rights as merely manifestations of a particular tradition is entirely at odds with the universalism implicit in the language of rights.

Other recent writers have gone yet further, arguing not simply that Enlightenment philosophy looks for foundations in the wrong place, but that it is a mistake to look for foundations at all. Thus, Richard Rorty insists that foundationalist theories of human rights are 'outmoded': they represent an understanding of the philosophic enterprise which cannot be sustained and instead of seeking foundations, we should instead look merely for the articulation and extension of our practices through the medium of sentimental story telling.[6]

Though divided in their diagnosis of the problem, both Rorty and MacIntyre are agreed that foundationalist understandings of human rights are doomed to fail. This may be because there is no such thing as distinctively human reason in which human rights can be grounded (rationality, and the rights which are alleged to spring from it, must always be context-dependent), or it may be because the search for foundations is intrinsically misguided. Either way, human rights are the product of a confused understanding of the possibilities available to philosophy.

A second, and more specific set of concerns about human rights is indicated in the quotation from Marx. Marx's concern, and it is one which has been widely shared in modern political philosophy, is that appeal to human rights presupposes a specific, and contentious, political ideology – the ideology of possessive individualism. Where human rights are asserted, they are asserted as claims *by individuals* and *against* the power of the state, or against other individuals. But to assume that rights are needed against the state is to assume that there must always be antagonism between the interests of the state and the interests of individuals, and this is a denial of the kind of ideal society envisaged by socialists and communitarians alike. Furthermore, to suppose that rights are needed against other individuals is, apparently, to endorse an

---

[6] R. Rorty, 'Human rights, rationality and sentimentality' in Shute and Hurley, *On Human Rights*, p. 119.

egoistic or selfish understanding of human nature and human flourishing. As Jeremy Waldron asks:

> Does self-respect and human dignity really depend upon being in a position to make strident, querulous, adversarial claims *against* other people? Is that what it really boils down to? This indeed would be a theory which not only leads me to see in others the limitation of my freedom; it would be a theory that leads me to see that my fulfilment, my freedom and my self-realization depend upon my muscular and self-assertive capacity to place limits on yours.[7]

This view of human fulfilment, if indeed it is that which is implicit in human rights, is starkly at odds with socialist or communitarian conceptions of the good society, and for that reason socialists have traditionally had a somewhat ambivalent attitude towards the language of human rights. Some have been anxious to re-interpret human rights in a way which avoids the 'muscular and self-assertive' implications referred to by Waldron. They have argued for the extension of rights to include social and economic rights in addition to the more familiar 'liberty' rights, and in doing so they evince their concern that rights should be more than a means of protecting individuals against the incursions of others; they should also be the socially provided mechanisms whereby people are enabled to realize their potential.

Others, however, have argued that rights are, at root, individualistic and, for that reason, inhospitable to socialist ideals. Moreover, and most troublingly, when rights are extended beyond the traditional rights of forbearance to include rights to the provision of goods necessary for individual flourishing, it becomes difficult to determine exactly which rights may properly be claimed, and exactly what action a commitment to rights demands of others. The point is eloquently expressed by Milan Kundera:

> the more the fight for human rights gains in popularity, the more it loses any concrete content, becoming a kind of universal stance of everyone towards everything, a kind of energy that turns all human desires into rights. The world has become man's right and everything in it has become a right: the desire for love a right to love, the desire for rest a right to rest, the desire for friendship a right to friendship, the desire to exceed the speed limit the right to exceed the speed limit, the desire for happiness the right to happiness, the desire to publish a book the right to publish a book, the desire to shout in the street in the middle of the night the right to shout in the street.[8]

The anxiety which is implicit in Kundera is that whilst the traditional rights, rights of forbearance, appear to make negligible demands on others, these more extensive rights, rights to provision, result in almost unlimited demands on others. It seems, then, that we are faced with a dilemma: if rights are simply rights of forbearance, then they may be satisfied but, so understood, they are vulnerable to Marx's criticism and do indeed imply egoism and individualism. They imply that we owe to others no more than forbearance and that showing care and compassion, if obligatory at all, is a much less pressing, or 'strict'

---

[7] Waldron, *Nonsense upon Stilts*, p. 196.
[8] M. Kundera, *Immortality* (London, Faber, 1991), p. 153.

obligation. But if we extend rights beyond rights of forbearance in an attempt to avoid the Marxist criticism, the consequence is that the list of rights grows uncontrollably, as does the list of demands made on others by the rights holder.

Morever, these two kinds of anxiety about rights are connected: Raymond Plant refers to human rights as 'providing foundationalist political philosophy with what is probably its greatest intellectual challenge',[9] and we are now in a position to see why this is so. Without foundations – a theological background, or stipulative metaphysics – human rights seem ontologically precarious and there is a danger that appeal to them will simply degenerate into Kundera's 'universal stance of everyone toward everything'. Yet the metaphysical or theological foundations which rights require are unavailable to us in the modern world: we eschew the metaphysical assumptions which would make rights talk legitimate. However, once the search for foundations has been abandoned, there appears to be no constraint on the list of rights which may be claimed: rights become merely an alternative way of referring to needs, interests or desires. A way, moreover, which is limitlessly costly in moral terms, but necessary if human rights are to be interpretable in a way which does not presuppose a specific political ideology, that of possessive individualism.

Constructions of Rights

In response to these anxieties about human rights, some modern political philosophers have abandoned the foundationalist approach in favour of what is known as a 'constructivist' account of human rights. This strategy attempts to renounce both foundationalism and appeal to raw intuition. One of its most familiar incarnations is in the early work of John Rawls, who aims to derive rights from assumptions about rationality without appealing either to a theological background or to implausibly rich metaphysical assumptions. Of course, in doing this, Rawls asserts what MacIntyre denies, namely that there is such a thing as human rationality – rationality independent of a tradition, and that the human capacity for rationality can provide the starting point, if not the foundation, of a defence of human rights.[10] By expounding his theory in this way Rawls aims to avoid the charge of metaphysical extravagance often levelled at rights theories. Equally, however, he also aims to avoid relativism, and to do so by emphasizing a conception of rationality which is thin enough to be plausibly asserted of all human beings. If successful, his theory will deliver rights which can be attributed to all human beings just insofar as they are rational, but it will not be a theory which supposes the existence of rights as strange quasi 'objects'. In this way, it aims to tread a path between realism and relativism: by renouncing the search for foundations, whether metaphysical or theological, it aims to avoid realism, and by insisting upon a conception of human reason which can be asserted of all human beings, it aims to avoid relativism. As Waldron puts the matter, 'to call them *human* rights is to characterize the scope of the claims being made rather than hint at anything about their justification. The term refers to universality and a commitment to equality and non-discrimination, particularly across races and peoples ... it

---

[9] R. Plant, *Modern Political Thought* (Oxford, Blackwell, 1991), p. 291.

[10] This is less true of Rawls' most recent writings, particularly 'The law of peoples' in Shute and Hurley, *On Human Rights*, pp. 41–82.

leaves open the question of justification'.[11] Thus, this understanding of human rights carries with it an understanding of the proper aspirations of political philosophy which is significantly different from that criticized by MacIntyre. It does not construe rights as justificatory entities, but as universal commitments, and in consequence it sees philosophy as being, in some part, a matter of articulating rather than justifying practical political policies: what is articulated is a universal rationality.

There are, however, serious problems associated with this understanding of human rights, and with the conception of philosophy which it implies. I shall mention only two such problems here. Firstly, and as has already been indicated, we may have reservations about whether there can be a conception of rationality thin enough to be attributable to all human beings, yet simultaneously rich enough to generate a theory of human rights. Put more directly, we may wonder whether there is, in fact, any space between realism and relativism which Rawlsian theory can inhabit. Critics like MacIntyre argue that Rawls' conception of rationality is no more nor less than an account of what we in modern Western liberal democracies deem rational and that therefore while Rawls' account may appeal to 'people like us', it can and should carry no weight with people who inhabit entirely different kinds of community. 'What' we may ask 'is the point of saying to a person quite unlike ourselves who has lived and whose ancestors have lived quite happily with some practice or other for generations, "This practice violates your human rights"?'.[12] Indeed, Rawls himself appears to have been moved by considerations of this sort, but the difficulty for him is that the more he is persuaded by these considerations, the more relativist his final position becomes, and the less compelling will his theory be as a justification of intervention in societies where human rights are, or appear to be, under threat. In order to justify intervention in alleged cases of rights violation, we need something stronger than an account of human rights premissed on a conception of rationality which applies only to 'people like us'. But the appeal to something stronger rapidly begins to look like an appeal to a metaphysics which is not officially available to Rawls.

The second problem which confronts a constructivist account of rights is that of specifying exactly which rights there are. Just as the socialist attempt to extend rights beyond the traditional rights of forbearance generated a difficulty about proliferation of rights claims, so here there is a comparable problem of specifying the set of rights implied by a constructivist theory. For example, Rawls' theory aims to identify a set of rights which secures maximal liberty for each compatible with equal liberty for all, but it is not clear that maximal liberty can be uniquely and uncontentiously identified nor, for that reason, that a set of rights which secures maximal liberty can be specified: 'there is no unique way of accommodating different rights. There are indefinitely many ways of describing possible actions and hence indefinitely many ways of picking out sets of copossible, equal rights'.[13] Again, the rejection of the

[11] Waldron, *Nonsense upon Stilts*, p. 163. For a slightly different response to the problem of justification see Peter Jones, *Rights* (Basingstoke, Macmillan, 1995), pp. 115–9.

[12] Waldron, *Nonsense upon Stilts*, p. 168.

[13] Onora O'Neill, 'Children's rights and children's lives' in Onora O'Neill, *Constructions of Reason* (Cambridge, Cambridge University Press, 1989), p. 197. Rawls has attempted to meet this criticism in 'The basic liberties and their priority' in *Political Liberalism* (Columbia, Columbia University Press, 1993), pp. 289–372. I am grateful to Peter Jones for drawing this to my attention.

metaphysical and theological premisses originally associated with rights theories renders problematic any attempt to specify exactly which rights there are – and why.

What conclusions are then to be drawn from this rather dispiriting parade of anxieties and reservations about human rights in political theory? As an attempt to justify political practice, human rights do indeed seem at best 'outmoded': we lack, or reject, the metaphysical and theological premisses which made a justificatory account of rights plausible, and the aspiration of political philosophy to provide a foundation from which political practice could be entirely justified to all people at all times has been fatally damaged by that lack, or loss, of faith. But this conclusion is primarily a conclusion about the pretensions of a certain sort of political philosophy, not a conclusion about the political practice of appealing to human rights: it tells us that insofar as philosophy ever aspired to provide a complete *justification* of or *foundation* for political practice, and aimed to fulfil that aspiration through a theory of human rights, it was doomed to fail. Or at least that, in the conditions of modernity, it can no longer serve that purpose.

In response, writers such as Rawls and Gewirth have argued for a constructivist account of human rights, one which eschews metaphysical and theological baggage, but which nevertheless aims to go beyond the purely stipulative. Such an account begins from human reason, or agency, and attempts, not so much to justify as to articulate what reason implies in the realm of political practice. However, this project too is flawed, since it is not clear that there is the requisite space between realism and relativism (that the 'us' can be specified in a way which is neither restricted to specific cultures nor implicitly committed to transcendental or metaphysical foundational assumptions). Again, this conclusion is a conclusion about the aspirations of political theory, but it is more worrying than the previous one, for it suggests that human rights are problematic on either understanding of what philosophy can do. Understood as a set of claims about the foundations of political practice, philosophy reveals that we no longer have, and maybe never did have, such foundations; but understood as an attempt to articulate what we believe, philosophy reveals that human rights are just that – they are what *we* in Western liberal democracies believe. They are not, as they purport to be, universal and timeless, nor do they justify intervention in the practices of others. Either way, political theory appears to lead to the conclusion that we are not entitled to the conception of human rights which political practice requires.

In the remainder of this paper I want to suggest some ways in which the language of human rights may nevertheless survive these anxieties. The first part of my argument will be largely negative, and will take the form of a set of reservations about the criticisms of theories of rights. The second part will take a slightly different form. It will suggest that, in order to understand both the political importance and the philosophical credentials of human rights, we should begin from the political world, not from a set of assumptions about the task of philosophy. In this sense, the argument concurs with Richard Rorty's claim that philosophy has no special privileged status: it is not 'foundational'. However, I aim to resist the conclusion that, in that case, we can do nothing beyond sentimental story-telling in our attempts to articulate the importance of human rights. Put differently, the first, and negative, part of my argument will be that the critics of human rights themselves make implicit appeal to implausibly realist assumptions. Since this is so, the second part of the argument suggests, we may do better if we begin not with an account of how human rights may be justified, but rather with an account of what we stand to lose both politically and philosophically if we renounce the language of human rights. We should begin, not with a theoretical anxiety about the nature and origin of rights, but rather with a political question about what protection rights afford us. Additionally, this strategy of beginning with the political itself makes a statement about what political theory can and should aspire to.

Reconstructing Rights

In *Modern Political Thought* Raymond Plant states that human rights express our conviction that the boundaries of nations are not the boundaries of moral concern.[14] And so they do. This, indeed, is one reason why human rights present foundationalist political philosophy with its greatest intellectual challenge. In asserting that there are human rights, we aspire to transcend political and cultural boundaries and to declare some things right (or wrong) irrespective of what is required by specific cultures or within specific nations. Now if we begin from political *theory*, the task which faces us is to explain exactly how we can be entitled to transcend those boundaries and, as we have seen, that task appears Herculean. However, if we begin from *politics* – if, that is, we emphasize the facts of the political world – the very nature of the boundaries between nations, or between cultures, is itself problematic, and this fact is significant for theories of human rights.

In political theory, it is often assumed that there are (comparatively clear) boundaries between nations and cultures and that our task is to explain how moral claims may transcend them. But in the political world, the boundaries between nations and cultures are not always clear or given. Sometimes they are the subject of acrimonious dispute, but often they are fluid and indeterminate: the cases of Israel, Ireland, and the former Yugoslavia bear testimony to the contentiousness of boundaries, while the case of modern Europe bears testimony to their fluidity. In both cases, the philosophical aspiration to transcend boundaries assumes a clarity which is contradicted by the political facts.

In partial response to this problem, it is sometimes suggested that national boundaries reflect cultural distinctions. The basic idea behind a cultural justification of political boundaries is the thought that cultural identities are deep, singular and permanent in a way that political structures are not. But even this thought is contentious: identities are frequently multiple and fluid. At some times different aspects of identity are easier to harmonize than at others, and even in those contexts where identity is assumed to be single and fixed, that assumption may be more a convenient philosophic fiction than a reflection of the realities of people's lives. Onora O'Neill refers to the first point in noting that 'once upon a time it was easy to be German and Jewish; once upon another time it became impossible. Once upon a time it was easy to be Irish and British; latterly it has been easy (and even then not wholly easy) only for those of Irish origin living in Britain'.[15] Similarly, Amy Gutmann notes the

---

[14] Plant, *Modern Political Thought*, p. 290.
[15] Onora O'Neill, 'Permeable boundaries' (unpublished paper).

potentially deceptive nature of assumptions about the fixity and homogeneity of identity within a specific culture. Taking the example of the Mormons, who are characteristically understood as having 'a *total* system of belief and behaviour, dedicated to particular hopes, dreams and interpretation', she notes that this characteristic understanding is false to the reality of Mormon life and teaching:

> In 1890, twelve years following the Supreme Court decision in *Reynolds v. United States* that upheld state prohibition of polygamy, the Mormon church officially reversed course and prohibited polygamy, again on doctrinal grounds. Yet approximately 30,000 Mormons today, so called Mormon fundamentalists, still believe in polygamy and practice it despite plenty of pressure to the contrary ... none of these views represents *the* Mormon understanding of kinship because there is no single such social understanding endemic to Mormonism, either today or for any significant period of Mormon history, despite the fact that Mormonism has long been seen by outsiders as a nonpluralistic, monolithic culture.[16]

What these social and historical facts suggest is that criticisms of rights theories often depend for their force upon a simplistic understanding of the political. It is argued that appeal to human rights reflects our desire to transcend boundaries, but that that desire requires allegiance to a transcendentalism which is no longer available to us. However, on inspection, the belief that there are boundaries to be transcended is itself suspect. Partly because we all now live in 'global village', the sheer ability to retain monolithic cultures has become more difficult. But Gutmann's reference to the history of Mormonism suggests that the assumption of homogeneity never was true to the reality of Mormon life: even within the most monolithic of cultures there always was, and remains, a high degree of pluralism in interpretation of scripture and in understandings of the way to live. In some sense, therefore, it is misleading to refer to human rights as reflecting an aspiration to transcend national or cultural boundaries. Moral concerns do indeed transcend such boundaries, but the boundaries themselves are fluid and indeterminate even when they are premissed on assumptions about cultural identity.

If we take these social and historical facts seriously, then we may understand human rights as representing an acknowledgement of the contentiousness of boundaries and identities. Rights begin from the political and social realities of all our lives, and address problems about the forms which negotiation may take in circumstances where such boundaries are disputed, or identities fragmented. Put differently, they set limits to the ways in which one identity, or set of identities, may be reconciled with others, and they raise doubts about the optimism implicit in questions such as 'what is the point of saying to a person quite unlike ourselves who has lived and whose ancestors have lived quite happily with some practice or other for generations, "this practice violates your human rights"?'.[17] For while it is not impossible that there are such people, attention to the fluidity of national boundaries, and the fragmentation of cultural identities suggests that they will be the exception rather than the rule.

---

[16] Amy Gutmann, 'The challenge of multiculturalism in political ethics' in *Philosophy and Public Affairs*, 22.3 (1993), 171–206, pp. 175–6.
[17] Waldron, *Nonsense upon Stilts*, p. 168.

The harsh realities of political life show us, not that boundaries are fixed and identities determinate, but rather that boundaries are at best fluid, at worst disputed, and identities fragmented and often conflictual.

My second, and connected, suggestion takes its cue from the interesting fact that defences of human rights in political theory tend to take the form of story-telling, or imaginative hypotheses. As we have seen, when we begin with a question about what the philosophic enterprise can achieve, human rights appear doomed. Foundationalist, intuitionist, stipulative and constructivist accounts all lead to the general conclusion that human rights cannot bear the philosophical weight which is put on them. In that sense, it is perhaps unsurprising that defenders of human rights begin, not with the theoretical aspects of political theory, but with its political dimension. They ask what would a society without human rights look like, or what kind of society is envisaged by the proponents and opponents of human rights respectively.[18] Sometimes, as with Lukes and Feinberg, these stories take the form of imaginative hypotheses, but often they take the form of discussions of actual history (Gutmann). In one way, as has been said, this is unsurprising. But in another way, it is very surprising indeed: defenders of human rights are regularly accused of operating with concepts which are abstract and distant from the realities of life. And rights themselves have come under attack as strange, quasi-metaphysical entities, abstractions from the real world. Against this background, we may wonder why those who seek to defend human rights should begin, if not with the real world, then with detailed story-telling about possible worlds.

Richard Rorty has argued that there are, in the end, two kinds of thinker: those who believe that beneath the contingent clutter of the world there is something called 'Truth' or 'Geist' or 'the Good' (the philosophers); and those who believe that the contingent clutter of the world is all that there is (the poets).[19] Advocates of human rights have traditionally been associated with the former kind of thinker, but inspection of some of the most prominent literature on human rights suggests that it is precisely in the contingent clutter of the real world that people find appeal to human rights most necessary. Pace Rorty, it is not the philosophical desire for Truth which motivates appeal to rights, but rather reflection on the practicalities of actual political and moral life. Rorty's distinction between philosophers and poets thus suggests a different, but connected distinction: the distinction between optimism and pessimism, or between what Stuart Hampshire calls innocence and experience. Hampshire writes:

> If one follows the liberal tradition of Mill, Sidgwick, G. E. Moore, and John Rawls, one is liable to think of great public evils as a falling away from the pursuit of justice or of the good, whether it be happiness, or good states of mind, or the realization of primary goods, such as liberty: as if we had to understand those actions and policies which we consider purely evil as being the loss of those things which we consider just or good. But it is

---

[18] See, for example, J. Feinberg, 'The nature and value of rights' in J. Feinberg, *Rights, Justice and the Bounds of Liberty: Essays in Social Philosophy* (Princeton, Princeton University Press, 1980), pp. 143–58, and S. Lukes, 'Five fables about human rights'.

[19] R. Rorty, 'The contingency of selfhood' in *Contingency, Irony and Solidarity* (Cambridge, Cambridge University Press, 1989), pp. 23–43.

equally possible to interpret, and to understand, the things we consider
primary goods as being the prevention of great evils ... Illiberal moralists,
and particularly the greatest of them, Machiavelli and Hobbes, still retain
their hold on us, because they convey a vivid sense of the forces of
destruction which are always at large and which have to be diverted and
controlled if any kind of decent civilized life is to continue.[20]

Earlier in the paper, I suggested that there might be something politically
naive in the relativist criticism of rights which enjoins us to ask 'what is the
point of saying to a person quite unlike ourselves who has lived and whose
ancestors have lived quite happily with some practice or other for
generations, "This practice violates your human rights"?'. The political,
and indeed historical, naiveté lay in the assumption of cultural homogeneity
on which the question is premissed. However, Hampshire's distinction
between engendering and preventing suggests a second, and slightly different,
kind of assumption inherent in the question. This is the assumption that
human rights are the bearers of goods, rather than bulwarks against evil. If
we assume that evil is simply the loss of those things which we consider good,
then there is indeed something odd about saying to a person who lives
perfectly happily with different practices 'this practice violates your human
rights'. For there is, *ex hypothesi*, no loss of anything considered good *by that
person* and therefore no obvious work for the appeal to human rights to do.
But reflection upon the realities of social life, both contemporary and
historical, suggests that this situation is a somewhat implausible construct,
partly because of the assumption of homogeneity which is implicit in it, but
also because it neglects the extent to which 'the forces of destruction are
always at large'. Hampshire's argument draws attention to the emphasis
which moral and political philosophy place upon the pursuit of good to the
near exclusion of the avoidance of evil, and he urges a rediscovery of evil as
something distinct from the absence of good. In this reorientation lies, I
believe, the beginning of an understanding of the role of human rights in
political theory, and also a richer understanding of the tasks of political
theory itself.

In order to make good this claim, I shall consider two very recent accounts
of the role and importance of human rights in political theory. The first is
Richard Rorty's discussion in his Amnesty Lecture, 'Human Rights,
Rationality and Sentimentality', and the second is Stephen Lukes' discussion, in his Amnesty Lecture, 'Five Fables about Human Rights'. Rorty's
central theme is that foundationalism about human rights is outmoded and, as
part of this claim, he emphasizes the movement in modern political theory
from questions about man's nature to questions about what we can make of
ourselves. Part of his aim is to indicate the diminishing emphasis on ontology
or theories of human nature in modern political philosophy, but a further, and
more wide-ranging, aim is to suggest that by distancing ourselves from
ontological questions and questions about human nature, we have simultaneously become more interested in the malleability of human beings. He writes:
'There is a growing willingness to neglect the question "what is our nature?"

---

[20] S. Hampshire, *Innocence and Experience* (St Ives, Penguin, 1989), pp. 67–8.

and to substitute the question "What can we make of ourselves?"' and he concludes:

> Nowadays, to say that we are clever animals is not to say something philosophical and pessimistic but something political and hopeful, namely: If we can work together, we can make ourselves into whatever we are clever and courageous enough to imagine ourselves becoming. This sets aside Kant's question "What is Man?" and substitutes the question "What sort of world can we prepare for our great-grandchildren?"[21]

In addition to being anti-foundationalist, Rorty's account is also fundamentally optimistic and forward looking: it emphasizes the good which we may do for the future via our cleverness and courage. It is this optimism, or what Hampshire terms 'innocence' which I wish to concentrate on here, and it may be emphasized by contrasting Rorty and Lukes.

Lukes's discussion takes the form of five 'fables' about possible societies (Utilitaria, Proletaria, Communitaria, Libertaria and Egalitaria) and their attitudes to human rights. Of these five, only two (Libertaria and Egalitaria) allow room for human rights, and only Egalitaria, in Lukes's view, takes human rights sufficiently seriously. Even Egalitaria is defective, however, because ultimately it is unattainable and unmaintainable – a mirage, built upon the implausible hope that the inhabitants can 'view anyone, including themselves, impartially, seeing everyone's life as of equal worth and everyone's well-being and freedom as equally valuable'.[22] As Lukes points out, a casual glance around the world tells us that this is not the way people are in fact inclined to view one another. Virtually overnight, Yugoslavs turned into Croats and Serbs, it matters deeply to some Canadians that they are Quebeçois, and to some Czechoslovaks that they are Slovaks. Contemporary politics is, for Lukes, the ground of pessimism rather than optimism, and it is in the philosophical doctrine of human rights that we may find such comfort as there is. Since for Lukes it is futile to expect people actually to take the impartial view of each other, to see everyone's life as of equal worth, hope for the future lies in adherence to a philosophical theory of rights which can serve as a bulwark against the worst deliverances of practical politics: 'to defend human rights is to defend a kind of "egalitarian plateau" on which political conflicts and arguments can take place'.[23] It is to allow cultural identity without committing oneself to cultural superiority or, worse, to cultural cleansing. In this context, philosophical theory is a nice thought prompted by a demonstrably nasty world.

For Rorty, by contrast, the hope must lie in an attempt, via story-telling, to enlarge the sympathies of people for one another, to encourage people to see the differences between themselves and others as fewer, and less important, than the similarities. Lukes, we may say, is a pessimist and Rorty an optimist. Or, rather differently, Lukes takes the side of experience, in Hampshire's sense, and Rorty the side of innocence. What are the costs attached to an adherence to innocence, and what view of political philosophy (political theory) is encapsulated in a commitment to human rights borne of an acknowledgement of experience?

---

[21] Rorty, 'Human rights, rationality and sentimentality', pp. 121–2.
[22] Lukes, 'Five fables about human rights', p. 36.
[23] Lukes, 'Five fables about human rights', p. 39.

The contrasts between Lukes and Rorty may be traced through three themes, each of which is instructive in the context of a discussion of human rights and which, when taken together, may provide a new perspective on the role of human rights in political theory. Firstly, we may contrast Rorty's emphasis on the future with Lukes' awareness of the past. Where Rorty enjoins us to consider what we may become, if we can work together, Lukes emphasizes the fact that what we may become is always circumscribed by our understanding of who we are. And who we are is, in part, a retrospective not a prospective matter. Thus, he writes:

> Consider the idea of fraternity. Unlike liberty and equality, which are conditions to be achieved, who your brothers are is determined by the past. You and they form a collective in contradistinction to the rest of mankind, and in particular to that portion of it that you and they see as sources of envy or resentment.[24]

More generally, in looking forward, we must always look from where we now are, and where we now are is a matter which is 'given' or partly determined by the past. Secondly, and connectedly, this emphasis on the past will influence our ability and willingness to follow Rorty's injunction to 'see others as like ourselves'. Without a theory of human nature, or an answer to Kant's question 'What is man?', the optimism inherent in Rorty's account appears ungrounded, and the cultural and social importance of history, or of what is 'given' will serve to undermine attempts to see differences as fewer and less important. We need to ask 'by what criterion are the differences fewer and less important?', and again, without implicit appeal to a theory of human nature, that question lacks an obvious answer. These two sets of considerations lead to a third, which is that appeal to human rights might best be understood as a set of rules, prompted by political considerations, for the accommodation of difference, rather than justifications for the assertion of similarity. Rorty implies that, since we cannot answer Kant's question, we must simply attempt, through sentimental story-telling, to diminish the number and significance of differences between ourselves and others. But perhaps there is a more important task to perform – that of setting limits to the ways in which we may treat others, whilst acknowledging the differences between ourselves and them. Gutmann's discussion of the Mormons, and O'Neill's discussion of boundaries, both suggest that these differences may be less permanent and more fluid than is often supposed. These considerations are the grounds of optimism. At the same time, however, Lukes' discussion suggests that, where such differences occur, they are likely to be accorded great significance in the lives of individuals, and indeed to be partly constitutive of people's own self-understanding. These considerations, therefore, are the grounds of pessimism. The role of human rights is not to promote a false optimism by implying that there is a single human nature which underlies the differences between people, but rather to temper pessimism both by acknowledging the fluidity of boundaries, and by using the facts of fluidity to construct rules which will guide attempts to see others as like ourselves.

Since boundaries between nations are less clear and fixed than is often supposed, and since the boundaries between different cultures are less complete

---

[24] Lukes, 'Five fables about human rights', p. 37.

and rigid than is often supposed, we may be led in the direction of hypostatizing human rights as a kind of universal grammar, a statement of what is common to all the different and diverse nations and cultures. Or, following Rorty, we may be led to an optimistic assumption about the possibility of generating solidarity between otherwise different people via a prospective account of what we might become. Attention to the fluidity of boundaries, or to a prospective philosophy inspire optimism. But attention to the past – to the significance of culture in people's lives – generates pessimism: if we are to create solidarity and minimize differences, then that must be done in a way which does not drive out local allegiances and loyalties. And this, in turn, seems to thwart attempts to appeal to human rights. My suggestion therefore is that human rights should be construed as an attempt to specify the conditions under which prospective optimism can legitimately be pursued in political theory. They constitute an acknowledgement of the limits to the possible discovery or creation of solidarities between diverse people.

In the literature, theories of human rights are commonly thought to betray one or both of the following beliefs: that there is a single human nature, common to all people, however different they may appear; and that that human nature may serve as the justifying ground for a political theory which dictates what is right (or wrong) across the boundaries of nations and cultures. Thus construed, human rights theories are expressions of philosophical optimism, even arrogance, and this is true both of traditional theories and of Rorty's anti-foundationalist account. By contrast, my suggestion is that human rights be seen as an expression, not of philosophical optimism, but of political pessimism: they imply no commitment to a thick theory of human nature, but serve rather as a warning against overenthusiastic attempts to create solidarity. It may be said that the specification of those constraints will, in itself, imply a theory of human nature, and perhaps that is so. However, such a theory will be very 'thin' and will require only minimal agreement about what is evil, not any agreement about what constitutes 'the good for man', nor any commitment to the possibility of creating similarity or solidarity amongst diverse people. On this understanding, human rights are bulwarks against evil, borne of an acknowledgement of difference, not harbingers of goods consequent upon a commitment to similarity, whether created or discovered.

What, finally, does this suggestion imply for the role of human rights in political theory, and for the aspirations of political theory itself? It implies that human rights should be seen not as appeals to universal and timeless goods, but as acknowledgements of the diverse and fluid. As such, they do not reflect an understanding of philosophy as the pursuit of Truth, or the discovery of similarity, but neither do they subscribe to an understanding of philosophy as a matter of creating similarity. Rather, the philosophical task is to acknowledge both the fact and the fluidity of difference: both the fact that there are boundaries between nations and the fact that those boundaries are subject to change. So understood, philosophy neither creates nor discovers similarity. On the contrary, it acknowledges the ineliminability of difference, couples that with a recognition that specific differences may change from time to time and from place to place, and then proposes human rights as regulatory devices for the accommodation of difference, not justifications for the assertion of similarity.

All this, however, must be read against a political background, for the world contains not merely difference, but also evil, and the political impetus for human rights comes from the recognition of evil as a permanent threat in the world. Therefore, when philosophy is sceptical about a common human nature it must be careful not to allow that scepticism to render it impotent in the face of real and palpable evil. Where philosophy sees difference to be accommodated, politics sees evil to be eliminated. The real trick lies in showing how we can do both simultaneously: how in the political world we may act against evil without becoming tyrannical, and how in the philosophical realm we may accommodate difference without denying that some differences are manifestations of evil. Philosophers often tell us that in this area there is no Truth to be discovered, but politics reminds us that we cannot afford to believe that that is so.

Are there Collective Human Rights?

MICHAEL FREEMAN*

The Problem of Collective Rights in Political Theory

The doctrine of human rights affirms two fundamental principles of Western liberalism. The first is that the human individual is the most fundamental moral unit. The second is that all human individuals are morally equal. These two principles express a commitment to egalitarian individualism. Yet the doctrine belongs to an international discourse which also affirms two collectivist principles. The first is that states are the primary agents of international relations. The second is that states represent nations. Liberal theory and international law reconcile the claims of individuals and states by affirming that states are obliged to respect the human rights of individuals. The status of nations is less clear. The common Article 1 of the two international human-rights covenants of 1966 declares that all *peoples* have the right to self-determination. This proposition has generally been interpreted to mean that the populations of colonial territories have the right to form nation-states. It has, however, also been cited to express the aspirations of various national and ethnic minorities, and of indigenous peoples. The logical and practical relations between these collective claims and individual human rights is uncertain.

The problem inheres in liberal-democratic theory. The classical liberal theory of Locke held that every individual equally had a set of natural rights, and that government was legitimate only if it was based on the consent of the governed and protected the fundamental rights of all. In such political communities the majority had the right to bind the rest.[1] Thus Locke derived from the premises of equal and individual rights conclusions about collective rights of majorities.

In the republican democratic tradition associated with Rousseau sovereignty is placed not in the majority but in the general will. Rousseau maintained that this will was indivisible. If it was to prevail, there must be no partial associations in the state.[2] Locke and Rousseau both located the problem of political authority in the relation between the individual and the state. Minorities in Locke's theory and partial associations in Rousseau's had no role in legitimate government. This approach to the problem of political authority was introduced into world-historical politics when the French Revolution proclaimed individual rights and the sovereignty of the nation, while manifesting its hostility towards minorities and partial associations.

* I should like to thank other contributors to this volume, especially David Beetham and Allan Rosas, for their helpful comments on an earlier version of this paper, and Will Kymlicka for stimulating exchanges of views on this subject and for references to Canadian sources.

[1] J. Locke, *The Second Treatise of Government* (Cambridge, Cambridge University Press, 1970), para. 95.

[2] J. J. Rousseau, *The Social Contract* (London, Dent, 1966), Book II, chs 2 and 3.

Classical liberalism normally took the culturally homogeneous nation-state for granted. The republicanism of Rousseau and the French Revolution was explicit about the need for a civil religion.[3] John Stuart Mill held that free institutions required a united public opinion and were 'next to impossible' in a country made up of different nationalities.[4] John Rawls has continued the tradition of nation-state liberal individualism.[5] Lord Acton, by contrast, argued that the association of the state with the nation violated the 'rights of nationality' by subordinating all nationalities not associated with the state.[6]

The principles of equal individual rights and majority rule have provided the theoretical basis of liberal-democratic nation-states. The concept of a ruling majority, however, implies that of a subordinate minority. Liberal-democratic theory treats such minorities as sets of outvoted individuals. Their situation is legitimate because their individual rights are guaranteed, because these rights give them the opportunity to become part of the majority from time to time, and because it is the outcome of the rules of the democratic game. In this system there is majority rule, but no minority problem.

The construction of modern nation-states has, however, been accomplished partly by the domination and attempted assimilation of traditional communities. Many contemporary nation-states also contain minorities produced by immigration. Modern societies therefore include collectivities bound by common values that may be distinct from those of the majority. Such collectivities may form permanent minorities whose interests are persistently neglected by the majority. The state and the cultural majority may form a hegemonic bloc. Many social groups – for example, women, gays and the disabled – may be structurally disadvantaged in liberal democracies, and may require special rights in order to achieve equal citizenship. These rights might be collective (for example, quotas in the political representation of women) but the claims of these groups can generally be met by implementation of the individual right to be free from arbitrary discrimination and appropriate measures of positive discrimination. Because ethnic groups have common comprehensive cultures and national groups a sense of political distinctiveness, they raise special problems for nation-state political cultures based on the principle of majority rule. The doctrine of equal and universal rights may support the hegemony of the majority culture over various subordinated cultures.[7]

The problem of collective rights, therefore, arises in two ways. It arises firstly because the concept of individual human rights has been introduced into an international discourse committed to various forms of collectivism. It arises secondly because liberal-democratic theory and practice have traditionally concerned themselves with the relation between individual rights and the collective rights of nation-states. It is a mistake to believe that liberal democracy has favoured the individual over the collective. Rather, it has given

[3] Rousseau, *The Social Contract*, Book IV, ch. 8.

[4] J. S. Mill, *Considerations on Representative Government* (London, Dent, 1910), pp. 361–2.

[5] J. Rawls, 'The law of peoples' in S. Shute and S. Hurley (eds), *On Human Rights: The Oxford Amnesty Lectures 1993* (New York, Basic, 1993), pp. 41–82.

[6] Lord Acton, *Essays in the Liberal Interpretation of History: Selected Papers* (Chicago, University of Chicago Press, 1967), p. 157.

[7] V. Van Dyke, *Human Rights, Ethnicity, and Discrimination* (Westport CN, Greenwood, 1985), pp. 7–8, 59–60, 145–6, 220.

the individual a special status within a particular collectivity, the nation-state. It is precisely collectivities systematically unrepresented by states that are anomalies in liberal-democratic theory. Do such groups have moral (as distinct from positive, legal) rights? If they do, how are these rights logically related to individual human rights?

Collective Rights in International Politics and Law

The protection of minority rights by treaty has been practised for centuries. Such protection has been exceptional, however, since international law has normally recognized the sovereign power of states: it was, indeed, sovereign states that made treaties to protect minorities. The most extensive system of minority-rights protection was that of the League of Nations. This system recognized collective rights of various kinds (for example, equal rights for individual members of minority collectivities, special rights for minority collectivities and collective rights to cultural autonomy) and thereby weakened the dogma of state sovereignty in favour of human-rights concerns. It was, however, neither universal in principle nor effective in practice, and it vanished with the League.[8]

After the Second World War the UN adopted its Universal Declaration of Human Rights. Almost every right in this declaration is expressed as an individual right (for example, Article 3 states that 'everyone' has 'the right to life, liberty and security of person'). The Declaration does, however, have some collectivist features. Individuals have rights to participate in collective practices (Articles 20 and 27); families have the right to protection by society and the State (Article 16); parents have the right to choose the kind of education that shall be given to their children (Article 26); the 'will of the people' is the basis of the authority of government (Article 21); everyone is entitled to a social and international order in which the rights set out in the Declaration can be fully realized (Article 28); and all rights are subject to such limitations as are determined by law to meet 'the just requirements of morality, public order and the general welfare in a democratic society' (Article 29).

Attempts were made to include an article on minority rights. The Representative of the USSR said that minority rights were 'fundamental human rights'. The Representative of the USA opposed the inclusion of a minority-rights article, stating that the best solution of the problem of minorities was to encourage respect for human rights. There was therefore a conceptual disagreement as to whether minority rights were human rights or whether human rights did not include minority rights but were the means to solve minority problems. The Universal Declaration does not mention minorities. The UN Human Rights Commission did establish a Sub-Commission on the Prevention of Discrimination and the Protection of Minorities, but the theoretical and practical relations between the prevention of discrimination and the protection of minorities has remained unclear.[9] The most important minority-rights provision of international law, Article 27 of the International Covenant on Civil and Political Rights, declares that *persons*

---

[8] P. Thornberry, *International Law and the Rights of Minorities* (Oxford, Clarendon, 1991), Part I.

[9] Thornberry, *International Law*, Part III.

belonging to certain minorities shall not be denied the right, *in community with others*, to participate in the culture of their group. Some commentators have argued that Article 27 bears a collectivist interpretation, but the extent to which it does, if any, is uncertain.[10]

The different policies of the League and the UN towards minority rights can be explained to a considerable extent by their different beliefs about the implications of minority rights for the stability of nation-states and of the international order. The League believed that its minority-rights regime would contribute to peace as well as to justice. UN state élites have considered minority rights to be threats to national unity, territorial state integrity, peace and economic development.[11] In the face of increasingly insistent minority demands and violent ethnic conflicts, however, cautious changes have taken place. Article 1 of the UN Declaration on Minority Rights of December 1992, for example, imposes on states the obligation to protect the existence and identity of minorities.[12]

A number of so-called peoples' rights have also been introduced into international law. There is an African Charter on Human and Peoples' Rights. Article 25 of the International Covenant on Economic, Social, and Cultural Rights recognizes 'the inherent right of all peoples to enjoy and utilize fully and freely their natural wealth and resources'. Other people's rights include those to self-determination, international peace, economic, social and cultural development, and a satisfactory environment.[13] The conceptual character of these rights is unclear and their relation to individual human rights uncertain.

Towards a Theory of Individual and Collective Rights

The concepts of individual rights and collective rights have a similar history and a similar general theoretical rationale. Individuals and collectivities have been oppressed throughout history and in the modern period protection has been sought in the form of institutionalized rights. Collective rights as such are not controversial: associations and corporations clearly can have moral and legal rights and duties. However, some human-rights theorists have insisted that only individuals can have *human* rights. Others have argued for collective human rights. To analyse this disagreement, we need to consider the nature and justification of human rights.

I propose to defend a conception of collective human rights. In order to show that these collective rights *are* human rights, I shall argue that some collective rights have the same nature and justification as well-established human rights. To this end I shall argue that a particular conception of rights – the 'interest' conception – must and can be defended against some plausible criticisms. I shall then argue that the interest conception of *human* rights must and can be defended against communitarian and relativist objections. I shall conclude by presenting the argument for collective human rights, while

[10] P. Thornberry, 'International and European standards on minority rights' in H. Miall (ed.), *Minority Rights in Europe: the Scope for a Transnational Regime* (London, Pinter, 1994), p. 15.

[11] Thornberry, *International Law*, pp. 47–8, 122, 129, 136–7, 202, 206.

[12] A. Phillips and A. Rosas (eds), *The UN Minority Rights Declaration* (Turku, Åbo, 1993), p. 124.

[13] J. Crawford (ed.), *The Rights of Peoples* (Oxford, Clarendon, 1988).

identifying some problems raised by the attempt to reconcile individual and collective human rights.

The Nature of Rights

It is generally agreed that rights are constituted by norms that govern relations between those who have rights and those who have duties arising from those rights. These norms impose constraints on the actions of the duty-bearers.[14] There are said to be two competing views of how these relations should be analysed. The *interest* conception of rights is said to hold that the *grounds* of rights are the *interests* of the rights-holders, whereas the *choice* conception maintains that a right *exists* when the necessary and sufficient condition of imposing or relaxing the constraint on the duty-bearer is the right-holder's choice to this effect.[15] The two conceptions are, however, not necessarily mutually incompatible, for the interest conception emphasizes the *justification* of rights-constituting norms, whereas the choice conception is concerned with the *identification* of such norms. Thus, an *interest* of A may *justify* attributing to A the right to *x*, and we may *know* that A *has* the right to *x* because the correlative duty of B may be enforced or waived by the *choice* of A. The two conceptions may nevertheless have different and even mutually incompatible implications.

The concept of human rights appears to presuppose the interest conception. Article 3 of the Universal Declaration, for example, states that everyone has 'the right to life, liberty and security of person'. The *justification* of such rights surely relies on our intuition that everyone normally has a legitimate *interest* in life, liberty and security.

Steiner has, however, argued that the interest conception of rights should be rejected in favour of the choice conception. His principal argument is that, since interests can conflict, the interest conception entails conflicts of rights. If rights conflict, so do their correlative duties. And if duty-bearers have conflicting duties, they cannot carry out all their duties. Those duties that they cannot carry out cannot really be duties. So their correlative rights cannot really be rights. The interest theory of rights is therefore incoherent, he concludes.[16]

Interests certainly can conflict and the interest conception of rights entails that rights can conflict. But conflicting rights do not entail incompossible duties. Conflicting rights entail duties to balance rights. A government that discharges its duty to protect the right to privacy by limiting the right to freedom of speech is not violating its duty to respect the right to freedom of speech but fulfilling its duty to balance these rights. The problem of balancing conflicting rights may not have a determinate rational solution, but this does not mean that particular solutions are necessarily unreasonable. Steiner's critique of the interest conception is therefore not persuasive, for it rests on the rational unacceptability of indeterminacy. Conflicts of rights, with their consequent indeterminacy, are, however, stubborn facts of human-rights politics. Steiner's attempt to sacrifice the interest conception for the sake of

[14] H. Steiner, *An Essay on Rights* (Oxford, Blackwell, 1994), pp. 56–7.

[15] Steiner, *An Essay on Rights*, pp. 56–8, 61, 73.

[16] Steiner, *An Essay on Rights*, pp. 80–1, 92.

complete logical coherence is to accord priority to logic over (moral and political) experience.

The interest conception of rights has been systematized by Raz. He suggests that A has a right to *x* only if the *interest* A has in having *x* is *a sufficient reason* for imposing a duty on B. Conceptions of interests are determined by *ultimate values*. Thus, rights are dependent on ultimate values, which, Raz allows, are contested. Although those with different values may agree on certain rights, nevertheless rights claims will remain vulnerable to disagreement deriving from conflicting ultimate values.[17] Despite this weakness, however, Raz's analysis is useful in several ways. Firstly, in grounding rights in *interests*, it captures a central feature of the concept of natural or human rights in the classical tradition from Locke to the UN. Secondly, it provides a systematic framework for relating ultimate values, interests, rights and duties. Thirdly, by providing this framework, it makes possible a systematic analysis of the relation between individual and collective rights. *Since value-based interests ground rights, the conceptual relations between individual and collective rights depend on the kinds of values and interests that may ground the putative rights.*

Raz's account thus allows for the derivation of both individual and collective rights from fundamental interests. Individuals, he argues, have an interest in living in communities. Communities can have collective interests, such as the interest in self-determination. There is, however, no *individual* right to collective self-determination, because the realization of collective self-determination imposes far-reaching constraints on the actions of others: the interests of no individual are sufficient reasons for imposing such heavy burdens on others. But nations can have such rights. Raz suggests two reasons why nations and other collectivities may have rights that are not reducible to individual rights. The first is that only the interests of collectivities are of sufficient *weight* to justify the imposition of the correlative duties. The second is that some interests are interests in *collective goods* – such as the interest in collective self-determination – and only collectivities may be the holders of rights to collective goods.[18] Moreover, there is no general rule giving either individual rights or collective goods priority in cases of conflict.[19] Raz thus does not recognize that individual human rights have the special status in relation to collective goods that they are given in international law; and he leaves individual rights more vulnerable to violation by governments claiming to promote the common good than is permitted by human rights considerations.

Raz's analysis is useful in identifying interests as the grounds of rights and in giving a coherent account of the conceptual relation between individual and collective rights. He fails to give a plausible account of *human* rights, however, because he gives no sort of priority to individual rights over collective goods and because he grounds rights in contestable values. Thus, Raz is too 'communitarian' and too 'relativist' to provide theoretical support for the idea of universal human rights.

[17] J. Raz, *The Morality of Freedom* (Oxford, Clarendon, 1986), pp. 166, 180–1.
[18] Raz, *The Morality of Freedom*, pp. 174, 190, 194, 207–9, 288–9.
[19] Raz, *The Morality of Freedom*, pp. 216, 250–7, 308–13.

Universal Human Rights

Human rights are universal: *everyone* has, for example, the right to life, liberty and security. Raz derives rights from interests and values and thereby leaves the universality of human rights in question. Gewirth, in contrast, derives *universal* human rights from what he claims to be a universal feature of morality. All moralities, he holds, impose duties on individuals, and thereby require *actions*. Because 'ought' implies 'can', duties presuppose *rights* to the generic requirements of action: freedom and well-being. There are therefore universal human rights to freedom and well-being.[20]

Gewirth can recognize collective rights but collective rights are necessarily derivative from individual human rights. This attempt to derive the priority of individual human rights logically from a supposedly universal conception of morality attempts to prove too much. Those moralities that do not recognize individual rights but only duties to the collective good are not logically incoherent. Even if they must logically recognize that each individual has the right to the freedom and well-being necessary to do his or her duty, they are not *logically* required to recognize the priority of individual human rights over the collective good. Gewirth attempts to establish the universality of human rights and the priority of individual rights by claiming that a liberal conception of agency is implicit in all moralities. This claim is implausible.

Donnelly defends universal individual human rights but rejects the concept of collective human rights. He holds that one has human rights because one is a human being. Only individual persons are human beings, so that only individuals can have human rights. In the area defined by human rights the individual has prima facie priority over social interests. Yet he acknowledges that individuals must be members of social groups if they are to lead worthy lives. Individuals, therefore, have duties to society and society has correlative rights. Societies may legitimately constrain the exercise of many human rights, and should balance individual rights with individual duties. But it does not follow that society or any other social group has human rights, in his view.[21]

Donnelly's position leads him to make some inconsistent judgments. On the one hand he admits that the exercise of human rights may sometimes destroy groups. In such cases, human rights should ordinarily be given priority. It is morally preferable that groups disappear as a consequence of the exercise of the human rights of their members than that they should be protected by enforcement of group membership.[22] On the other hand, some societies do not recognize human rights, but protect many of the interests that are protected by human rights. The introduction of human rights into such societies might diminish the prospects for a dignified life. In such situations Donnelly accords priority to the collective good.[23]

Donnelly therefore allows the collective good to 'trump' individual human rights in some normal and some extraordinary situations, and yet would protect individual human rights even at the expense of *group survival*. Because

---

[20] A. Gewirth, *Reason and Morality* (Chicago, University of Chicago Press, 1978) and *Human Rights: Essays on Justification and Applications* (Chicago, University of Chicago Press, 1982).
[21] J. Donnelly, *Universal Human Rights in Theory and Practice* (Ithaca, Cornell University Press, 1989), pp. 1, 9, 16, 19–21, 57–8, 68–9, 90, 143–5.
[22] Donnelly, *Universal Human Rights*, pp. 58–9, 70, 151–2.
[23] Donnelly, *Universal Human Rights*, pp. 59, 67, 151–3.

he lacks a coherent theory of individual and collective rights, he arbitrarily rejects the concept of *collective human rights* while according considerable weight to *the collective social good*. The concept of collective human rights, he believes, is especially dangerous when it is proposed as a *prerequisite* for other human rights.[24] But it cannot plausibly be denied that there are collective preconditions for the protection of individual human rights, and that, while collective rights may be dangerous for individual human rights, it may be important to recognize collective human rights as the preconditions for other human rights.

Donnelly and Gewirth both attempt to escape the implicit relativism of Raz's conception of rights. Donnelly, however, fails to maintain consistently the priority of individual human rights over the collective good, or to acknowledge that, whatever their dangers, some collective human rights are a precondition for individual ones. Gewirth for his part consistently treats collective rights as derivative from individual human rights, but does so only by implausibly claiming that a liberal conception of agency is presupposed by all moralities. The inadequacy of both positions highlights the need for a coherent account and an effective reconciliation of individual and collective human rights. We must now see whether this is possible.

Collective Human Rights

Van Dyke maintains that doctrines that recognize only individual rights are not universally relevant to contemporary political problems. Many societies are characterized by radical cultural heterogeneity and can function only on the basis of collective rights. States have collective rights. Sub-state collectivities may rightly become states and they do not acquire moral rights only when they become states.[25] Liberal theory accords collective rights to nation-states but not to nations without states. However, nation-states have rights because they protect interests. Collectivities within nation-states have rights for the same reason, he concludes.[26]

Equally, we could argue, collective rights may be necessary to protect individual rights. The individualistic, egalitarian form of democracy in ethnically plural societies may lead to the violation of the human rights of members of minority collectivities.[27] The targets of many of the worst human-rights violations since 1945 have been ethnic groups as such.[28] These violations are often conceived by the perpetrators and perceived by the victims in collective terms. Victim-groups often plausibly believe that such collective problems require collective solutions. Since the problem consists of attacks on groups, the solution requires the defence of groups. Since the injustice is

---

[24] Donnelly, *Universal Human Rights*, pp. 146–7.

[25] V. Van Dyke, 'The individual, the state and ethnic communities in political theory', *World Politics*, 29 (1976–77), 343–369, pp. 355, 357, 364, 367; Van Dyke, *Human Rights, Ethnicity, and Discrimination*, pp. 195, 207–8; Van Dyke, 'Collective entities and moral rights: problems in liberal-democratic thought', *Journal of Politics*, 44 (1982), 21–40, p. 25.

[26] Van Dyke, *Human Rights, Ethnicity, and Discrimination*, pp. 119, 207.

[27] Van Dyke, *Human Rights, Ethnicity, and Discrimination*, pp. 14–6, 129, 205, 206, 219, 222–3; 'Collective entities and moral rights', p. 24.

[28] T. R. Gurr and J. R. Scarritt, 'Minorities at risk: a global survey', *Human Rights Quarterly*, 11 (1989), 380.

promoted by hostile attitudes towards groups, the solution requires the promotion of the dignity of groups.[29] This argument locates the human-rights problematic not only in individual–state relations but also in the relations among groups and in state–group relations.

If collectivities have rights, they surely have the right to exist. General Assembly Resolution 96 (I) declared genocide to be 'a denial of the right of existence of entire human groups'. The UN Genocide Convention is intended to protect groups from physical destruction. However, if groups have the right to exist, they surely have the right to be protected from economic and cultural destruction.[30] Yet cultural groups have no right to state support if their decline is the outcome only of a set of free choices. Whether they have a right to protection from the results of previous assimilationist policies is not certain.[31] Rights of such groups to state aid are certainly subject to the condition that protection of their culture does not violate important rights of others.[32]

If we look at actual practice, we can see a widespread recognition of collective rights, as well as the difficulties which they pose. States often adopt policies, such as affirmative action or positive discrimination, to provide special advantages to members of groups that have suffered from historic injustice. Such policies accord priority to the collective rights of favoured groups over individual rights to equality of opportunity of those who are not members of these groups.[33] These are collective-rights policies of which only some individual members of the favoured collectivities are the beneficiaries. They have generally been accepted as permitted, if not required by human-rights principles.

The interests of collectivities may justify special representation in government, even though this violates the principle of individual equality of citizenship. The constitutions of many ethnically divided societies provide for proportional ethnic representation. These are designed to protect the individual human rights of members of minority groups, to protect collective interests of such groups, and to maintain peace.[34] Similar collective rights are recognized where constitutions provide for political devolution to sub-state regions in which national minorities are regional majorities.[35] A dilemma arises when a community that has a plausible rights-claim to self-government to protect some important rights of its members has political traditions which

[29] R. Kuptana, 'The universality of human rights and indigenous peoples: new approaches for the next millennium', Rights and Humanity Roundtable, *Strengthening Commitment to the Universality of Human Rights* (Amman, Jordan, April 1993), pp. 4, 10.

[30] Van Dyke, *Human Rights, Ethnicity, and Discrimination*, pp. 20, 84, 130; V. Van Dyke, 'Justice as fairness: for groups?', *American Political Science Review*, 69 (1975), 607–614, p. 609.

[31] Thornberry, *International Law*, Part II, pp. 176–7; 'The UN Declaration on the rights of persons belonging to national or ethnic, religious and linguistic minorities: background, analysis and observations', in Phillips and Rosas (eds), *The UN Minority Rights Declaration*, pp. 22–3; D. Sanders, 'Collective rights', *Human Rights Quarterly*, 13 (1991), 370; Van Dyke, *Human Rights, Ethnicity, and Discrimination*, pp. 80–1.

[32] Sanders, 'Collective rights', p. 378; J. Waldron, 'Minority cultures and the cosmopolitan alternative', *University of Michigan Journal of Law Reform*, 35 (1992), 751–93.

[33] Van Dyke, *Human Rights, Ethnicity, and Discrimination*, pp. 134–6, 153–4, 157–8.

[34] Van Dyke, *Human Rights, Ethnicity, and Discrimination*, pp. 10–1, 14–5, 26–8, 55–6, 76–7, 96–7, 101, 125–6, 139.

[35] V. Van Dyke, 'Human rights and the rights of groups', *American Journal of Political Science*, 18 (1974), pp. 730, 734–5.

violate some other human rights, including the equal right to political participation.[36]

Recent proposals for the recognition of peoples' rights to development, peace, a satisfactory environment, etc., are undoubtedly aimed at protecting important human interests, but they also raise several conceptual problems: the subjects of the rights are uncertain; potential conflicts between peoples' rights and individual human rights are not addressed; and the holders and the nature of the correlative duties are unclear. The formulation of these rights may have the merit of drawing attention to the structural dimensions of human-rights violations, but it is conceptually unsatisfactory and potentially dangerous insofar as it encourages states to violate individual human rights in the name of people's rights.[37]

The problems raised by some collective rights-claims, however, do not refute the case for the recognition of the concept of collective human rights. Van Dyke argues that liberal democracies in fact recognize collective rights and they are right to do so because collective rights may be necessary to protect individual rights and collective interests, and to maintain peace among groups. He calls for a balance between individual and collective rights, but his empirical and pragmatic approach to rights leaves the supporting theory unclear. Can we identify any principle(s) to help determine how this balance should be struck?

Raz suggested that the most fundamental human interest is in the quality of life. One important element in the quality of life is well-being, which refers to the goodness of a life *from the point of view of the person living it*.[38] Kymlicka argues similarly that the value of human lives derives not only from their conformity to external standards of the good but also from the beliefs of the individuals who lead them that they are good. Communities are necessary to good individual lives, but individuals must have some autonomy from the communities of which they are members to choose specific forms of good life.[39]

Individuals *have* autonomy (i.e., the capacity to choose) because community cultures are not fixed and homogeneous, and there are often internal differences over their interpretation. Individuals *should have* autonomy (i.e., the right to choose) because communities can be oppressive. Communities are also often stratified. Individuals who are required to conform to the community are required to conform to the wills of those with the most power in the community. It is obviously question-begging to assume that this power is legitimate.[40]

Individuals have a fundamental interest in leading good lives, and in those rights necessary to good lives, including the right to live in communities that support good lives. The rights of individuals should be limited by the duty to

[36] *Native Women's Assn of Canada* v. *Canada, Dominion Law Reports* (Fourth Series), 95 (1993), 106–27.

[37] Crawford, *The Rights of Peoples.*

[38] Raz, *The Morality of Freedom*, p. 289.

[39] W. Kymlicka, *Liberalism, Community and Culture* (Oxford, Clarendon, 1989), pp. 10–11; *Contemporary Political Philosophy: an Introduction* (Oxford, Clarendon, 1990), pp. 203–5, 207–9, 210–1; 'Liberalism, individualism, and minority rights' in A. C. Hutchinson and L. J. M. Green (eds), *Law and the Community: the End of Individualism?* (Toronto, Carswell, 1989), pp. 188–94, 197–8.

[40] Kymlicka, *Liberalism, Community and Culture*, pp. 89, 95; *Contemporary Political Philosophy*, pp. 223–4, 228.

support communities of this kind. Kymlicka argues that communities and their cultures should be protected only for the sake of individuals, but cultures should be protected when such protection is necessary to maintain the basic rights of individuals, and that the protection of group cultures may be inconsistent with an absolute individual right to equal citizenship.[41] Where a set of individuals requires *a particular culture* for its chosen way of life, it has a right to have it protected against certain actions of outsiders. The exercise of certain rights may enable a majority to destroy the culture, and thereby the opportunity for a good life of a minority. Since individual rights are justified by their contribution to good lives, there is here a conflict of rights, and rights that are helpful but not necessary to good lives should yield to rights that are necessary.[42] Some restriction of the individual rights of insiders may also be justified to prevent actions that would undermine communities which are necessary for autonomous choices. What makes this justification of community restriction of individual rights liberal is that its purpose is to protect a rights-supporting community.[43]

The Problem of Toleration

Kymlicka proposes a liberal theory of collective rights. It is liberal because it assumes that individuals have an interest in autonomy. It recognizes collective rights because it holds that such rights may be necessary conditions of individual autonomy. The theory is attractive because it provides a clearer and more coherent solution than any rival to the problem of reconciling collective and individual human rights. The collective rights that Kymlicka defends are human rights because they are grounded in the same *individual* human interest in self-determination that grounds individual human rights.

The liberal theory of collective rights has, however, been criticized for endorsing cultural imperialism and thereby violating the liberal principle of toleration. Liberal societies have been historically imperialistic, and those who are still fighting the results of liberal imperialism sometimes characterize the vocabulary of human rights as an alien discourse. Subject peoples, it is said, are forced to use the master's conceptual weapons to combat the master's domination. Indigenous peoples, for example, appeal to the discourse of human rights, but only because the terms of discourse are themselves set by liberal hegemony. From the point of view of the oppressed, oppression can be adequately characterized only in terms of their own cultures. The discourse of individual rights subverts collectivist cultures. Liberal societies may be 'tolerant', but dominant liberalism sets the terms of toleration. The discourses of liberal rights and those of non-liberal communities are incommensurable, and thus the imposition of the former is part of the liberal imperialist project.[44]

---

[41] Kymlicka, *Liberalism, Community and Culture*, pp. 24, 64–6, 78, 80, 82, 162–3, 165–6, 175, 177–8, 231, 254; 'Liberalism, individualism, and minority rights', pp. 193–4, 196–8, 200, 202.

[42] Kymlicka, *Liberalism, Community and Culture*, p. 226.

[43] Kymlicka, *Liberalism, Community and Culture*, pp. 151, 169–71, 189, 200, 239–40, 242; *Contemporary Political Philosophy*, p. 232.

[44] B. Parekh, 'Decolonizing liberalism' in A. Shtromas (ed.), *The End of 'Isms?* (Oxford, Blackwell, 1994), pp. 85–103; M. E. Turpel, 'Aboriginal peoples and the Canadian *Charter*: interpretive monopolies, cultural differences', *Canadian Human Rights Yearbook*, 6 (1989–90), 3–45.

This argument is too strong. It treats pre-colonial cultures as authentic and considers appeals to human rights as distortions imposed by liberal hegemony. In fact imperialism produces various responses in traditional communities, and it is arbitrary to treat only the most conservative as authentic. The liberal theory of collective human rights may be 'alien' to traditionalists, but it may be well suited to protect the collective interests of communities and the fundamental interests of individuals under contemporary conditions. The appeal to the value of cultural difference that supports the critique of imperialism can also support the defence of individual rights against oppressive communities.

The anti-liberal critique of collective human rights is not, therefore, a plausible solution to the problem of defending collective and individual interests. Kymlicka's liberal theory of collective rights has, however, also been criticized on the ground that its conception of the good life is too narrow. Some individuals, it is said, may have a conception of the good that requires them to conform to the norms of communities that do not value autonomy. Liberalism promotes an adversarial and competitive culture and it is not irrational to prefer one that is co-operative and solidaristic. Kymlicka requires communities to respect individual autonomy. On this view liberal societies are justified in imposing their values on communities that have chosen other values.[45] Kukathas, in contrast, argues that liberals should tolerate communities that do not value autonomy, provided that they recognize a right of exit and certain basic human rights.[46]

There are two important issues here. The first concerns the right of exit. Individuals have the right to leave communities that they find oppressive. The community certainly has a correlative duty not to use force to prevent an individual from leaving. It is less clear whether the community may use social pressure to the same end. There is no general solution to this problem, since social pressure can vary from allowable friendly persuasion to intolerably oppressive sanctions. The right of exit may also be nullified by the denial of the information and skills that are necessary to make such a choice. Communitarians are likely to emphasize the right of the community to socialize its members into its values.[47] Liberals may well hold that education for autonomy is necessary for an effective right to exit.[48] Liberal theory generates a dilemma because it endorses collective and individual rights here that may be mutually incompatible.

The second issue is that of liberal imperialism. This charge is overstated in two ways. Firstly, the term 'imperialism' implies the self-interested use of overwhelming power, which is not typical of human-rights enforcement. Secondly, supporters of human rights normally seek to defend the weak against the strong. The charge of unjust domination can therefore be turned back by liberals against illiberal communitarians.

---

[45] J. Chaplin, 'How much cultural and religious pluralism can liberalism tolerate?' in J. Horton (ed.), *Liberalism, Multiculturalism and Toleration* (Basingstoke, Macmillan, 1993), pp. 39–46.

[46] C. Kukathas, 'Are there any cultural rights?', *Political Theory*, 20 (1992), 105–39, pp. 113, 114, 116, 120, 122, 124, 128.

[47] C. Kukathas, 'Cultural rights again: a rejoinder to Kymlicka', *Political Theory*, 20 (1992), 674–80, pp. 677–8.

[48] D. Fitzmaurice, 'Liberal neutrality, traditional minorities and eduction' in Horton, *Liberalism, Multiculturalism and Toleration*, pp. 67–8.

It is now commonly suggested that the liberal principle of toleration requires that conflicts between liberals and illiberal communities should be settled by dialogue.[49] However, dialogue is an inadequate solution for two reasons. The first is that it begs the question of the right to participate in the dialogue. The second is that, if the community perpetrates serious violations of the rights of its members, the liberal state should enforce those rights. Anti-imperialist values cannot plausibly be advanced to defend tyrannical communities. Most liberals value individual autonomy and cultural pluralism. Individuals may, however, choose illiberal cultures. The liberal state may intervene in illiberal communities for the sake of individual rights or tolerate a partly illiberal pluralism in order to keep the peace between different communal conceptions of the good.[50]

Liberals from Locke to the UN have held that respect for rights is conducive to peace.[51] Kymlicka, however, objects to the argument that minority rights should be recognized for the sake of peace on the ground that it sacrifices the requirements of justice to those of power and would given the fewest rights to the weakest minorities, who need rights most.[52] It is surely right to distinguish between what is required by power and what by justice. However, peace, too, has a moral value, which derives in part from the fact that human rights are better protected in peace than in war. The dilemma is that giving priority to peace can be a thugs' charter, while giving priority to justice can be utopian. There are, however, empirical grounds for believing that well-judged collective-rights policies are conducive to peace.[53]

The question of collective human rights therefore leads to the familiar problem of toleration in liberal theory. The problem arises because some, though not all, versions of liberalism are committed to a pluralism of values that may conflict with each other.[54] In particular, liberals may be committed to some degree of toleration of communities that do not respect autonomy and human rights. Contemporary liberal theory has not found a coherent resolution of the dilemma of choosing between liberal imperialism and illiberal collaborationism.[55] Raz's value of individual well-being suggests that toleration should be extended to some forms of life in which autonomy is not valued and human rights are imperfectly recognized. This is a liberal principle of toleration because it holds the fundamental interests of individuals to be ultimate values. But the same values suggest that autonomy and individual human rights are normally of the first importance and that liberals should have

[49] Parekh, 'Decolonizing liberalism', p. 103; W. Kymlicka, 'The rights of minority cultures: reply to Kukathas', *Political Theory*, 20 (1992), pp. 143, 145. Kymlicka's position on the enforcement of the liberal rights of individuals in illiberal minority communities is ambiguous. At times he favours judicial enforcement of individual rights, for example to protect women against discrimination: 'Liberalism, individualism, and minority rights', pp. 187–8.

[50] Kukathas, 'Are there are cultural rights?', pp. 112, 117–8; 'Cultural rights again', p. 680.

[51] Locke, *Second Treatise*, para. 224; Thornberry, 'The UN Declaration', pp. 25–6, 36–7; Phillips and Rosas, *The UN Minority Rights Declaration*, p. 123.

[52] Kymlicka, *Liberalism, Community and Culture*, pp. 215–6.

[53] T. R. Gurr, *Minorities at Risk: a Global View of Ethnopolitical Conflicts* (Washington DC, United States Institute of Peace Press, 1993).

[54] G. Crowder, 'Pluralism and liberalism', *Political Studies*, 42 (1994), 293–305; I. Berlin and B. Williams, 'Pluralism and liberalism: a reply', *Political Studies*, 42 (1994), 306–9.

[55] For a strikingly incoherent attempt to resolve this dilemma by a leading liberal philosopher, see Rawls, 'The law of peoples'.

the courage to be intolerant of disregard of these values except when such disregard is necessary to individual well-being.

Conclusions

Collective human rights are rights the bearers of which are collectivities, which are not reducible to, but are consistent with individual human rights, and the basic justification of which is the same as the basic justification of individual human rights. Some human-rights theorists argue either that there are no collective human rights or that there are collective human rights but all such rights are derivative from individual human rights. I have argued that there are non-derivative collective human rights which are justified by the grounding value of the interest that individuals have in the quality of their own lives.

Dworkin has proposed that the ground of those individual rights that should 'trump' ordinary claims of the common good is the right to equal concern and respect.[56] I have argued elsewhere that this is the most plausible ground for the theory of human rights.[57] I wish now to suggest that the right to equal concern and respect is itself grounded on the interest every individual has in the quality of his or her own life. We have seen that the doctrine of human rights and the associated liberal value of autonomy have been criticized on the ground that they fail to recognize that individuals can lead worthy lives in societies which do not recognize the claims of human rights and which do not value autonomy.[58] However, such defences of heteronomous forms of life appeal to principles of concern and respect for persons and of the interest that individuals have in the quality of their lives which are similar to those that form the bases both of individual and collective human rights. The principles that support individual and collective human rights, therefore, make plausible moral claims both in societies that value autonomy and in those that do not, and consequently have considerable cross-cultural force.

The conditions under which, and the forms in which collective human rights should be recognized are, nevertheless, contingent. This is because the conditions under which the recognition of collective rights is necessary to protect individuals are contingent. For example, the interests of individual members of dominant ethnic groups may be adequately protected by their individual human rights. By contrast, the interests of indigenous peoples or of immigrant minorities and those of their individual members may require the protection of collective rights, such as the right to collective cultural goods. The contingency of collective rights does not, however, distinguish them sharply from individual human rights. For, on my account, rights protect value-based interests from threats, and the interests to be protected and the threats from which they are to be protected must be at least in part subject to contingency. The right to privacy is a good example of an individual human right, the precise formulation of which should vary in different circumstances.

Yet collective human rights have important features that distinguish them from individual human rights. Social collectivities are highly complex, and the

---

[56] R. Dworkin, *Taking Rights Seriously* (London, Duckworth, 1977), p. xii.

[57] M. Freeman, 'The philosophical foundations of human rights', *Human Rights Quarterly*, 16 (1994), 491–514.

[58] Kukathas, 'Are there any cultural rights?'; Parekh, 'Decolonizing liberalism', p. 101; Turpel, 'Aboriginal peoples and the Canadian *Charter*', p. 36, footnote 77.

interrelations among collectivities, and between collectivities and individuals, are consequently also very complex. The practice of proclaiming lists of individual rights has been criticized for its insensitivity to the fine grain of social and political life. The project of drafting declarations of collective rights, on which the international community is now embarked, has great potential for conceptual confusion and political danger. The implication of this is not that the concept of collective human rights should be rejected, but that the conceptual and practical relations between collective and individual human rights should be made as clear as possible.

The most difficult problem raised by the concept of collective human rights is how to reconcile the recognition of such rights with individual human rights and other individual human interests, such as the interest in autonomy. Collectivities can violate individual human rights.[59] The recognition of a 'right to identity' that is now associated with minority rights in international relations may be well-intentioned, but is potentially dangerous.[60] For individuals to lead good lives in a complex world, a set of rights more sensitive than the crude 'right of exit' from oppressive groups is required.[61]

This problem is related to another, which is the difficulty of identifying the subject of collective rights. Membership of groups can be fluid and uncertain. International law has experienced great difficulty in defining 'minorities'.[62] Collective identities can be manipulated and/or coercively imposed, and they can form the basis of unjust demands. Liberal individualism has often been characterized as egoistic and collectivism as altruistic. This is quite mistaken, for individualism can emphasize responsibility as well as rights and collectivism can be ruthlessly selfish.[63] Recognition of collective rights may fix collective identities too rigidly and thus oppressively.[64] Identity formation is a complex process, usually involving the interactions of different collectivities and individuals. Communities and cultures are not static, so that the interplay of identity, difference and rights should not be arbitrarily terminated for the sake of some hegemonic interpretation of community.

Collective human rights are, however, not reducible to individual human rights. The right to collective self-determination is not reducible to any set of individual human rights, though it may be *dependent on* and *necessary for* such rights.[65] Liberal individualism has traditionally failed to recognize its own

[59] T. Isaac, 'Individual versus collective rights: aboriginal people and the significance of *Thomas v. Norris*', *Manitoba Law Journal*, 21 (1992), 618–30; S. Poulter, 'Ethnic minority customs, English law and human rights', *International and Comparative Law Quarterly*, 36 (1987), 589–615; Native Women's Association of Canada, Press Statement, *Native Women, The Charter and the Right to Self Government* (Ottawa, 9 May 1992).

[60] Thornberry, 'The UN Declaration', pp. 19, 38; Phillips and Rosas, *The UN Minority Rights Declaration*, pp. 124–5.

[61] Waldron, 'Minority cultures'.

[62] Gurr, *Minorities At Risk*, pp. 10–3; Thornberry, 'The UN Declaration', p. 33.

[63] G. Hofstede, 'Foreword', in U. Kim *et al.* (eds), *Individualism and Collectivism: Theory, Method, and Applications* (Thousand Oaks CA, Sage, 1994), p. xiii.

[64] A. Phillips, 'Democracy and difference: some problems for feminist theory', *Political Quarterly*, 63 (1992), pp. 85, 87; R. G. Wirsing, 'Dimensions of minority protection' in R. G. Wirsing (ed.), *Protection of Ethnic Minorities: Comparative Perspectives* (New York, Pergamon, 1981), pp. 7–8.

[65] Julia Tao has suggested that the right to freedom of the press is a collective right that is not reducible to a set of individual rights: personal communication, 22 September 1994. A similar idea is expressed in Raz, *The Morality of Freedom*.

dependence on the assumption that nation-states have collective rights. This lacuna in liberal-democratic theory is manifested by the problematic status of indigenous peoples, who are *nations without states*, and who have been variously conceptualized by liberal states as alien peoples, as minorities with special rights, and as aggregates of individuals, but rarely with respect for either their collective values or the rights of their individual members. The egalitarianism of both the liberal and republican theories of democracy has also encouraged the neglect or even the oppression of *intra-national minority communities*. These problems have now been recognized in international relations, but international law has so far failed to produce a coherent account of individual and collective rights.

Collective human rights are necessary in some situations for justice and peace. There is, however, a tension between these two objectives of collective-rights policy because the desire for peace may encourage capitulation to collective demands that are unjust. This problem is, however, only one kind of manifestation of the general problem that power is often unjust. This problem lies at the heart of all politics. The theoretical concept of collective human rights cannot solve the practical problems posed by unjust collectivities. It can, however, solve an important problem of political theory, and this may have beneficial practical consequences. Recognition of collective human rights and the reconciliation of collective with individual human rights blur the distinction between individualist and collectivist conceptions of rights. This does not abolish all disagreements of value and policy between individualists and collectivists, but it does create a 'third space' in which supporters of these two kinds of value-system can engage in dialogue, and recognizes the value of both individual autonomy and collective solidarity. The concept of collective human rights, therefore, helps to reconcile the values of liberal universalism and cultural pluralism, and thereby provides a theoretical framework for practical policies that might reconcile justice and peace.

What Future for Economic and
Social Rights?

David Beetham

It is a commonplace of discussions about human rights that economic and social rights, like the poor themselves, occupy a distinctly second class status.[1] When human rights are mentioned, it is typically civil and political rights that spring to mind. When Western governments include the promotion of human rights in their foreign policy goals, it is the freedoms of expression and political association, the right to due process and the protection from state harassment that principally concern them rather than, say, access to the means of livelihood or to basic health care. And when the role of human rights NGOs is discussed, it is the work of organizations such as Amnesty International or civil liberties associations that we tend to think of. By the same token, our paradigm for a human rights violation is state-sponsored torture or 'disappearance' rather than, say, childhood death through malnutrition or preventable disease.

This disparity between the two sets of rights was acknowledged by the UN Committee on Economic, Social and Cultural Rights itself, in its statement to the Vienna World Conference of 1993:

> The shocking reality ... is that states and the international community as a whole continue to tolerate all too often breaches of economic, social and cultural rights which, if they occurred in relation to civil and political rights, would provoke expressions of horror and outrage and would lead to concerted calls for immediate remedial action. In effect, despite the rhetoric, violations of civil and political rights continue to be treated as though they were far more serious, and more patently intolerable, than massive and direct denials of economic, social and cultural rights.[2]

A number of reasons can be advanced as to why this disparity persists, despite the repeated assertions of human rights protagonists that the human rights agenda is 'indivisible'. One reason is intellectual. Ever since the Universal Declaration of 1948, the idea of social and economic rights has been subjected to sustained criticism. It is argued, typically, that the list of so-called 'rights' in the Declaration and in the subsequent International Covenant on Economic, Social and Cultural Rights (hereafter ICESCR) can at most be a statement of aspirations or goals rather than properly of *rights*. For an entitlement to be a human right it must satisfy a number of conditions: it must be fundamental

---

[1] This article will concentrate on economic and social, rather than cultural, rights for reasons of space. I am grateful to the other contributors, especially Susan Mendus, for comments on an earlier draft.

[2] UN Doc. E/C.12/1992/2, p. 83.

and universal; it must in principle be definable in justiciable form; it should be clear who has the duty to uphold or implement the right; and the responsible agency should possess the capacity to fulfil its obligation. The rights specified in the Covenant do not satisfy these conditions, it is argued.[3]

Indeed, they would seem to fail on every count. They confuse the fundamental with the merely desirable, or that which is specific to the advanced economies (holidays with pay, free higher education, the right of everyone to the continuous improvement of living conditions),[4] Even those that are fundamental cannot in principle be definable in justiciable form. At what level can the deprivation of nutrition, sanitation or health care be sufficient to trigger legal redress? And whose duty is it to see that these 'rights' are met – national governments, international institutions, the UN itself? If it is governments, can they be required to provide what they do not have the means or capacity to deliver? Since 'ought' entails 'can', since to have an assignable duty entails a realistic possibility of being able to fulfil it, can the positive requirements of the Covenant be reasonably expected of impoverished and less than fully autonomous regimes? While we may reasonably require them to *refrain* from torturing their citizens, it is not obvious that we can equally require them to guarantee them all a livelihood, adequate accommodation and a healthy environment. Moreover for them to do so, it is contended, would require a huge paternalist and bureaucratic apparatus and a corresponding extension of compulsory taxation, both of which would interfere with another basic right, the right to freedom.[5]

Such are the arguments that have been repeatedly advanced against the idea of economic and social rights. And it must be said that these arguments have had a certain echo within UN procedures themselves, with the initial division between the two separate human rights covenants, the weaker monitoring procedures of the ICESCR, its distinctive formula that states should 'take steps' towards the 'progressive achievement' of the rights according to available resources, and the distribution of responsibility for the ESCR agenda between different specialist agencies (FAO, WHO, UNICEF, UNESCO, ILO, UNDP), as well as a human rights committee.[6]

---

[3] See M. Cranston, 'Human rights, real and supposed', in D. D. Raphael (ed.), *Political Theory and the Rights of Man* (London, Macmillan, 1967), pp. 43–52; M. Cranston, *What Are Human Rights?* (London, Bodley Head, 1973). The most frequent objections are summarized in P. Alston and G. Quinn, 'The nature and scope of states parties' obligations under the ICESCR', *Human Rights Quarterly*, 9 (1987), 157–229, pp. 157–60; A. Eide, 'The realisation of social and economic rights and the minimum threshold approach', *Human Rights Law Journal*, 10 (1989), 35–51; G. J. H. van Hoof, 'The legal nature of economic, social and cultural rights: a rebuttal of some traditional views' in P. Alston and K. Tomasevski (eds), *The Right to Food* (Dordrecht, Martinus Nijhoff, 1990), pp. 97–110.

[4] These examples are from the ICESCR articles 7, 11 and 13 in I. Brownlie (ed.), *Basic Documents on Human Rights* (Oxford, Oxford University Press, 3rd ed., 1992), pp. 114–24.

[5] This last is a standard neo-liberal objection; see R. Nozick, *Anarchy, State and Utopia* (Oxford, Blackwell, 1974), pp. 30–3.

[6] For the establishment of the committee, see P. Alston, 'Out of the abyss: the challenges confronting the new UN Committee on Economic Social and Cultural Rights', *Human Rights Quarterly*, 9 (1987), 332–81. A repeated complaint of the Committee since its inception has been 'the continuing separation of human rights and social development issues' in UN development programmes. See the Statement by the Committee of May 1994 to the World Summit on Social Development (typescript), p. 1.

—However, it would be mistaken to attribute the disparity of status between the two sets of rights to intellectual and institutional factors alone, and not also to political ones. There is a general agreement among commentators on economic and social rights that for them to be effectively realized would require a redistribution of power and resources, both within countries and between them. It is hardly surprising that many governments should be less than enthusiastic about such an agenda, and should resort to the alibi of 'circumstances beyond their control', and to the ready-made language of 'taking steps', 'available resources', etc., of the ICESCR itself. Indeed, this very language, and the procedural limitations of the Covenant, owe as much to political inspiration as to intellectual or institutional requirements.[7]

While the above could have been written at almost any time during the past thirty years, developments from the 1980s onwards have made the position of economic and social rights even more precarious. First are developments in the international economy itself. The normal processes of the international market, which tend to benefit the already advantaged, have been intensified by the effects of deregulation and the cutting of welfare provision, to the further disadvantage of the deprived in many societies. There has indeed been a politics of redistribution at work, but it has been a redistribution from the poor to the well-off, within and between countries: an upwards flood rather than a 'trickle down'.[8] In the process the capacity of governments to control their own economic destinies has been significantly eroded, as collective choice has been displaced by market forces, and economic policy has been conducted under the scrutiny of what 'average opinion' in financial circles 'believes average opinion to be'.[9]

A second development has been the demise of the USSR and the Communist model as a viable alternative to capitalism. Although in theory the end of the Cold War could have provided an opportunity for ending the sterile opposition between the two sets of human rights, in practice it has reinforced the priorities of the USA, the country which has been most consistently opposed to the idea of economic and social rights.[10] And the more general loss of credibility of socialism in any form has deprived the poor everywhere of an organizing ideology for political struggle and the politics of redistribution. This is not to mention the more specific effects that the end of Communism has had for the peoples of the former Soviet Union and other Communist states: the collapse of social security systems, and the extension of the zone of civil war to include the Balkans and central Asia.

In face of this depressing litany of developments, two alternative responses are possible. One is to conclude that the incorporation of economic and social rights in the human rights canon is simply spitting in the wind, when hundreds of millions suffer from malnutrition and vulnerability to disease and

---

[7] H. Shue, *Basic Rights* (Princeton, Princeton University Press, 1980), p. 158.

[8] For the widening global gap between rich and poor see United Nations Development Programme (UNDP), *Human Development Report 1992* (New York, Oxford University Press, 1992), ch. 3; for the UK see Rowntree Foundation, *Inquiry Into Income and Wealth*, 2 vols (York, Joseph Rowntree Foundation, 1995), vol. 2, ch. 3.

[9] J. Eatwell, 'A global world demands economic coordination', *New Economy*, 1 (1994), 146–150, p. 148.

[10] The USA has still not ratified the ICESCR.

starvation.[11] Worse, it is an insult to them to insist on their 'human rights' when there is no realistic prospect of these being upheld. It was precisely for confusing the promise with its actualization, the desire to have a right with having one, that Bentham denounced the fictional 'rights' of the French Declaration: 'want is not supply, hunger is not bread'.[12] It is one thing to describe the victim of an armed robbery as having been deprived of his or her rights, when these are normally upheld and legal recourse is available; quite another where such insecurity has become the norm. And this is the situation with food security in many parts of the world.

The opposite response is to insist that human rights most urgently need asserting and defending, both theoretically and practically, where they are most denied. Indeed the language of rights only makes sense at all in a context where basic requirements are vulnerable to standard threats (could we imagine a 'right' to clean air in a pre-industrial society?). The human rights agenda has therefore necessarily an aspirational or promotional dimension; but it is not mere rhetoric. The purpose of the two covenants and their monitoring apparatus is to cajole state signatories into undertaking the necessary domestic policy and legislation to ensure their citizens the protection of their rights in practice. This promotional aspect of the human rights agenda is not only addressed to those whose responsibility it is to secure the rights in question. It also serves as a legitimation for the deprived in their struggles to realize their rights on their own behalf, by providing a set of internationally validated standards to which they can appeal.

The purpose of this paper is to offer a defence of the second of these responses against the first. More particularly, it seeks to provide a defence of economic and social rights as human rights against the many different objections levelled against them. The first section deals with their definition and justification; the second outlines a theory of corresponding duties; the third assesses objections on the grounds of practicality; the final section evaluates the purpose of the economic and social rights agenda in an imperfect world.

Definition and Justification

The idea of economic and social rights as *human* rights expresses the moral intuition that, in a world rich in resources and the accumulation of human knowledge, everyone ought to be guaranteed the basic means for sustaining life, and that those denied these are victims of a fundamental injustice. Expressing this intuition in the form of human rights both gives the deprived the strongest possible claim to that of which they are deprived, and emphasizes the duty of responsible parties to uphold or help them meet their entitlement.

Those who do not share the intuition articulated above, or who believe that it conflicts with a more fundamental one they hold, are unlikely to be persuaded by anything written in this paper. Many who do share it, however,

---

[11] For a recent assessment of global poverty see World Bank, *World Development Report 1990* (New York, Oxford University Press for World Bank, 1990).
[12] J. Bentham, 'A critical examination of the Declaration of Rights' in B. Parekh (ed.), *Bentham's Political Thought* (London, Croom Helm, 1973), pp. 257–90, p. 269.

are unconvinced that the framework of human rights is the most appropriate vehicle for giving it expression. Here we might distinguish between strategic and specific objections. 'Strategic' objections are those which urge the superiority of an alternative moral framework for giving effect to the above intuition: the theory of justice,[13] say, or of Kantian obligation,[14] or of basic needs,[15] or human development.[16] There is not the space here to explore all these possible alternatives. Suffice to say, however, that the contrast between these other frameworks and a human rights perspective has been considerably overstated. Human rights theory itself embodies a theory of justice (albeit a partial or incomplete one);[17] it entails an account of obligation and of duties corresponding to the rights claimed;[18] and it presupposes a conception of human needs and human development.[19] Moreover, among strategic considerations for embracing a particular moral framework, it is not evident that philosophical claims should have *sole* place, to the exclusion of institutional or political considerations. This is a point I shall return to at the end of the paper.

Here I shall concentrate on what I call 'specific' objections to economic and social rights, which question whether they can meet the requirements of a human right, for the kinds of reason outlined earlier. If to have a right means to have a justifiable entitlement to x (the object of the right), by virtue of y (possession of the relevant attribute), against z (the agent with the corresponding obligation to meet the entitlement);[20] then this formula establishes both the criteria that have to be satisfied for a human right, and also an order of argument for the consideration of objections. Starting with questions of definition and justification, we can proceed to an examination of the corresponding duties, and of their practicability. Although these

[13] Although John Rawls' theory of justice (J. Rawls, *A Theory of Justice*, Oxford, Oxford University Press, 1972) is a rights based theory, there is doubt among human rights theorists whether his 'difference principle' of social distribution provides a sufficiently robust defence of basic economic and social rights, in the light of its lower lexical ordering, and the fact that it can be interpreted to justify 'trickle down' economics, or merely marginal improvements in a desperate situation. 'The Rawlsian difference principle can be fulfilled while people continue to drown, but with less and less water over their heads', Shue, *Basic Rights*, p. 128. For his part, however, Rawls agrees with Shue that 'subsistence rights are basic', since they are a condition of exercising liberty: J. Rawls, 'The law of peoples' in S. Shute and S. Hurley (eds), *On Human Rights* (New York, Basic, 1993), pp. 41–82, note 26.

[14] Onora O'Neill rejects the language of 'manifesto rights' and the 'rancorous rhetoric of rights' for its lack of underpinning by a theory of obligation. O. O'Neill, *Faces of Hunger* (London, Allen and Unwin, 1986), chs 6 and 7.

[15] Paul Streeten rejects giving basic needs the status of human rights on the grounds of scarcity of resources. See 'Appendix: basic needs and human rights', in Paul Streeten and associates, *First Things First: Meeting Basic Needs in Developing Countries* (New York, Oxford University Press for World Bank, 1981), pp. 184–192.

[16] UNDP distinguishes the material dimensions of human development from human rights, which it interprets exclusively as civil and political; see e.g. UNDP, *Human Development Report 1992*, p. 9.

[17] Its principle can be simply stated: securing basic economic and social rights takes priority over other distributional principles, whatever these happen to be.

[18] Shue, *Basic Rights*, ch. 2.

[19] Johan Galtung, *Human Rights in Another Key* (Cambridge, Polity, 1994), ch. 3; F. Stewart, 'Basic needs strategies, human rights and the right to development', *Human Rights Quarterly*, 11 (1989), 347–74.

[20] This is Gewirth's well-known formulation, A. Gewirth, *Human Rights* (Chicago, University of Chicago Press, 1982), p. 2.

elements are all interconnected, they can be treated separately for analytical purposes.

So I start with the definition of social and economic rights. Can they be defined in such a way that they meet the criteria for a human right of being fundamental, universal and clearly specifiable? That they should be *fundamental* conforms to the idea of the human rights agenda as being to protect the means to a minimally decent, rather than maximally comfortable, life; and to the perception that the seriousness of this purpose is compromised if the list of rights confuses the essential with the merely desirable.[21] The same conclusion can be reached from the standpoint of *universality*: human rights should be applicable to all, regardless of the level of development a country has reached. That they should be clearly *specifiable* follows from the fairly elementary requirement that we should be able to ascertain whether a right has been upheld or not, and when it has been infringed or violated.

From the standpoint of these criteria the text of the ICESCR suffers from its attempt to define the rights in a way that, on the one hand, serves to protect the social achievements of the advanced economies, and use them as a standard for best practice; and, on the other, to prescribe a necessary minimum that is within the capacity of all. This uneasy conjunction of a minimum and maximum agenda is apparent in many of the articles (e.g. Article 7 on conditions of work, Article 13 on education), and the language of 'progressive achievement as resources allow' stems partly from the attempt to bridge the two. With hindsight it might have been better if the original text had concentrated on establishing a minimum agenda, while leaving it to regional charters to develop their own formulation of rights which might be more ambitious than, yet consistent with, the universal one.

It should be said that the body charged with monitoring the Covenant (since 1987 the UN Committee on ESCR) is itself painfully aware of this problem, and has set itself the task of defining a minimum 'core' under each right, which should be guaranteed to all regardless of circumstances. As its current Chairman, Philip Alston wrote: 'The fact that there must exist such a "core" would seem to be a logical implication of the use of the terminology of rights ... Each right must therefore give rise to an absolute minimum entitlement, in the absence of which a state party is to be considered to be in violation of its obligations'.[22] This process of 'norm clarification' on the part of the Committee, and the monitoring procedures associated with it, constitute a serious attempt to deflect some of the recurrent objections to the ICESCR on the grounds of its lack of universalizability.

What, then, should be the minimum 'core' of economic and social rights? This question cannot be answered independently of the question of how human rights in general come to be *justified*. Such justification requires a number of different steps. Its starting point lies in identifying the grounds on which all humans deserve equal respect, or merit treating with equal dignity, whatever

---

[21] J. W. Nickel, *Making Sense of Human Rights* (Berkeley, University of California Press, 1987), ch. 3.

[22] Alston, 'Out of the abyss', pp. 352–3. Compare the pronouncement of the Committee itself in its 5th Session: 'A minimum core obligation to ensure the satisfaction of, at the very least, minimum essential levels of each right is incumbent upon every state party ... If the Covenant were to be read in such a way as not to establish such a core obligation, it would be largely deprived of its *raison d'être.*' UN Doc. E/C.12/1990/8, p. 86.

the differences between them. Although these grounds are contestable,[23] reference to some feature of distinctive human agency is unavoidable, such as: the capacity for reflective moral judgement, for determining the good for one's life, both individually and in association with others, for choosing goals or projects and seeking to realize them, and so on. These can be summed up in a concept such as 'reflective moral and purposive agency'.[24] A further step would then be to specify the most general preconditions for exercising human agency over a lifetime, whatever the particular goals, values or conceptions of the good that might be embraced. Such preconditions include physical integrity or security, the material means of existence, the development of capacities, and the enjoyment of basic liberties.[25] These necessary conditions of human agency constitute the basis of human rights.[26]

If on the one side, then, the specification of any list of human rights takes its justification from the general conditions for effective human agency, on the other side it is also grounded in a distinctively modern experience, both of the characteristic threats to the realization of these conditions, and of the means required to protect against such threats. It is the potentially (and historically experienced) absolute and arbitrary power of the modern state that has come to determine much of the content of the civil and political rights agenda. It is the insecurity generated by the unfettered market economy, and the threats to health produced by widespread urbanization and industrialization, that have likewise determined much of the economic and social rights agenda. At the same time, it is the historically acquired knowledge of the means to protect against these threats, that enables the human rights agenda to be defined as rights, rather than as utopia.

This conjunction of the universal with the historically specific helps explain some of the confusion about the universality of human rights. They are universal in that they rest on assumptions about needs and capacities common to all, and the rights apply to all humans alive now. Yet they are also distinctly historical in that any declaration of human rights has only been possible in the modern era. At a theoretical level, the idea of human rights could only be entertained once the status distinctions and privileges of traditional society had been eroded, and people could be defined as individuals independently of their birth-determined social statuses. From this viewpoint, an anti-discrimination clause can be seen as the most fundamental of human rights articles. At a practical level, it was precisely the same breakdown of traditional society, with its personalized guarantees and mutual responsibilities, that made the agenda of human rights *necessary*, in face of the depersonalizing forces of the modern state and market economy. Those who complain that their traditional societies managed perfectly well without any conception of human rights may be perfectly correct. It does not follow that they can continue without them, given the globalization of the forces that have made them both possible and necessary.

[23] M. Freeman, 'The philosophical foundations of human rights', *Human Rights Quarterly*, 16 (1994), 491–514.

[24] See A. Gewirth, 'The basis and content of human rights', in Gewirth, *Human Rights*, ch. 1.

[25] Gewirth summarizes these as 'freedom and well-being', Gewirth, *Human Rights*, p. 47.

[26] For a defence of this general structure of argument against both neo-liberals and communitarians, see R. Plant, *Modern Political Thought* (Oxford, Blackwell, 1991), chs 3 and 7; also L. Doyal and I. Gough, *A Theory of Human Need* (London, Macmillan, 1991), chs 1–5.

In the light of the above, a minimum agenda of economic and social rights will aim to secure those basic material conditions for human agency that modern experience has shown to be both necessary and effective. These are not that remarkable actually. Both the defenders of a 'basic needs' approach within development economics and human rights theorists would converge on a minimum core of rights such as the following: the right to food of an adequate nutritional value, to clothing, to shelter, to basic (or primary) health care, clean water and sanitation, and to education to at least primary level.[27] Although there may be other things to be added to this list (see below), it provides the foundation, together with the crucial principle of non-discriminatory access. All of those mentioned above concern the satisfaction of elementary physical needs, except for education; here the evidence suggests that the latter is a direct prerequisite for the others, since, in the absence of knowledge about what causes illness, or how to make the best use of available food, an otherwise adequate supply may prove insufficient to meet basic needs.[28]

If the rights in the above list can meet the criteria of being both fundamental and universally applicable, can they also meet the test of specificity, such that it is possible to specify a level below which a given right can be said to be denied? Even the level of necessary nutrition, which seems to be the most objectively definable, will vary according to person and circumstance. The level of clothing or shelter needed will vary according to the climate. And the need for health care and education, as is well known, is almost infinitely expandable as knowledge increases. Here there will inevitably be a *certain* arbitrariness about defining the required standard for a human right as that of primary health care and education, although that standard is based upon a general agreement that these constitute significant thresholds. That some minimum standards need to be established, however, is necessary to the idea of a 'core' of rights, and to the assumption of the UN Committee on ESCR that such rights can increasingly be justiciable, and amenable to individual petition and complaint.[29] In any case, the methods needed are perhaps not that complex for determining when girls are discriminated against in access to education, when children die through lack of food or clean water, or when people sleep rough because they have no access to housing; nor for deciding on the kind of comparative statistics – on infant mortality rates, life expectancy rates, literacy rates, school attendance rates, etc., – which can serve as evidence of rights denials.

On the supposition, then, that a minimum core of economic and social rights can be given appropriate specificity, they can also be defined in sufficiently general terms to allow differing approaches to their realization, whether through market or non-market mechanisms, or various mixtures of the two. The literature on basic needs from the outset emphasized its ideological neutrality as between politico-economic systems, and supported this with evidence that a profile of basic needs was being met by a number of developing

[27] Shue, *Basic Rights*, pp. 22–9; F. Stewart, *Planning to Meet Basic Needs* (London, Macmillan, 1985), chs 1 and 6; Streeten, *First Things First*, ch. 6; UNDP, *World Development Report 1992*, 'criteria of human deprivation', pp. 132–3. For a fuller list, which also includes the above, see Doyal and Gough, *A Theory of Human Need*, ch. 10.

[28] Streeten, *First Things First*, pp. 134–5. All these items are in fact interdependent requirements for health.

[29] For the Committee's proposal for an individual complaints procedure, see Annex IV of the 7th Session of the Committee, UN Doc. E/C. 12/1992/2, pp. 87–108.

countries with market-led, state-run and mixed economies, and at different levels of development.[30] What mattered, the argument ran, was that meeting basic needs should be targeted as a specific goal of policy, and not be assumed to follow as an automatic by-product of aggregate economic growth. In similar vein, the UN Committee on ESCR has insisted that 'in terms of political and economic systems the Covenant is neutral, and its principles cannot accurately be described as being predicated exclusively upon the need for, or desirability of, a socialist or capitalist system, or a mixed, centrally planned or laissez-faire economy, or upon any other particular approach'.[31] In legal terms, the duties undertaken by parties to the Covenant are duties of 'result' more than duties of 'conduct', of ends more than means.[32]

However, the ideological neutrality of the Covenant is more apparent than real, in two key respects. First, from a human rights perspective, it cannot be a matter of indifference if the institutions involved in the attainment of basic economic rights are also systematically engaged in the violation of civil and political liberties, as was typical of ruling Communist parties. The argument that one set of rights has to be sacrificed for the other is now thoroughly discredited; and historical experience shows that economic and social rights themselves cannot be guaranteed over time, if people are deprived of information about the effects of economic policies, and have no influence over their formulation or implementation.[33] It is in this sense that the two sets of rights are 'indivisible', and that democracy constitutes a necessary condition for the sustained realization of economic and social rights.[34] On the other hand, as the UN Committee insists, 'there is no basis whatsoever to assume that the realization of economic, social and cultural rights will necessarily result from the achievement of civil and political rights', or that democracy can be a *sufficient* condition for their realization, in the absence of specifically targeted policies.[35]

The insistence on the indivisibility of the two sets of rights should lay to rest the charge often levelled against the Covenant that it presents the bearers of economic and social rights as the passive recipients of paternalist state welfare, rather than as active providers for their own needs; and should discourage any simple division between 'welfare' and 'liberty' rights. Apart from any necessary provision of collective goods by public authority, most people prefer to have the opportunity to meet their own needs through their own efforts, whether through access to land for subsistence farming, through a fair price for the goods they produce, or through a sufficient wage for the labour they supply. It is only in the event of their inability to provide for themselves that 'welfare' in a narrow sense becomes necessary. By the same token, people also require the

[30] Stewart, *Planning to Meet Basic Needs*, pp. 70–3; Streeten, *First Things First*, ch. 5.

[31] UN Doc. E/C.12/1990/8, p. 85.

[32] For a discussion of this distinction see G. S. Goodwin-Gill, 'Obligations of conduct and result' in Alston and Tomasevski, *The Right to Food*, pp. 111–8.

[33] R. E. Goodin, 'The development-rights trade-off: some unwarranted economic and political assumptions', *Universal Human Rights*, 1 (1979), 31–42; R. Howard, 'The full-belly thesis: should economic rights take priority over civil and political rights?', *Human Rights Quarterly*, 5 (1987), 467–90.

[34] The UN Committee is thus somewhat disingenuous when it claims that the ICESCR 'neither requires nor precludes any particular form of government', since it immediately proceeds to add: 'provided only that it is democratic'! UN Doc. E/C.12/1990/8, p. 85.

[35] UN Doc. E/C.12/1992/2, pp. 82–3.

freedom to organize collectively to protect and improve the conditions for the provision of their needs, whether as groups of peasants, the landless, the self-employed, the unemployed, as well as wage workers. In this context, the more narrowly defined trade union rights of the ICESCR can be seen as a special case of the general right of association protected under the International Covenant on Civil and Political Rights; here more than anywhere there is an overlap between the two, and the case for their separation is most clearly indefensible.

If on one side, then, the achievement in practice of economic and social rights as *human* rights can now be seen to exclude the instrumentality of a command economy, on the other it is also incompatible with untrammelled private property rights and the unrestricted freedom of the market. Certainly the rights discussed above entail some property rights; and both private property and the market are useful instruments through which basic economic needs can be met. But the institution of private property, which depends upon a socially recognized principle of exclusion or limitation of freedom, cannot be defended as a 'natural' right, any more than the market can be construed as a 'natural' rather than a socially constructed and validated institution.[36] If their primary justification as social institutions lies in their effectiveness in securing people's means of livelihood, then their justifiable limitation (of accumulation and use in the one, of freedom to exchange in the other) must lie at the point of their failure to do so. To this extent the agenda of economic and social rights is necessarily at odds with a neo-liberal approach to the market and private property.[37]

In this section I have sought to defend a minimum agenda of economic and social rights which will meet the criteria of being fundamental, universal and specifiable. The agenda comprises a list of rights necessary to meet basic human needs (rights to food, clothing, shelter, primary health care, clean water and sanitation, and primary education), combined with the right of association necessary to the collective protection and promotion of these rights by the bearers themselves. I have also argued that, though much of the literature presents the achievement of these rights as ideologically neutral, or non institution-specific, their realization is in practice incompatible with both ends of the ideological spectrum.[38]

Corresponding Duties

Among the most substantial objections which the theory of human rights has to face is that it is impossible to specify the duties which correspond to the rights claimed, to show who should fulfil them or to demonstrate that they can

---

[36] For the argument that private property constitutes a major restriction on freedom see G. Cohen, 'Freedom, justice and capitalism', in Cohen, *History, Labour and Freedom* (Oxford, Oxford University Press, 1988), pp. 286–304.

[37] In effect the principle of basic economic and social rights, together with whatever compulsory transfers are necessary to secure them, constitutes a modern version of the original Lockean limitation on the duty to respect private property in land: that its enclosure did not prejudice the livelihood of others, because 'enough and as good' was left for them. J. Locke, *Two Treatises on Government*, P. Laslett (ed.), (Cambridge, Cambridge University Press, 1988), p. 291.

[38] This conclusion is similar to that reached by Doyal and Gough, *A Theory of Human Need*, ch. 13; see also M. Ramsay, *Human Needs and the Market* (Aldershot, Avebury, 1992).

realistically be fulfilled. In the absence of a satisfactory theory of obligation, it is urged, human rights must remain merely 'manifesto' claims, not properly rights. This objection is held to be particularly damaging to economic and social rights, which require from individuals and governments, not merely that they refrain from harming others or undermining their security, but that they act positively to promote their well-being.[39] This requirement not only presupposes resources which they may not possess. It also contradicts a widely held moral conviction to the effect that, while we may have a general negative duty not to harm others, the only positive duties we have are *special* duties to aid those to whom we stand in a particular personal, professional or contractual relationship. There can be no general duty to aid unspecified others; and, insofar as it presupposes such a duty, the inclusion of economic and social rights in the human rights agenda is basically flawed.

This formidable charge-sheet rests, I hope to show, on a number of fallacies. Easiest to refute is the assumption of a principled difference between the two sets of rights in the character of the obligations each entails, negative and positive respectively. As many commentators have shown, this difference will not hold up.[40] Certainly the so-called 'liberty' rights require the state to refrain from invading the freedom and security of its citizens. However, since governments were established, according to classical liberal theory itself, to protect people from the violation of their liberty and security at the hands of one another, it requires considerable government expenditure to meet this elementary purpose. Establishing 'the police forces, judicial systems and prisons that are necessary to maintain the highest achievable degree of security of these (sc. civil and political) rights ... is enormously expensive and involves the maintenance of complex bureaucratic systems'.[41]

Henry Shue has developed this argument furthest in his distinction between three different kinds of duty that are required to make a human right effective. There is, first, the duty to *avoid* depriving a person of some necessity; the duty to *protect* them from deprivation; and the duty to *aid* them when deprived. All three types of duty, he argues, are required to secure human rights, whether these be civil and political, or social and economic. Personal security, for example, requires that states refrain from torturing or otherwise injuring their citizens; that they protect them from injury at the hands of others; and that they provide a system of justice for the injured, to which all equally have access. Similarly, subsistence rights require that states do not deprive citizens of their means of livelihood; that they protect them against deprivation at the hands of others; and that they provide a system of basic social security for the deprived. The examples are entirely parallel. The difference is not between

---

[39] For the distinction between positive and negative rights see C. Fried, *Right and Wrong* (Cambridge MA, Harvard University Press, 1978), pp. 108–13; H. A. Bedau, 'Human rights and foreign assistance programs' in P. G. Brown and D. MacLean (eds), *Human Rights and US Foreign Policy* (Lexington, Lexington Books, 1979), pp. 29–44; Cranston, 'Human rights, real and supposed'.

[40] S. M. Okin, 'Liberty and welfare: some issues in human rights theory' in J. R. Pennock and J. W. Chapman (eds), *Human Rights: Nomos XXIII* (New York, New York University Press, 1981), pp. 230–56; R. Plant, 'A defence of welfare rights', in R. Beddard and D. M. Hill (eds), *Economic, Social and Cultural Rights* (Basingstoke, Macmillan, 1992), pp. 22–46; Plant, *Modern Political Thought*, pp. 267–86; Shue, *Basic Rights*, ch. 2.

[41] Okin, 'Liberty and welfare', p. 240.

different categories of *right*, but between different types of *duty* necessary to their protection, Shue concludes. 'The attempted division of rights, rather than duties, into forbearance and aid ... can only breed confusion. It is impossible for any basic right – however "negative" it has come to seem – to be fully guaranteed unless all three types of duties are fulfilled.'[42]

Shue's argument is persuasive. However, two opposite conclusions can be drawn from it. One (the conclusion which Shue, and others who argue similarly, invite us to draw) is that economic and social rights have to be considered as equally solid as civil and political rights, since there is no difference of principle between the state's provision of security for the vulnerable and of social security for the deprived. Those who are prepared to defend the one have to treat the other with equal seriousness. The opposite response, however, is to conclude that Shue's argument makes civil and political rights every bit as precarious as economic and social ones. If the most that can realistically be required from governments with limited resources, as from individuals with limited moral capacities, is duties of restraint or avoidance of harm to others; and if these negative duties are on their own insufficient to guarantee any human rights, as Shue has ably demonstrated: then no human right can be regarded as secure, since they all remain unanchored by the full range of corresponding duties. In other words, to make the case for human rights it is not enough simply to show what range of duties *would be* required to make the rights effective; it has also to be shown that these are duties which appropriate agents can reasonably be expected to fulfil.

The argument has therefore to be engaged at a deeper level, and a second assumption – that we have no general duty to aid others – needs examination. This is particularly important to economic and social rights, because the suspicion remains, despite all Shue's endeavours, that the two sets of rights are not after all symmetrical. More seems able to be achieved comparatively in the civil and political field by government abstention; and more seems required comparatively in the economic and social sphere by way of positive aid and provision. Moreover, while the provision of defence and law and order can readily be presented as a public good, from which all benefit, key elements of a basic economic and social agenda more readily assume the aspect of a particular good, which benefits definable sections of the population through transfer from the rest. Examining the logic of duties, therefore, is particularly necessary in respect of economic and social rights.

The argument that the only general duties we owe to unspecified others are negative ones, to refrain from harming them, not positively to give aid, is rooted not merely in liberal categories of politics, which prioritize non-interference, but also in a basic moral intuition about what we can reasonably be held responsible for. The objections to holding people responsible (and therefore morally reprehensible) for all the good that they could do, but do not, as well as for the harm they actually do, are twofold. Whereas the latter, sins of commission, are clearly assignable (to *our* actions), and to avoid them entails a clearly delimited responsibility (we can reasonably be required to take care not to harm others, and it is usually evident what this involves), a general duty to aid others is both potentially *limitless*, and also *non-assignable* (why us rather

---

[42] Shue, *Basic Rights*, p. 53.

than millions of others?). By contrast, special duties to give aid – to family, friends, clients, etc. – derive their moral weight precisely from the fact that they are both clearly assignable and delimited, and in this they share with the general negative duty to avoid harming others the necessary characteristics of *circumscription* for a duty which a person can reasonably be required to fulfil.[43]

There is much force in these considerations. Most of us remain unconvinced by philosophical arguments which show that inaction is simply another form of action, and omissions therefore as culpable as commissions. A morality which requires us to go on giving up to the point where our condition is equal to that of the poorest of those we are aiding is a morality for saints and heroes, perhaps, but not for ordinary mortals; and not one, therefore, on which the delivery of basic rights can rely. However, it does not follow from these arguments that there can be *no* general duty to aid the needy, or that such a duty cannot be specified in a form sufficiently circumscribed to meet the criteria outlined above.

Consider an elementary example. All would surely agree that children have a variety of needs which they are unable to meet by themselves, and that a duty therefore falls on adults to aid and protect them. In most cases this responsibility is fulfilled by their parents or other close relatives as a 'special' duty by virtue of their relationship. However, where there is no one alive to perform this duty, or those who have the responsibility are incapable of meeting it, then it falls as a general duty on the community as a whole. Here is an example of a general duty to aid the needy, whose ground lies in the manifest needs of the child.[44] Yet it is neither limitless nor unassignable. It is not a duty to aid all children, but only those for whom no one is able to care as their 'special' duty; they are, so to say, a residual rather than a bottomless category. And the duty falls upon members of the society in which they live as those most appropriately placed to help, just as when someone is in danger of drowning those most appropriately placed to help, and therefore with the duty to do so, are those present at the incident. In the case of children, however, those responsible will typically fulfil their duty, not as individuals in an *ad hoc* manner, but collectively, by establishing arrangements whereby the children are placed in the care of professionals or foster parents, and paid for by a levy on all members capable of contributing. A publicly acknowledged duty so to aid those in need, with whom we stand in no special relationship, forms one of the principles of the modern welfare state.[45]

It is mistaken therefore to assume that, if there is a general duty to aid those in need, it can only be unlimited and unassignable, and so must be either unrealistically burdensome or inadequate to guarantee any universal rights. We incur general duties to aid the needy in a social world already structured with special relationships and special duties, and in which most people meet their

[43] See P. Foot, *Virtues and Vices* (Oxford, Blackwell, 1978); H. L. A. Hart, 'Are there any natural rights?', *Philosophical Review*, 84 (1955), 3–22.

[44] For a thoroughgoing defence of the principle that duties to aid derive from the vulnerability of those aided, not from self-assumed obligations, see R. E. Goodin, *Protecting the Vulnerable* (Chicago, University of Chicago Press, 1985).

[45] Goodin, *Protecting the Vulnerable*, pp. 134–44; see also Plant, *Modern Political Thought*, pp. 284–5.

basic needs for themselves either individually or collectively. As Henry Shue argues in a more recent article:

> One should not leap from universal rights to universal duties ... On the side of duties there can be a division of labour ... For every person with a right, and for every duty corresponding to that right, there must be some agents who have been assigned that duty and who have the capacity to fulfil it. We have no reason to believe, however, that everyone has burdensome duties toward everyone else even if everyone else has meaningful rights.[46]

As the ICESCR recognizes, it is governments that have the overarching duty to ensure a division of labour in the matter of positive duties, and one that is both appropriate to their own societies and sufficient to ensure that the rights are effectively secured. This is an obligation on all states, but one with quasi-legal or contractual status for the 130 (as of 1994) that have ratified the Covenant. As the so-called Limburg principles of interpretation of the Covenant insist, states are 'accountable both to the international community and to their own people for their compliance with the obligations under the Covenant'.[47] In other words, the obligations corresponding to the rights are not merely derivable from a general moral duty, on the part of both individuals and governments, to aid those in need; they are also publicly acknowledged by international agreement.

But what if states are unable to meet their obligation to realize a minimum agenda of basic rights? Whose duty does it then become to assist them, and to aid the deprived to realize their rights? By a logical extension of the general duty to aid those in need, and the principle of a division of labour in fulfilling that duty, it clearly falls to other governments with the resources to do so, coordinated by an international body such as the UN and its agencies. A prior duty to aid those within our own country – whether we argue this on the 'kith and kin' principle, or, more plausibly, from the logic of a world organized into territorial citizenships[48] – does not absolve us of any wider duty. This is indeed publicly acknowledged in internationally agreed aid targets for the developed countries, in their contributions to UN agencies, in the continuous public support for the work of NGOs, in the massive (if spasmodic) public response to emergency appeals, and so on. These may be all insufficient, but the duty is at least generally acknowledged.

A clear answer can thus be given to the objection that economic and social rights remain unanchored by any corresponding duties. The ground of the duty is the same as for the rights themselves: in human needs. The general duty to aid those in need is, however, neither unlimited nor unassignable. It falls in the first instance upon governments, from societal resources, to ensure that basic rights are realized where individuals, families or groups prove insufficient by themselves; and to the international organizations in turn, from the resources of the developed world, to support this effort where national resources prove insufficient. Such duties are widely acknowledged. But are they realizable in practice?

---

[46] H. Shue, 'Mediating duties', *Ethics*, 98 (1988), 687–704, p. 689.
[47] UN Doc. E/C.4/1987/17, Annex, principle 10.
[48] R. E. Goodin, 'What is so special about our fellow countrymen?', *Ethics*, 98 (1988), 663–86.

Practicalities

The question of the practicability of the corresponding duties is for many the chief stumbling block to a theory of economic and social rights. If the requisite duties cannot be fulfilled, either because the size of the task continually outstrips the resources, or because of constraints on the way existing institutions operate, or both, then the claim that the rights are, or could effectively be made, universal must fail. We may still acknowledge the duties, but only be able to fulfil them in a partial or unpredictable manner, and one that is insufficient to guarantee the relevant claims as *rights*. Moreover, the incommensurability between duty and possible fulfilment may simply erode the will to action or the sense of responsibility altogether.

In addressing this question of practicability, it is difficult not to become schizophrenic. From one point of view – the technical-economic – a joint programme on the part of the international community and national governments to ensure that everyone's basic rights are met, and on a continuing basis, appears eminently practicable. From another point of view – the politico-economic – the difficulties seem equally insuperable. It is this conjunction of the eminently practicable with the seemingly impossible that renders judgements about the feasibility of guaranteeing basic economic and social rights so contradictory, depending upon the standpoint taken.

Let me take each of them in turn. From the technical-economic standpoint, there are now many studies which show that sufficient resources and economic and technical knowledge exist to ensure that the basic rights of practically everyone in the world could be guaranteed within a decade or so, and without huge cost to taxpayers in the developed world. A comparison of the World Bank study of basic needs published in 1981 with the UNDP Human Development Reports from 1990 onwards reveals important continuities over the past decade, as well as changes of emphasis in terminology, proposed methods of resourcing and administrative reforms required.[49]

As far as technical knowledge is concerned, the conclusions of the World Bank's systematic study of experience from different countries about how the basic needs (for food, shelter, primary health care, etc.) of the world's poorest could be met were summarized in its 1981 volume. Meeting these basic needs, it concluded, has to be the subject of specific policy initiatives; each is more effectively addressed in combination with the others than on its own; appropriate technologies have to be selected; policies must be formulated in consultation with the potential beneficiaries; a decentralized administrative structure with effective central support works best. Of the individual 'sectors', shelter, clean water, sanitation and primary health care are the cheapest to guarantee, given the use of appropriate technologies. Food is the most complex, since it involves interactions between agrarian policy, the structure of prices and wages, the form in which the residual guarantee of food security is assured, and other factors. Education is the most expensive, but at the same time the most important for ensuring the effectiveness of the others, and is especially effective when directed at women. In sum, enough experience has been accumulated in many countries and contexts, including problems of

[49] Streeten, *First Things First* for the 1981 World Bank study; UNDP, *Human Development Report, 1990, 1991, 1992, 1993, 1994* (New York, Oxford University Press). Of these the 1992 Report deals with the international context of development.

transition and 'reflexivity', for a programme not to be unattainable through lack of knowledge.[50]

As far as *resources* are concerned, although the funds required to finance such a programme are huge in absolute terms, they are also minuscule when expressed as a percentage of the GNP of the developed economies. The World Bank study put the figure required, if the OECD countries were to fund 50% of the cost, as requiring only an increase in aid from 0.35 to 0.45% per annum of their GNP (i.e. well below the already agreed aid 'target' of 0.7%), if existing aid were progressively redirected towards a basic needs programme.[51] The UNDP report of 1992, while regarding any new resources from OECD taxation as unrealistic, also concludes that a basic programme to meet 'essential human development targets' could be financed from a redirection of existing aid towards the poorest countries and poorest groups, if combined with a progressive conversion of military to development aid, the opening up of OECD markets to Third World goods, and a write-down of international debt.[52]

Sufficient evidence also exists to refute two common misconceptions about a programme to meet basic needs or 'essential human goals'. One is that it would undermine economic growth in the LDCs by redirecting resources to current consumption. Some developing countries are themselves sceptical about setting minimum economic rights standards on the ground that development is a progressive concept, and that the acknowledged 'right to development' cannot imply static levels of attainment.[53] However, the evidence suggests that securing a minimum platform and aiming for progressive levels of development are more likely to be mutually reinforcing than contradictory, in view of the contribution to growth made by investment in human capital. What a basic rights programme does is to alter the pattern of growth and the distribution of its benefits, rather than to undermine it.[54]

A second common misconception is that a strategy to meet basic rights could never keep up with population growth. Again, the evidence suggests that the most effective combination of policies to control population involves the ready availability of contraceptive facilities within a primary health care programme, improved education opportunities for girls, and greater confidence on the part of parents in their children's survival and their own economic security. These are precisely what a basic rights programme would be designed to secure.[55]

From one point of view, then, a programme to guarantee basic economic and social rights looks eminently feasible. From a politico-economic standpoint, however, it looks equally impossible. The structures of power and interest and the forces at work in the international economy and within developing countries themselves pull remorselessly in the opposite direction to

[50] Streeten, *First Things First*, chs 6 and 7.

[51] Streeten, *First Things First*, pp. 174–5.

[52] UNDP, *Human Development Report 1992*, pp. 9 and 89–90; cp. UNDP, *Human Development Report 1994*, pp. 77ff.

[53] R. L. Barsh, 'The right to development as a human right: results of the global consultation', *Human Rights Quarterly*, 13 (1991), 322–38.

[54] Goodin, 'The development-rights trade-off', pp. 33–5; N. Hicks, 'Growth vs. basic needs: is there a trade-off?', *World Development*, 7 (1979), 985–94; Streeten, *First Things First*, ch. 4.

[55] Shue, *Basic Rights*, ch. 4, esp. pp. 101–4.

a basic rights agenda.[56] The relevant features have been frequently rehearsed, and can merely be enumerated here.

1. *International.* The structure and terms of international finance and trade systematically favour the North at the expense of the South, especially of those countries which are heavily dependent on the export of a few primary commodities.[57] The institutions which regulate the international economy (IMF, World Bank, GATT) are controlled by the North, and work to protect the interests of their banks, investment funds and multinational companies. Although the effects of the structural adjustment programmes of the 1980s are hotly contested, the least that can be said of them is that they have failed to protect the poorest from the harmful side-effects of adjustment; the worst, that they have served to intensify the flow of resources from South to North, and to further the erosion of the economic and social rights of the poorest.[58]

2. *Domestic.* The capacity of states in many developing countries to effect basic needs programmes is further constrained by internal factors. Huge inequalities of wealth, especially of landownership, and of access to the state skew policies towards the already advantaged.[59] In many countries a weakly developed sense of public interest renders the state vulnerable to those seeking to use it for merely private benefit. The interests of state personnel themselves bias public expenditure towards prestige projects and military hardware at the expense of basic services. As a consequence the poor often regard the state not merely as indifferent, but actively hostile, to their needs, even under a nominally democratic regime.

From the second standpoint, then, what from the first standpoint seems eminently practicable, appears simply impossible, because none of the responsible agents is sufficiently in control of the factors which would need to be changed for a basic rights programme to be agreed, let alone effectively implemented. Instead these factors provide a cast-iron alibi for each party's inability to meet its obligations. 'The North blames corrupt regimes and poor planning for economic disvelopment, the South blames the World Economic Order.'[60]

In the face of such an impasse, the strategy adopted by the UN Committee on ESCR is to occupy the moral high ground, and expose beneath the evidence

[56] 'Resources are quite adequate to end destitution immediately ... if those in power were determined to do so.' D. Seers, 'North–South: muddling morality and mutuality', *Third World Quarterly*, 2 (1980), 681–93, p. 684.

[57] Even a relatively market-friendly document such as the UNDP *Human Development Report 1994* acknowledges that 'where world trade is completely free and open – as in financial markets – it generally works to the benefit of the strongest. Developing countries enter the market as unequal partners, and leave with unequal rewards' (p. 1). At the same time it points out the market *restrictions* which work to the disadvantage of developing countries (p. 67).

[58] The issue is partly how to assess claims that countries would have been even worse off without structural adjustment. For World Bank studies see L. Squire, 'Poverty and adjustment in the 1980s', *World Bank Policy Research Bulletin*, 2.2 (March–April 1991), 1–5. For a more critical assessment see the Oxfam reports on Africa and Latin America: *Africa: Make Or Break* (Oxford, Oxfam, 1993); *Structural Adjustment and Inequality in Latin America* (Oxford, Oxfam, 1994). For a range of assessments of structural adjustment in Africa see W. van der Geest (ed.), *Negotiating Structural Adjustment in Africa* (London, James Currey for UNDP, 1994).

[59] For comparative figures on inequality of landownership see UNDP, *Human Development Report 1993*, pp. 28–9.

[60] Barsh, 'The right to development as a human right', p. 324.

of inability a deficiency of will. Its many pronouncements recall the signatories of the Covenant to their duty to uphold a minimum agenda of rights regardless of circumstances. 'States parties are obligated, regardless of the level of economic development, to ensure respect for the minimum subsistence rights for all.'[61] The Committee 'draws attention to the obligations devolving upon States parties under the Covenant, whatever their level of development'. 'A State party in which any significant number of individuals is deprived of essential foodstuffs, of essential primary health care, of basic shelter or housing, or of the most basic forms of education is, prima facie, failing to discharge its obligations under the Covenant.'[62] In the absence of the IFIs from the dock, however, since they are not signatories to the Covenant, the Committee is unable to be completely evenhanded in its strictures.

The task of the political theorist at this point is perhaps to exchange the hortatory for the analytical mode, and to explore what might be termed the moral low ground: how people in practice come to acknowledge a responsibility to others through the convergence of duty with self-interest. Behind institutions stand people. If institutions, whether Northern or Southern states or IFIs, are unable to fulfil their responsibilities it is partly because not enough of the people to whom they are accountable are sufficiently convinced of any obligation to aid those in need. How they might become convinced is a complex question; but the history of the development of the welfare state suggests it is a matter of incentives as much as of exhortation or moral leadership.[63]

Two different processes of convergence between duty and self-interest suggest themselves. One, the 'insurance principle', occurs when the same insecurity that afflicts the poor penetrates sufficiently deeply into the ranks of the contented for the latter to discover that they share a common interest in developing or sustaining a system of collective insurance against misfortune or destitution.[64] It may be that a process of rediscovery is now taking place in the advanced economies, as the insecurity generated by the latest phase of capitalism spreads more widely.

If the first process involves an extension of sympathy through the prospect of shared experience, the second is based more on fear. This is the 'boomerang effect', whereby neglect of the deprived returns, through direct or indirect effects, to threaten the interests of the rest. The classic example is the fear of contagion in early Victorian Britain, which fuelled the public health movement, as the wealthy discovered that disease was no respecter of housing zones.[65] Other examples are the discovery that widespread unemployment among young males produces a chronic surge in crime against property and the

---

[61] UN Doc. E/C.4/1987/17, principle 25.

[62] UN Doc. E/C.12/1990/8, pp. 41, 86.

[63] See R. E. Goodin, *Motivating Political Morality* (Oxford, Blackwell, 1992). For Richard Rorty, posing the motivational issue as one of tension between duty and interest (even group interest) is wholly mistaken. His solution lies in a combination of 'sentimental story-telling' and avoiding 'having children who would be like Thrasymachus and Callicles'. R. Rorty, 'Human rights, rationality, and sentimentality' in Shute and Hurley, *On Human Rights*, pp. 111–34.

[64] Goodin, *Motivating Political Morality*, ch. 3.

[65] E. C. Midwinter, *Victorian Social Reform* (London, Longman, 1968), p. 24. Cf. Carlyle's account of the Irish woman in Edinburgh who was refused help from all charitable institutions, but went on to infect a whole street with typhus. 'She proves her sisterhood: her typhus-fever kills *them*.' T. Carlyle, *Past and Present* (London, Chapman and Hall, 1893), p. 128.

person, which no expansion of the police or the prisons can contain; or that neglect of education retards economic development in a way that affects even the educated to their detriment.[66]

Then there is the 'heavy boomerang', the prospect of social revolution, which did much throughout the past century to reconcile the advantaged to social reform, through fear of something worse. With the collapse of Communism that fear has now subsided, much to the disadvantage of social democracy, for all that the practice of 'actually existing socialism' appeared to discredit it also. Whether new forms of revolutionary movement or social uprising will take place in the future, to provide the spur to reform, is an open question. Equally unpredictable is the point at which the more ruthless strategies of the rich to seal themselves off from the effects of destitution on their own doorstep become politically unsustainable.[67]

Both the processes discussed above, whether operating through fear or the extension of shared experience, have been effective in the past in producing a convergence of principle and self-interest *within* countries. Can they also operate *between* them, across frontiers and at long distances? At present the spillover effects of war, of environmental degradation or pollution, of population increase and migration, may seem too remote and uncertain to convince people of their interdependency at the international level. Yet the fact that these global interdependencies are increasing suggests that the pressures to develop a new global compact and a corresponding reform of international economic institutions to meet the demands of basic economic and social rights will themselves increase rather than diminish in the future, for all their apparent impracticality in the present.

Conclusion

In this paper I have sought to provide a defence of the idea of economic and social rights against its critics, by defining and justifying a minimum agenda of basic rights, and by showing that the corresponding duties are assignable, delimited and, from one point of view at least, practicable. There remains the huge gulf between the promise and its fulfilment. It is here that philosophical critics from Bentham onwards have tended to lose patience with the protagonists of human rights, for trading on an inherent ambiguity in the language of a 'right': between having a morally justifiable entitlement, and having that entitlement legally recognized and enforced. The human rights agenda is not based on sloppy thinking, however, but constitutes a self-conscious project for moving the rights in question from the first status to the second. A final issue to consider is whether the language of human rights itself can be effective as a *persuasive political discourse* in this process.

Compared with other approaches, couching the basic economic and social requirements for human agency, human self-realization, or human develop-ment, in the language of *rights* not only has the advantage that such rights enjoy the authority of international recognition and agreement. They also correspond to conceptions widely held among the poor themselves. As Pierre Spitz shows in his historical survey of laws regulating food supply, the concept

---

[66] For the UK see W. Hutton, *The State We're In* (London, Cape, 1995), ch. 7.
[67] J. K. Galbraith, *The Culture of Contentment* (London, Sinclair-Stevenson, 1992), ch. 14.

of a basic entitlement to food has been widespread in many historical cultures.[68] Similarly, James Scott has shown in his comparative studies of peasant attitudes to exploitation that the guarantee of basic subsistence is much more central to peasant conceptions of justice than the precise percentage of crop appropriated by landlords.[69] Framing such intuitions in terms of human rights provides a language that is both more urgent and more authoritative than alternative discourses of 'human security' or 'basic welfare goals'. It also identifies the deprived as themselves the potential agents of social change, as the active claimants of rights, and thus offers an 'empowering potential which is far greater than any of the "new" terms that seem (temporarily) so compelling to many development specialists ... but which are devoid of any power of mobilization or transformation'.[70]

Expressing basic economic and social requirements in the language of human rights, then, does more than emphasize the obligations of governments or international agencies and their respective publics, or provide a challenge to legal experts to develop justiciable norms to assist their effective implementation; it also offers an internationally authorized discourse to the deprived, to legitimate their own struggles for their realization.

---

[68] P. Spitz, 'Right to food for peoples and for the people: a historical perspective', in Alston and Tomasevski, *The Right to Food*, pp. 169–86. Spitz points out that in the rarely quoted French Declaration of Rights of 1793, article 21 contained a specific economic right that was absent from the 1789 version: 'society has the duty to ensure the sustenance of the poor either by providing them with work or by giving the means of livelihood to those who are unable to work' (p. 174).

[69] J. C. Scott, *The Moral Economy of the Peasant* (New Haven, Yale University Press, 1976).

[70] Statement by the UN Committee on ESCR, May 1994, to the World Summit on Social Development (typescript), p. 3.

State Sovereignty and Human Rights: towards a Global Constitutional Project

ALLAN ROSAS

The Landmarks of 1945 and 1948

In the international human rights system of today, the Universal Declaration of Human Rights of 1948[1] stands out as a foundation and symbol of pivotal importance. The establishment three years earlier of the United Nations with its legal framework, the UN Charter, had laid the basic institutional structure. The Charter also came to include some general references to the protection of human rights and fundamental freedoms. According to the Preamble of the Charter, the peoples of the United Nations were 'determined ... to reaffirm faith in fundamental human rights, in the dignity and worth of the human person, in the equal rights of men and women and of nations large and small'.[2] The Universal Declaration was meant to give more concrete substance to such rather sweeping formulations.[3]

Some commentators saw the new emphasis on human rights in the Charter, as supplemented by the Universal Declaration, as an almost revolutionary achievement. Others were more sceptical.[4] Until recently, most general standard courses and textbooks of public international law have paid secondary if any attention to human rights.[5] In political science and the study of international

---

[1] UN General Assembly resolution 217 A (III) of 10 December 1948.

[2] See also Article 1, para. 3, and ch. IX (Articles 55–60) of the Charter.

[3] On the status, significance and content of the Universal Declaration see e.g. A. Verdoodt, *Naissance et signification de la Declaration Universelle des Droits de l'Homme* (Louvain, Editions Nauwelaerts, 1964); J. P. Humphrey, *Human Rights & the United Nations: a Great Adventure* (Dobbs, Ferry, New York, Transnational, 1984), pp. 1–77; A. Eide, G. Alfredsson, G. Melander, L. A. Rehof and A. Rosas, *The Universal Declaration of Human Rights: a Commentary* (Oslo, Scandinavian University Press, in co-operation with Oxford University Press, 1992).

[4] See, in particular, H. Lauterpacht, *International Law and Human Rights* (London, Stevens, 1950), pp. 424–8, with references. Lauterpacht himself stressed a new paradigm based on human rights and the notion of the individual as a subject of international law: 'International law, which has excelled in punctilious insistence on the respect owed by one sovereign State to another, henceforth acknowledges the sovereignty of man. For fundamental human rights are rights superior to the law of the sovereign State' (p. 70). He was sceptical with respect to the specific importance of the Universal Declaration, however, arguing that it lacked legally binding force, (pp. 394–428).

[5] In D. P. O'Connell, *International Law* (London, Stevens, 2nd ed., 1970), 20 pages (Vol. II, pp. 742–61) out of a total of 1123 pages (i.e. less than 2 per cent) deal with 'personal jurisdiction: human rights' in a Part on 'jurisdiction'. In I. A. Shearer, *Starke's International Law* (London, Butterworths, 11th ed., 1994), 10 pages (pp. 328–38) out of a total of 597 pages (again less than 2 per cent) deal with 'human rights and fundamental freedoms'. Cf. I. Brownlie, *Principles of Public International Law* (Oxford, Oxford University Press, 4th ed., 1990), which already contains a somewhat more elaborate chapter (XXIV) of some 50 pages (of a totality of 748 pages) on 'the protection of individuals and groups: human rights and self-determination'.

relations, human rights have been an even odder figure. Especially for the realist paradigm, human rights, and the Universal Declaration as their basic normative exposition, have been largely irrelevant, except perhaps as a rhetorical device for expressing disguised state and other interests.[6]

Gradually human rights have nevertheless crept into foreign policy, international relations and theories about them.[7] The 1980 and 1990s have witnessed an unprecedented upsurge of human rights concerns and activities, as witnessed by the proliferation of international treaties and institutions, both universal and regional. Of particular importance are the two International Covenants of 1966[8] (entered into force in 1976), which completed the so-called International Bill of Rights (consisting of the Universal Declaration and the two Covenants). If International Labour Organisation and other special conventions, regional conventions and bilateral treaties are included, the number of human rights treaties can be counted in the hundreds rather than in the tens.[9]

The 1993 World Conference on Human Rights in Vienna[10] and the subsequent establishment of a UN High Commissioner for Human Rights[11] are perhaps small but still significant further steps in an evolving institutional and normative framework. According to the Vienna Declaration and Programme of Action, the universal nature of human rights and fundamental freedoms 'is beyond question' and human rights 'are the birthright of all human beings'. Hence their protection and promotion 'is the first responsibility of Governments'.

These developments are historically grounded in the UN Charter and the Universal Declaration. But the power of these instruments does not seem to be limited to forming a historical basis for an enlarged agenda of international relations. The Universal Declaration offers a paradigmatic challenge to the Hobbesian strand of the Westfalian legacy, which has seen the international system as a horizontal inter-state system based on the sovereign equality of states. This is because the Universal Declaration:

> – concerns matters between the state and its own population (*vertical* approach) rather than inter-state relations

---

[6] For a survey of the relation between human rights and different theories of international relations, see e.g. R. J. Vincent, *Human Rights and International Relations* (Cambridge, Cambridge University Press, 1986), pp. 111–28.

[7] The foreign policy of the US Carter administration (1977–81) was – in retrospect – a significant precedence. On this period in US foreign policy, see e.g. B. M. Rubin and E. P. Spiro (eds), *Human Rights and U.S. Foreign Policy* (Boulder CO, Westview, 1979); D. P. Kommers and G. D. Loescher (eds), *Human Rights and American Foreign Policy* (Notre Dame, Indiana, University of Notre Dame Press, 1979). See more generally, Vincent, *Human Rights and International Relations*.

[8] International Covenant on Economic, Social and Cultural Rights and International Covenants on Civil and Political Rights (the latter with two Optional Protocols, the first of 1966 establishing a system of individual complaints).

[9] The texts of the most important treaties and other instruments are published, e.g. in *Human Rights: a Compilation of International Instruments*, Vol. I, Parts 1–2 (New York, United Nations, 1994), Vol. II (forthcoming).

[10] On 25 June 1993, representatives of 171 states adopted by consensus the Vienna Declaration and Programme of Action of the World Conference on Human Rights, UN doc. A/CONF.157/23. The previous World Conference was held in Teheran in 1968.

[11] UN General Assembly resolution 48/141 establishing the High Commissioner was adopted by consensus. The establishment of this post had been a contentious question for more than twenty years. Ambassador José Ayala Lasso of Ecuador has been appointed the first High Commissioner.

– concerns all *human beings*, who in the words of Article 1 of the Declaration 'are born free and equal in dignity and rights', rather than the nationals (citizens) of a given state
– is a proclamation and interpretation of *universal values* rather than a negotiated compromise between different wills (interests) of states.[12]

To uncover the potential revolution behind these observations, it is worth taking a brief look at the Westfalian system as it evolved between 1648 and 1948. The essence of state sovereignty has to be explained in socio-legal terms and the Universal Declaration and its follow-up related to this conceptualization. This should lead to an assessment of the post-1945 international human rights system as a process. Is it part of a development leading to a new historical system, based on global constitutionalism? While the emphasis here is on paradigmatic, normative and institutional developments, we should not lose sight of the realist point of view. Are, after all, the Universal Declaration and its normative follow-up merely to be reckoned among those covenants which, to quote Thomas Hobbes,[13] are 'but words, and of no strength to secure a man at all'?

The Legacy of 1648

The essence of our understanding of the Westfalian system, as it has gradually unfolded since 1648, is the principle of the sovereign equality of states, still highlighted as the first of seven principles listed in Article 2 of the UN Charter.[14] This horizontal and inter-state system can be visualized (see Figure 1).[15] The sovereign states (S1, S2 ...) are markedly territorial entities, with defined borders. Internal sovereignty means the supreme power to exert jurisdiction (legislative, judicial and administrative competence) over a given piece of territory, while external sovereignty implies freedom from interference in this competence and the formal equality of states in their dealings with each other. To put it in more socio-economic terms, one can say that a national economy is regulated and protected by autonomous state institutions, being able to call upon the national standing army as a last means of enforcement.

The prevailing doctrine is the liberal theory of the state.[16] States are seen as being like individuals, equal and autonomous, enjoying a right to self-

---

[12] True, the Universal Declaration was adopted by the UN General Assembly, an inter-state body, and its text was worked out by the intergovernmental Commission on Human Rights and its sub-bodies. Yet, the text of the Declaration and the circumstances surrounding its preparation and adoption take it far beyond a traditional inter-state contract. On this aspect of both the UN Charter and the Universal Declaration see e.g. G. Sperduti, 'La Souveraineté, le droit international et la sauvegarde des droits de la personne' in Y. Dinstein (ed.), *International Law at a Time of Perplexity: Essays in Honour of Shabtai Rosenne* (Dordrecht, Martinus Nijhoff, 1989), pp. 879–85, p. 881.

[13] T. Hobbes, *Leviathan, or the Matter, Forme, & Power of a Common-Wealth Ecclestiasticall and Civill* (London 1651/C. B. Macpherson (ed.), London, Penguin Classics, 1985), p. 223, ch. XVII.

[14] Article 2 begins as follows: 'The Organization and its Members, in pursuit of the Purposes stated in Article 1, shall act in accordance with the following Principles: 1. The Organization is based on the principle of the sovereign equality of all its Members'.

[15] From A. Rosas, 'The decline of sovereignty: legal perspectives' in J. Iivonen (ed.), *The Future of the Nation State in Europe* (Aldershot, Edward Elgar, 1993), pp. 130–58, p. 131.

[16] On the relation between sovereignty and liberal theory see M. Koskenniemi, *From Apology to Utopia: the Structure of International Legal Argument* (Helsinki, Finnish Lawyers', 1989), pp. 56–73. Cf. Vincent, *Human Rights and International Relations*, pp. 113–8, who speaks about the 'morality of states'.

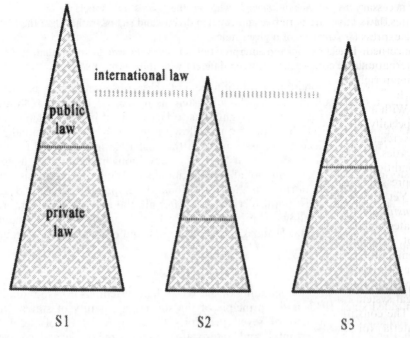

Figure 1. The post-1648 inter-state system.

determination. Thus the Preamble of the UN Charter, quoted above, refers in one stroke to the 'equal rights of men and women and of nations large and small'. But if nations, independently of their size, are both sovereign and equal, it is difficult to see how human beings could be equal, except within each nation-state. Thus our conceptions of equality and justice have been strongly linked to the contexts of nation-states.[17]

The governing concept of law in the Westfalian system has been legal positivism, teaching that the law emanates from the state and its will.[18] Values or laws of nature cannot constitute legal norms, unless they are recognized as such by the state. To put it in blunt terms, a law is not law because it is valuable

---

[17] For instance, J. Rawls, *A Theory of Justice* (Cambridge MA, Belknap, 1971), pp. 7–8, limits his theory of justice to domestic societies: 'The conditions for the law of nations may require different principles arrived at in a somewhat different way' (p. 8). A brief explanation of this 'law of nations' (pp. 377 et seq.) follows the liberal paradigm: 'The basic principle of the law of nations is a principle of equality. Independent peoples organized as states have certain fundamental equal rights. This principle is analogous to the equal rights of citizens in a constitutional regime', (p. 378).

[18] Already Hobbes, *Leviathan*, p. 527, was at pains to demonstrate that we should disregard commands of 'any Minister of Christ' which were contrary to the command of the King, or another sovereign representant of the Commonwealth. The Hobbesian conception was of course also based on the principle that the sovereign was above the law (e.g. p. 367). Rousseau stressed popular sovereignty but the individual, being a member of a state community, must be subordinated to the law as being an expression of the general will, J.-J. Rousseau, *Du contrat social ou principes du droit politique* in Oeuvres choisies (Paris, Garnier Frères, Libraires-éditeurs), p. 250, ch. VII: 'Afin donc que ce pacte social ne soit pas un vain formulaire, il renferme tacitement cet engagement, qui seul peut donner de la force aux autres, que quiconque refusera d'obéir à la volonté générale, y sera contraint par tout le corps: ce qui ne signifie autre chose sinon qu'on le forcera à être libre'.

or necessary but because it is anchored in the sovereign will of the state. Within states, laws have been enacted unilaterally. Between states, laws have required the express (treaties) or implied (customary law) consent of the parties (states) concerned. There has been no norm of general international law requiring that international law is automatically part of domestic law. Thus, international human rights are the law of the land only if the state has recognized them as such.

With a stronger emphasis on national constitutionalism and the rule of law especially since the nineteenth century, the harsh consequences of Hobbesian sovereignty were mitigated. Moreover, an emerging regime of international treaties, starting with treaties regulating warfare and later also peacetime conditions such as social questions and the status of national minorities,[19] expressed some common principles and values.

Yet the sovereignty of states continued to imply what can be termed *constitutional independence* of other states and the international community.[20] States could enact and amend their constitutions, and in doing so they were not, from the point of view of the international system, obliged to uphold a democratic system or any other particular system of governance.[21] By contrast, the European Union or local governments cannot by themselves amend their 'constitutions'.[22] (The term 'constitution' of course here refers to the politico-legal system rather than to a specific formal text.)

The constitutional independence of the state can be linked to the classical criteria for statehood, namely defined territory, permanent population, government, capacity to enter into relations with other states, and so on.[23] As to defined territory, this has been a question of effective control and governance (based on historical titles, wars, etc.) and commensurate provisions in domestic law (usually restrained by the territorial claims of other states) rather than international regulation. The population has been defined by constitutional and other provisions on nationality, citizenship and aliens' right

[19] The codification of the laws and customs of war, later to be branded international humanitarian law, started with the Paris Declaration respecting Maritime Law of 1856. The promotion of social rights and minority protection advanced with the establishment in 1919 of the International Labour Organisation and the League of Nations, respectively.

[20] R. H. Jackson, *Quasi-states: Sovereignty, International Relations, and the Third World* (Cambridge, Cambridge University Press, 1990), p. 32, observes that sovereignty in international relations 'signifies constitutional independence of other states'.

[21] F. R. Tesón, *Humanitarian Intervention: an Inquiry into Law and Morality* (Dobbs Ferry, New York, Transnational, 1988), p. 79, describes this constitutional independence as follows: 'While political theory and constitutional doctrine may support the idea that governments should be Lockean, or Kantian, to be internally legitimate, international law teaches that they need only be Hobbesian to become honorable members of the international community'. See also A. Rosas, 'International legitimacy of governments ' in G. Alfredsson and P. Macalister-Smith (eds), *The Living Law of Nations: Essays on Refugees, Minorities, Indigenous Peoples and the Human Rights of Other Vulnerable Groups in Memory of Atle Grahl-Madsen* (Kehl am Rhein, Engel, forthcoming).

[22] Rosas, the decline of sovereignty', pp. 133–4. The UN Charter can be amended by a qualified majority of its member states (which must include the five permanent members of the Security Council), but the sovereignty of recalcitrant members is preserved by the interpretation that they may in such a case withdraw from membership.

[23] The four criteria mentioned in the text appear in Article 1 of the Montevideo Convention on the Rights and Duties of States of 1933. Legal doctrine adds other criteria; the formulations may vary from author to author. See generally, J. Crawford, *The Creation of States in International Law* (Oxford, Oxford University Press, 1979), pp. 31 et seq.

of entry and residence. As to the criterion of government, what has been essential has been a system of government (a legal order) designed to maintain law and order but, as was noted above, not necessarily based on any particular material requirements (such as democracy). The requirement of capacity to enter into relations with other states and other similar criteria which have been mentioned in legal doctrine do not add much to this picture. All the criteria for statehood can be linked to the basic notion of constitutional independence with respect to a certain piece of territory.

Thus if the Westfalian order is to come to an end, it must be shown that these elements of constitutional power are being transferred to the international community level or at least that the sovereign power of the state is being seriously curtailed. In the following sections, we shall argue that this is indeed what is taking place, and that the legacy of 1948 rather than 1648 plays a significant role in such developments.

Law-making

It seems useful at this stage to distinguish roughly between three dimensions of the constitutional independence outlined above, namely law-making (the legislative power), adjudication (the judicial power) and enforcement (executive power). To start with law-making, can it be shown that the process of international norm-formation has an impact on national developments which is of constitutional significance? The following discussion will centre on international human rights norms, which seem to be of pivotal importance from a paradigmatic point of view. At the same time the reader should be reminded of the fact that the scope of international standard-setting is much wider.

As to the very level of constitution-making, it can easily be shown that there is no device in general international law and intergovernmental co-operation to actually amend national constitutions. What international law contains is first of all the fairly recent concept of *jus cogens*, meaning peremptory norms from which no derogation (even by concluding conflicting treaties) is possible.[24] The concept is quite indeterminate, but arguably includes a minimum protection of life, liberty and security of person and today perhaps also what has been called internal self-determination, that is, roughly a basic right to democracy.[25] In principle, a state cannot contract out of such basic obligations and treaties conflicting with peremptory norms are held to be null and void.[26] A step which would take us much further would be to hold national constitutions in contravention of *jus cogens* null and void as well; such a step has not been articulated and even less recognized internationally.

Secondly, the elaborate web of international human rights instruments, from an international law point of view, provide considerable constraints on the contents of national constitutions and other laws for those states that are

---

[24] L. Hannikainen, *Peremptory Norms (Jus Cogens) in International Law: Historical Development, Criteria, Present Status* (Helsinki, Finnish Lawyers', 1988).

[25] The latter point is open to argument, A. Rosas, 'Internal self-determination' in C. Tomuschat (ed.), *Modern Law of Self-Determination* (Dordrecht, Martinus Nijhoff, 1993), pp. 225–52. This point is further discussed below.

[26] Articles 53 and 64 of the Vienna Convention on the Law of Treaties of 1969 and Articles 53 and 64 of the Vienna Convention on the Law of Treaties between States and International Organizations.

bound by the instrument in question. They also contain positive obligations for the Contracting Parties to fulfil (requirements of penal and judicial systems, protection of privacy and private property, political rights, including periodic elections, etc.). There is even an evolving set of international minimum standards constraining states' freedom of action with respect to the definition of nationality and citizenship, one of the core elements of sovereignty.[27] The fact that a conflicting domestic provision is contained in the national constitution does not absolve the State Party concerned from international responsibility.

There are at least three counter-arguments to this limitation on state sovereignty.[28] First, there is as yet no rule of general international law requiring states to apply directly such international norms instead of their domestic laws (violations of these norms entail international responsibility but are not necessarily violations of domestic law). Secondly, states can opt out of the international instruments not only by refusing to adhere to new instruments or to accept parts of them (by making reservations) but also by withdrawing from instruments binding on the state. Thirdly, existing human rights treaties contain considerable leeway for national solutions. Outright derogations may be possible in times of public emergency,[29] limitation clauses leave room for restrictions in the public interest and national governments are sometimes left with a wide margin of appreciation in the application and interpretation of individual provisions. (A fourth counter-argument, the weaknesses of international enforcement mechanisms, will be considered later.)

Yet, with increasing interdependence and the move towards global and transnational markets and an increasing role for international institutions and co-operation, the right to 'opt out' is more and more becoming a fiction.[30] States do not withdraw from international human rights treaties. Instead, there is a continuing – albeit in the view of many human rights activists, painstakingly slow – flow of additional ratifications and accessions, the more popular conventions at present enjoying the formal support of more than 2/3 of all states.[31] A parallel phenomenon is the obvious reluctance of states to withdraw from membership of intergovernmental organizations. No state has

[27] A. Rosas, 'Nationality and citizenship in a changing European and world order' in M. Suksi (ed.), *Law under Exogenous Influences* (Turku, Turku Law School, (1994) vol. 1, no. 1, pp. 30–59.

[28] Rosas, 'The decline of sovereignty: legal perspectives', pp. 143–7.

[29] A. Rosas, 'Public emergency regimes: a comparison' in D. Gomien (ed.), *Broadening the Frontiers of Human Rights: Essays in Honour of Asbjørn Eide* (Oslo, Scandinavian University Press, 1993), pp. 165–99.

[30] J. A. Camilleri and J. Falk, *The End of Sovereignty? The Politics of a Shrinking and Fragmenting World* (Aldershot, Edward Elgar, 1992), p. 33.

[31] As of 1 January 1994, the number of State Parties for the 'top ten' was as follows: 1949 Geneva Conventions relative to the Protection of Victims of War: *185*; 1989 Convention on the Rights of the Child: *152*; 1965 International Convention on the Elimination of All Forms of Racial Discrimination: *137*; 1932 ILO Convention No. 29 concerning Forced Labour: *135*; 1979 Convention on the Elimination of All Forms of Discrimination against Women: *130*; Protocol I additional to the 1949 Geneva Conventions: *130*; 1966 International Covenant on Economic, Social and Cultural Rights: *127*; 1966 International Covenant on Civil and Political Rights: *125*; 1949 ILO Convention No. 98 concerning the Application of the Principles of the Right to Organize and Bargain Collectively: *122*; 1951 Convention relating to the Status of Refugees: *121*. See *Human Rights Law Journal*, 15 (1994), 56–64.

left the UN, and withdrawal from the Specialized Agencies has been scarce and usually then of temporary duration.[32]

While the formal applicability of these arrangements still depends on state consent, the powers of the UN Security Council are of a different breed. The revitalization of the Security Council, which began in 1990 with the Iraqi attack on Kuwait and was made possible by the collapse of the Eastern European communist system, has brought to the fore the legislative potential inherent in the powers of the Security Council in the context of enforcement actions. Thus, after having defined the existence of a threat to the peace, or (in the case of Iraq) a breach of the peace,[33] the Security Council has prohibited Iraq from possessing certain types of weapons, established a UN Compensation Commission to settle claims against Iraq, ordered Iraq to comply with a UN demarcation of the border between Iraq and Kuwait, ordered Libya to extradite its nationals to third countries in contravention of Libyan law, endorsed the use of military force for humanitarian purposes in the former Yugoslavia, Somalia and Rwanda, and established International Tribunals for the prosecution of persons responsible for serious violations of international humanitarian law committed in the former Yugoslavia and Rwanda.[34]

These measures have been taken following a determination of a situation as a threat to the peace or breach of the peace, with the objective 'to maintain or restore international peace and security' (Article 39 of the UN Charter). In addition, given the inherent indeterminacy of the notion of 'threat to the peace', the very decision to define a situation as a threat to the peace may have a legislative role. That the decisions of the Security Council include situations such as an alleged complicity in terrorism (Libya), human rights violations and humanitarian crises (the former Yugoslavia, Liberia, Somalia, Angola, Rwanda) and the continuation of an illegitimate regime (Haiti) indicates that a wide interpretation of the notion of threat to the peace has been favoured, to include situations which are far beyond the threat of inter-state war.

The sanctions against Haiti are particularly interesting, as they were based on the determination as a threat to the peace of a situation which involved an unlawful government, in combination with the existence of a humanitarian crisis. The express objective of these sanctions was to restore the lawful

---

[32] In 1965, Indonesia announced its intention to withdraw from the UN but this was in the following year interpreted as a temporary absence and Indonesia was not required to undergo a readmission procedure. South Africa's credentials were rejected by the UN General Assembly as from 1974 but the country never withdrew from the organization. At the time of writing, Serbia and Montenegro have been prevented from participating in the work of the General Assembly but the question of membership remains open. Of the Specialized Agencies, for instance the International Labour Organisation has witnessed four withdrawals but these have turned out to be of a temporary character (South Africa, Albania, Lesotho and the United States). See B. Broms, *The United Nations* (Helsinki, Annales Academiae Scientiarum Fennicae, 1990), pp. 149–52, 729–30.

[33] According to Article 39 of the UN Charter, the Security Council 'shall determine the existence of any threat to the peace, breach of the peace, or act of aggression and shall make recommendations, or decide what measures shall be taken in accordance with Article 41 and 42, to maintain or restore international peace and security'.

[34] Rosas, 'The decline of sovereignty: legal perspectives', pp. 141–2, 146; D. Caron, 'The legitimacy of the collective action of the Security Council, *American Journal of International Law*, 87 (1993), 552–88; A. Rosas, 'Whither sovereignty?', *Juridisk Tidskrift vid Stockholms Universitet*, 6 (1994), 312–8, p. 315. These sources do not refer to the most recent decision to establish the International Tribunal for Rwanda by Security Council resolution 955 (1994) of 8 November 1994.

Government elected in UN monitored elections of 1991.[35] In resolution 940 (1994) of 31 July 1994, the Security Council went so far as to authorize Member States to form a multinational force and, in this framework, 'to use all necessary means to facilitate the departure from Haiti of the military leadership, consistent with the Governors Island Agreement, to prompt return of the legitimately elected President and the restoration of the legitimate authorities of the Government of Haiti ...' (para. 4). To appease reluctant Member States, notably China, the Council did emphasize 'the unique character of the present situation in Haiti and its deteriorating, complex and extraordinary nature, requiring an exceptional response' (para. 2).[36] Such caveats cannot change the fact that the Security Council with the sanctions against Haiti has entered the minefield of democratic legitimacy and what has been called the right to democratic governance.[37] It should be added that the establishment of the Multinational Force, with strong US military and political backing, paved the way for the peaceful return of President Aristide on 15 October 1994 and the lifting of UN sanctions.[38]

True, there is no way that the Security Council could act in a consistent manner in taking such measures of 'democracy enforcement'. In particular, enforcement measures against one of its permanent members would apparently be voided by the use of the veto. This does not strip the Haiti actions of any value as a precedent, however. Moving from one historical system (state sovereignty) to another will of necessity imply a number of inconsistencies, constraints and setbacks over a considerable span of time.

There is another international normative development which, in a formal sense, is quite far from binding Security Council sanctions, but which serves a similar purpose in downplaying the requirement of state consent. We are thinking of the phenomenon of 'soft law', meaning standards which are not legally binding in the strict sense. Some soft law instruments, such as the political commitments undertaken in the framework of the Conference on Security and Co-operation in Europe (CSCE),[39] recently renamed the Organization for Security and Co-operation in Europe (OSCE),[40] are still based on consensus. Other instruments, such as indeed the Universal Declaration of Human Rights itself, have been adopted by majority decision-making. Yet other instruments are legally in the nature of private recommendations only. While soft law is not legally binding *per se*, it may add to the fabric of

---

[35] Security Council resolutions 841 (1993), 861 (1993), 862 (1993), 867 (1993), 873 (1993), 875 (1993), 905 (1994), 917 (1994), 933 (1994), 940 (1994), 944 (1994).

[36] See also resolution 841 (1993), preambular paragraphs 13 and 14.

[37] T. Franck, 'The emerging right to democratic governance', *American Journal of International Law*, 86 (1992), 46–91.

[38] See Security Council resolution 948 (1994) of 15 October 1994. In this resolution, the Security Council, *inter alia*, expressed its full support for efforts by 'President Aristide, democratic leaders in Haiti, and the legitimate organs of the restored government to bring Haiti out of crisis and return it to the democratic community of nations'. See also resolution 964 (1994) of 29 November 1994.

[39] These commitments abound with human rights and humanitarian standards. See the collection by A. Bloed, *The Conference on Security and Co-operation in Europe: Analysis and Basic Documents 1972–1993* (Dordrecht, Martinus Nijhoff, 1993). See also A. Heraclides, *Security and Cooperation in Europe: the Human Dimension* (London, Frank Cass, 1993).

[40] See the CSCE Budapest Document 1994: Towards a Genuine Partnership in a New Era, adopted in Budapest on 6 December 1994. The change in name became effective on 1 January 1995.

value-oriented principles derived from what a treaty clause of 1899 terms 'the laws of humanity, and the requirements of the public conscience'.[41]

In this context, it should also be noted that many international organizations not only issue soft law proclamations and recommendations, but also engage in a wide range of activities encouraging states to develop their constitutions and laws, with a view to strengthening the democratic system, the rule of law and respect for human rights.[42] Especially with respect to Central and Eastern European countries, the UN, the OSCE (CSCE), the Council of Europe and the European Union have performed a number of such advisory services. While the states concerned are legally free to disregard the advice given, a network of institutional mechanisms, political leverage and economic sticks and carrots tends to erode state sovereignty *de facto*.

The Council of Europe and the European Union also offer far-reaching cases of semi-supranational and supranational decision- and law-making. An important element is provided by the adjudicatory bodies of these organizations, the European Commission and Court of Human Rights in Strasbourg and the Court of Justice and the Court of First Instance of the European Communities in Luxembourg. In this context, the increasing constitutional role of human rights case-law should be emphasized. While the judgments of the European Court of Human Rights cannot, as such, entail amendments to national constitutions or laws, its case-law produces indirect effects in this respect.[43]

European Community law goes further in including the principles of supremacy, direct applicability and direct effect and forms in the words of the Court of Justice 'its own legal system'.[44] This 'permanent limitation' of the sovereign rights of the Member States of the European Union[45] is remarkable but could be explained as a special case of economic, legal and political integration which may ultimately lead to the creation of a new (federal) state. Be that as it may, what is worth stressing in this context is the creeping impact of human rights principles on Community law.[46] This implies that international human rights principles may, through Community law, become part

---

[41] This is the famous Martens Clause, contained in the ninth preambular paragraph of Convention (II) with Respect to the Laws and Customs of War on Land of 1899. See also the corresponding preambular paragraph of Convention (IV) respecting the Laws and Customs of War on Land of 1907 and Article 1, paragraph 2, of Protocol I of 1977 additional to the Geneva Conventions of 1949.

[42] There is an abundance of materials produced by international organizations within the framework of various assistance programmes and projects. As an example of a handbook focusing on elections and thus political rights can be mentioned Human Rights and Elections: a Handbook on the Legal, Technical and Human Rights Aspects of Elections, *Professional Training Series*, No. 2 (New York and Geneva, United Nations, Centre for Human Rights, 1994).

[43] Among the standard works on the European Convention and its implementation machinery can be mentioned P. van Dijk and G. J. H. van Hoof, *Theory and Practice of the European Convention on Human Rights* (Deventer, Kluwer Law and Taxation Publishers, 2nd ed., 1990) and A. H. Robertson and J. G. Merrills, *Human Rights in Europe: A Study of the European Convention on Human Rights* (Manchester, Manchester University Press, 3rd ed., 1993).

[44] The leading cases are Case 26/62, *Van Gend en Loos* [1963] ECR 12 and Case 6/64, *Costa v ENEL* [1964] ECR 593.

[45] Many commentators, such as J.-V. Louis, *The Community Legal Order* (Brussels, Commission of the European Communities, 2nd ed., 1990), p. 13, try to save the concept of sovereignty by speaking of a 'new concept of sovereignty', meaning divided or shared sovereignty. See also Rosas, 'Whither sovereignty?', p. 318.

[46] See, in particular, A. Clapham, *Human Rights and the European Community: a Critical Overview*. Vol. I of European Union: The Human Rights Challenge (Baden-Baden, Nomos, 1991);

of the law of the land in the Member States. This would become even more obvious should the Community settle for adhering formally to the European Convention on Human Rights, an issue which is again the subject of discussion and study.

Adjudication and Enforcement

It goes without saying that international standard-setting does not mean much if there is no way of checking compliance. It is a well-known fact that international law has not been at its strongest when it comes to implementation and enforcement. In traditional inter-state issues (for instance, the status of diplomats), the common interests of the states concerned have usually provided some checks and balances. As far as human rights matters are concerned, the principle of reciprocity may not work in the same way. States have often stood aloof when their neighbours have killed or maimed their own populations, as long as the nationals of the former have been spared. Matters of human rights interest have seldom reached the International Court of Justice, which is the leading international court to adjudicate inter-state disputes.

However, international adjudication is gradually entering the human rights field as well.[47] The most obvious cases are the European Court of Human Rights already referred to above, and the more recent Inter-American Court of Human Rights. These courts render legally binding decisions (including the award of compensation). The same goes for the Court of Justice of the European Communities, which, as was also noted above, may apply human rights as general principles of Community law.

At the universal level, there is of course no specific human rights court (although this option, too, has been discussed). But the Human Rights Committee acting under the International Covenant on Civil and Political Rights, despite the fact that it is an expert body without judicial status, is increasingly performing the functions of an adjudicatory body.[48] There are a number of other expert bodies which have supervisory functions with respect to particular conventions. And, as was noted above, the UN Security Council has established international criminal tribunals for two particular cases, namely the former Yugoslavia and Rwanda.[49] The fact that the UN International Law Commission has recently completed its work for a Draft Statute for a permanent International Criminal Court,[50] indicates that the Yugoslavia and Rwanda criminal tribunals may be followed by a more general and permanent institution. Moreover, the International Court of Justice, which has seen an

N. Neuwahl and A. Rosas (eds), *The European Union and Human Rights* (Dordrecht, Martinus Nijhoff, forthcoming 1995).

[47] For an overview of the international protection of human rights and various international supervisory and adjudicatory bodies see e.g. A. H. Robertson and J. G. Merrills, *Human Rights in the World: an Introduction to the Study of the International Protection of Human Rights* (Manchester, Manchester University Press, 3rd ed., 1992).

[48] See D. McGoldrick, *The Human Rights Committee: Its Role in the Development of the International Covenant on Civil and Political Rights* (Oxford, Oxford University Press, 1990); M. Nowak, *UN Covenant on Civil and Political Rights: CCPR Commentary* (Kehl am Rhein, Engel, 1993).

[49] See also T. Meron, 'War crimes in Yugoslavia and the development of international law', *American Journal of International Law*, 88 (1994), 78–87.

[50] UN doc. A/CN.4/L.491/Rev. 2 (Report of the Working Group on a Draft Statute for an International Criminal Court), 14 July 1994.

incoming flow of cases during the last ten or so years,[51] has been seized of some cases of a human rights interest.[52]

It is not possible within the confines of this paper to give an overview of all non-judicial monitoring, verification and control mechanisms that have been created during the last decades in such fields as arms control and disarmament, international economic law, human rights and international environmental law. Suffice it to note that the phenomenon of on-site inspections (*in situ*), which for obvious reasons constitutes an inroad into the internal sovereignty of the territorial state, has made considerable headway in the field of arms control and disarmament in particular.[53]

Similar arrangements have recently been established in the human rights and humanitarian field.[54] These include the right of a Committee established under the European Torture Convention of 1987 to visit all places of detention in State Parties to the Convention, and certain OSCE (CSCE) commitments under the so-called Human Dimension to allow OSCE missions of rapporteurs to enter the territory of a state. On a more voluntary basis, the UN and the OSCE have an elaborate system of rapporteurs, special representatives and working groups, including permanent missions, which carry out fact-finding and monitoring missions in a number of Member States. The recently established UN High Commissioner for Human Rights (1994) and the OSCE High Commissioner on National Minorities (1993) add to this picture.[55] Politically, it is becoming increasingly difficult for a state to refuse such missions entry.[56]

Yet, states and state-like entities may still refuse to co-operate with international monitoring and verification activities. That this is not a theoretical possibility only is illustrated by the problems facing international humanitarian, peace-keeping and peace-enforcement efforts in the former Yugoslavia, Somalia, Angola and other places. The fact that the UN Security Council, as was noted above, has included such situations in its conception of 'threats to the peace' has removed a legal obstacle to collective action. Moreover, the Council has resorted to economic and to some extent also

---

[51] K. Highet, 'The peace palace heats up: the world court in business again?', *American Journal of International Law*, 85 (1991), 646–54.

[52] See notably the case of Bosnia and Herzegovina v. Yugoslavia (Serbia and Montenegro), *Application of the Convention on the Prevention and Punishment of the Crime of Genocide, Provisional Measures*, Orders of 8 April and 13 September 1993, I.C.J. Reports 1993, pp. 3, 325.

[53] R. Hanski, A. Rosas and K. Stendahl, *Verification of Arms Control Agreements, with Special Reference to On-Site Inspections* (Helsinki, Finnish Ministry for Foreign Affairs, ARNEK A/10, 1991). A far-reaching international verification system will be established when the new Convention on the Prohibition of the Development, Production, Stockpiling and Use of Chemical Weapons and on Their Destruction, signed in January 1993, will enter into force.

[54] A general survey of monitoring and inspection mechanisms in the fields of human rights and humanitarian law is provided by A. Bloed, L. Leicht, M. Nowak and A. Rosas (eds) *Monitoring Human Rights in Europe: Comparing International Procedures and Mechanisms* (Dordrecht, Martinus Nijhoff, 1993).

[55] Since 1994, there is also a sub-regional Commissioner on Democratic Institutions and Human Rights, Including the Rights of Persons Belonging to Minorities, established by the Council of the Baltic Sea States. For the text of the mandate of this Commissioner, see H. Mikkola (ed.), *European Institutions: Basic Instruments* (Turku, Department of Law of the Åbo Akademi University, Compendia Series K, No. 11, 1994), ch. 14.

[56] This observation is partly based on the personal experience of the author in his capacity as an expert who follows closely UN, OSCE and Council of Europe human rights activities.

military sanctions against a number of countries (Iraq, former Yugoslavia, Libya, Liberia, Somalia, Haiti, Angola, Rwanda; previously also Rhodesia and South Africa). In the cases of the former Yugoslavia and Rwanda, this has been followed by the establishment of an international criminal tribunal. And, above all, the UN and other international organizations *are* present and playing a certain mitigating role in these conflicts.

Significant as these steps are, the overall effect of international sanctions and enforcement has so far been conspicuously ineffective in the case of the former Yugoslavia in particular. In some grave situations, such as the armed conflicts raging in various places of the former Soviet Union, the UN has abstained from sanctions altogether. It is a well-known fact that the UN is not independent of governments, in particular the five permanent members of the Security Council. There are many who see the actions against Iraq, Somalia, Haiti, etc. mainly as UN endorsed United States actions. Even if the endorsement, guidance and coordination offered by the UN in these situations has not been negligible, it is true that the UN still lacks a permanent military force to back up its decisions. International law during the present century has implied a radical curtailment of the national use of force, both between and within states.[57] But if Thomas Hobbes is right in saying that 'the sword' is necessary to give covenants practical relevance,[58] then international law is in need of a collective sword to back up its norms. This discussion is going on.[59]

This is not to say that compliance will necessarily always require military measures. Apart from the non-military sanctions (economic embargoes, etc.) recognized in Article 41 of the UN Charter and in the constitutions of many other international organizations, and the inter-state countermeasures based on general international law,[60] various informal punishments as well as rewards may induce states and other relevant actors to follow the rules. There is an on-going debate on what role development co-operation, and the international financial and trade organizations, should play in the furtherance of human rights and democracy.[61] In so far as respect for human rights, including the requirement of democracy, is increasingly seen as conducive to a stable international market and political environment,[62] reasons of long-term self-interest may also play a role.

Education and a global culture may assist actors to 'internalize' human rights norms and foster rule-following values.[63] For instance, there is an increasing transnational diffusion of domestic and international human rights

---

[57] Rosas, 'The decline of sovereignty: legal perspectives', pp. 135–43.

[58] Hobbes, *Leviathan*, p. 223.

[59] See e.g. A. Rosas, 'Towards some international law and order', *Journal of Peace Research*, 31 (1994), 129–35, where the establishment of an international armed police' is advocated.

[60] See e.g. L. Boisson de Chazournes, *Les contre-mesures dans les relations internationales économiques* (Paris, Pédone).

[61] See e.g. K. Tomasevski, *Development Aid and Human Rights Revisited* (London, Pinter, 1993).

[62] Note, for instance, the (in our view, well-substantiated) claim that pluralist democracies do not wage wars against each other, see e.g. M. W. Doyle, 'Kant, liberal legacies, and foreign affairs', *Philosophy & Public Affairs*, 12 (1983), 205–35, 323–53; N. P. Gleditsch, 'Democracy and peace: good news for human rights advocates' in D. Gomien (ed.), *Broadening the Frontiers of Human Rights: Essays in Honour of Asbjørn Eide* (Oslo, Scandinavian University Press, 1993), pp. 287–306.

[63] The expressions internalization and rule-following values are from F. Schauer, *Playing by the Rules: a Philosophical Examination of Rule-Based Decision-Making in Law and in Life* (Oxford, Oxford University Press, 1991), pp. 126, 133.

experiences and practices, also among national judges and civil servants. Such processes can build on an increasing awareness that war and human rights violations will not bring much 'gain' in the form of enduring resources and goods (since the most crucial resource is know-how, which will rather suffer in the midst of war or oppression) and that 'glory' may be better pursued by economic and technological advances, success in sporting contests, and so on.[64]

Concluding Observations

It is easy to deride, or at least question, the developments towards an international human rights regime and international regimes in general outlined above. The continuing and conspicuous reference to the principle of the sovereign equality of states in Article 2 of the UN Charter is a reminder of another reality. In order to calm Danish worries about national independence in the face of the Treaty on European Union (Treaty of Maastricht), the Heads of State and Government of the twelve Member States underlined, when meeting within the framework of the European Council in Edinburgh in December 1992, that the Union 'involves independent and sovereign States'.[65] If the Member States of the European Union insist on being 'sovereign', how could one contemplate an end of sovereignty at a universal level?

It is beyond doubt that the independent state will continue to play an essential role in the creation, application and interpretation, and implementation, of laws and policies. The purpose of this paper is not to demonstrate the end of the state. In fact, one cannot exclude the possibility that strengthening international and national human rights regimes may add to rather than threaten the legitimacy of the state.[66] The main point we make is that the basic Westfalian paradigm surrounding our conception of the state is changing, and that human rights play a crucial role in this paradigmatic change. The core of the human rights concept, as expressed in the Universal Declaration, is anathema to the horizontal Westfalian system.

There is furthermore no denying that the present stage of international relations have moved beyond the philosophical stage, as human rights and related concerns are now becoming more and more ingrained in a complex web of global, regional, interstate, transnational and local relations. For someone who, like the present author, has been following the international and national human rights scene, including its political dimensions, over a longer period of time, the developments of the last, say, ten years have been breath-taking. It will be noted that much of these developments are based on normative and institutional developments of the previous 40 years (the Universal Declaration, the two Covenants of 1966 and accompanying special conventions, the CSCE process, etc.) and are of world-wide scope. Thus, it is not merely a question of the collapse of communism and the end of the Cold War.

---

[64] This builds on Hobbes' discussion of the main sources of conflict ('So that in the nature of man, we find three principall causes of quarrell. First, Competition; Secondly, Diffidence; Thirdly, Glory. The first, maketh men invade for Gain; the second, for Safety; and the third, for Reputation', Hobbes, *Leviathan*, p. 185, ch. XIII, and on A. Ripstein, 'Hobbes on world government and the world cup', in T. Airaksinen and M. A. Bertman (eds), *Hobbes: War among Nations* (Aldershot, Avebury, 1989), pp. 112–9.

[65] Conclusions of the Presidency, Part B, Annex 1, OJ No C 348, 31.12.1992, p. 2.

[66] Vincent, *Human Rights and International Relations*, pp. 150–1.

The concept of state sovereignty will for some time continue to be hailed by political élites clinging to the old order but it is becoming less and less able to capture new realities.[67] At least it finds itself in troubled conceptual waters in the face of the insistence in the 1993 Vienna Declaration and Programme of Action, adopted by consensus by the UN World Conference on Human Rights, that the protection and promotion of human rights and fundamental freedoms is 'the first responsibility of Governments' and 'a legitimate concern of the international community'. These formulations strengthen the notion of the international accountability of states for human rights violations.[68]

The need to go further on this road stems from the inevitable globalization (and 'localization') of markets and cultures. For the enactment and enforcement of relevant laws, relying on individual states will not suffice. Morality, law and politics must adapt to new realities. Otherwise the power of the market will not be a just power. We have to transcend conceptions of justice within (national) societies and introduce visions of international justice.[69] A new concept of law, distancing itself from legal positivism but also moving beyond traditional schools of natural law, should take as one of its projects the promotion of a global constitution. This project, however, will not mean enacting 'the constitution' of the world, but a much more multifaceted endeavour. The world seems to become structured along different 'layers' of norm-formation involving, if we also take markets and civil societies into account, a patchwork of authorities (Figure 2).[70] The global constitutional project we have in mind should in some way or another take all these levels into account. One central objective must be to allocate power and jurisdictions among the various layers.[71] In our vision, the universal level, or indeed the European level, will not be served by labelling it either a confederation of independent states or a world state.[72] The emerging global constitution, and even the European Union, will escape such classifications based on the concept of the (modern) state.

While it will not be easy to construe an effective normative framework for such a multi-layered world, there are a few areas that have to be tackled. There must be norms on institutional development and jurisdictional allocation, on a universal Bill of Rights, and on international law-making and the sources of law.

Institutional development will have to build on what we have, namely the United Nations, the Specialized Agencies (including the financial institutions)

[67] In Rosas, 'Whither sovereignty?', p. 318, we concluded that 'even a revised concept of sovereignty may become a straitjacket, which hampers our search for duties beyond "national" time and space (the so-called national interest). We should transgress old frontiers and envisage duties towards future generations and duties towards humankind, rather than national duties'.

[68] See M. T. Kamminga, *Inter-State Accountability for Violations of Human Rights* (Philadelphia, University of Pennsylvania Press, 1992).

[69] C. Beitz, *Political Theory and International Relations* (Princeton NJ, Princeton University Press, 1979); J. Thompson, *Justice and World Order: a Philosophical Inquiry* (London, Routledge, 1992); J. Räikkä, *An Essay on International Justice* (Turku, Reports from the Department of Practical Philosophy, University of Turku, 1992).

[70] Rosas, 'The decline of sovereignty: legal perspectives', p. 151.

[71] Cf. Schauer, *Playing by the Rules*, pp. 231–2, who discusses the jurisdiction-allocation function of rules in general, including the need for a 'moral theory of jurisdictional separation'.

[72] Rosas, 'Whither sovereignty?', p. 318.

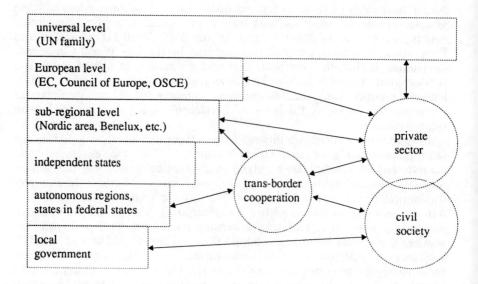

Figure 2. Layers of Public Decision-making.

and the World Trade Organization.[73] In the human rights context, a radical strengthening of the new High Commissioner for Human Rights as an early-warning institution, and open acknowledgement of the right and duty of other UN organs, including the Security Council, to act upon the advice of the High Commission, are among the ideas that merit attention. In the long run, something has to be done to increase the space for majority decision-making in intergovernmental organs.[74]

In an allocation of powers and jurisdictions, the universal level must be recognized as possessing the competence to lay down minimum rules for the attributes of statehood, namely territory (recognition of borders), population (determination of nationality) and government (requirement of pluralist democracy).[75]

A universal Bill of Rights already exists on paper. It is certainly in need of some development and brushing-up, especially in the field of economic, social and cultural rights,[76] but the main challenge concerns implementation and enforcement. The current process of tying the international human rights norms in concrete terms to institutional and jurisdictional developments

[73] Global trade will hopefully be better co-ordinated by the World Trade Organization, which has replaced the General Agreement on Tariffs and Trade (GATT). See the Agreement Establishing the Multilateral Trade Organization of December 1993 (the name of the organization was subsequently changed to World Trade Organization), 33 I.L.M. 13 (1994).

[74] On the need for a legislative capacity for international environmental matters see e.g. G. Palmer, 'New ways to make international environmental law', *American Journal of International Law*, 86 (1992), 259–83.

[75] Rosas, 'Whither sovereignty?', pp. 315–6.

[76] A. Eide, C. Krause and A. Rosas (eds), *Economic, Social and Cultural Rights: a Textbook* (Dordrecht, Martinus Nijhoff, 1995).

(early-warning and monitoring mechanisms, complaints procedures, etc.) should be strengthened. There is probably also a need for more linkage between trade on the one hand and human rights, social questions, and environmental concerns, on the other.

The system of norm-formation and law-making will inevitably be a pluralist and complex one. Treaties based formally on consensualism, binding majority decision-making, soft law pronouncements and other normative articulations will exist side by side.

The pluralistic nature and complexity of this evolving world legal order will be underlined by the plurality of law- and decision-makers and subjects of rights and obligations. The traditional human rights paradigm, according to which individuals are subjects of rights and states holders of obligations, does not fully reflect present-day tendencies. The concept of group rights, and the on-going discussions on the human rights obligations of international organizations[77] and of non-governmental actors,[78] are pointers to this.

In this multifarious context, there is an increasing need for a common legal *chapeau*, to increase a sense of universal community and togetherness and to promote a more coherent legal system. The concept of general principles of law[79] seems to offer the conceptual tool. At least some of these principles are at the same time peremptory (*jus cogens*) norms, from which no derogation is possible.[80] The concept of general principles of law can be seen as a bridge between 'hard law' based on consent and objective interests and values (including natural law considerations), and also between international law and domestic law. In fact, could one not view the Universal Declaration of Human Rights, together with the fundamental principles of the UN Charter, as an authoritative expression of such general principles of law, constituting a common legal denominator for all human activity?[81] It will be noted that the Universal Declaration expresses principles that are grounded in various national constitutional traditions and which could thus qualify as general principles of law even under a strict understanding of this notion.

---

[77] See e.g. Article F (2) of the 1992 Treaty on European Union, according to which 'the Union shall respect fundamental rights', as guaranteed by the European Convention on Human Rights and as they result from the constitutional traditions common to the Member States, 'as general principles of Community law' (note, however, that it is the three Communities rather than the Union itself which constitute legal persons).

[78] See e.g. the Turku Declaration of Minimum Humanitarian Standards, adopted by an expert meeting in Turku/Åbo, Finland, on 2 December 1990, UN doc. E/CN.4/-Sub.2/1991/55, which provides in Article 2 that 'these standards shall be respected by, and applied to all persons, groups and authorities, irrespective of their legal status and without any adverse discrimination'. For discussion, see T. Meron and A. Rosas, 'A declaration of minimum humanitarian standards', *American Journal of International Law*, 85 (1991), 375–81, pp. 376–7; A. Eide, T. Meron and A. Rosas, 'Background paper on declaration of minimum humanitarian standards', *American Journal of International Law*, 89 (1995) (forthcoming).

[79] Cf. Article 38, paragraph 1, of the Statute of the International Court of Justice, according to which the Court shall apply not only international conventions and international customary law but also 'the general principles of law recognized by civilized nations'.

[80] The specific relationship between general principles of law and peremptory norms is a moot question which cannot be developed here (it is more commonly assumed that norms of *jus cogens* can emerge as customary law, see e.g. Shearer, *Starke's International Law*, p. 49, while the general principles of law referred to in Article 38 of the Statute of the International Court of Justice are often associated with general principles developed in domestic law contexts).

[81] Cf. the way the Court of Justice of the European Communities has applied fundamental human rights as general principles of Community law.

Apart from such doctrinal issues, international enforcement is clearly in need of some more teeth. This need is underscored by the seemingly declining role of the state in law-making and law-enforcement. At least for the foreseeable future, some military backing, too, will be needed, maybe in the form of an international military police force.[82] Whether international law and order will in the more distant future be secured simply through technological and cultural developments rather than military force, is a question of images and mind processes which is still awaiting an answer.

---

[82] Rosas, 'Towards some international law and order', pp. 133–4.

Stock-taking on Human Rights: The World Conference on Human Rights, Vienna 1993

KEVIN BOYLE

Introduction

In June 1993, 171 states were gathered by the United Nations in Vienna to confer on human rights. Representatives of states and of international agencies were joined by an estimated 800 non-governmental organizations, making it the largest assembly ever on global human rights issues. The Vienna World Conference on Human Rights was only the second such international consultation focused exclusively on human rights in United Nations history. A similar conference had been held in Teheran in 1968 to mark the twenty fifth anniversary of the Universal Declaration of Human Rights.[1] International conferences are not a new phenomenon but historically a staple of great power diplomacy. But in a post-colonial world of now over 180 independent and formally equal states, such world wide UN inspired consultations, involving all governments and open to a degree of non-governmental participation and pressure, has a distinctly different significance. The World Conference on Human Rights in Vienna had been preceded by the Rio conference on Environment and Development, in 1992 and was followed in September 1993 by the UN conference on Population and Development held in Cairo. A conference on World Social Development will be held in March 1995 in Copenhagen, to be followed by the Fourth World Conference on Women in Beijing in September 1995. These global processes of consultation and participation and policy formation are likely to be a significant element in shaping the future international society.[2]

The idea of a world conference on human rights was first suggested in 1989, as the Cold War was coming to an end. The ideological competition between East and West which had long distorted United Nations processes was over. The thought was that a fresh start could be made in strengthening the United Nations to enable it to pursue a range of global challenges including its human rights mission.[3] The focus of the conference therefore was intended primarily

---

[1] See the Proclamation of Teheran, 13 May 1968 in, *Human Rights a Compilation of International Instruments* (New York, United Nations, 1988), p. 43.

[2] D. Held, *Democracy and the International Order* (London, Institute of Public Policy Research, 1993).

[3] Boutros Boutros Ghali, *An Agenda For Peace, Preventive Diplomacy Peacemaking and Peace-Keeping*, Security Council S/24111, 17 June 1992 (New York, United Nations).

as a review of the international system for promoting and protecting human rights.[4]

The conference when eventually held however, in June 1993, took place in an atmosphere with little of the euphoria and enthusiasm which had swept the world in 1989. Its agenda, only finally agreed through the intervention of the General Assembly, included more questioning of the basic principles of universal human rights and less focus on technical improvements than anticipated. The protracted process of preparing the conference and the bad tempered sessions at Vienna itself, were reminders of the deep uncertainties, confusion and regional tensions that have replaced the Cold War in international relations. The Conference was overshadowed by the shameful conflict in Bosnia Herzogovina, an hour's flight from Vienna and the failure it represented for the promise of a new era of international cooperation. But its defining feature was that it provided a major opportunity after decades of East–West ideological confrontation over human rights to address the most pressing of many global dilemmas: how can a common commitment to a single standard of human rights help transform relations between the developed minority world and the developing majority world?

The Conference did make a beginning in answering that question. It will be remembered for the acceptance by the North that the peoples of the South have a right to development and that guarantees of basic economic and social rights are necessary if political stability and respect for civil and political rights are to be ensured. It will be remembered also for the acceptance by the South that the pursuit of sustainable development requires a democratic society, not measured alone in the holding of elections, but in the full participation of the entire population men and women, in decisions effecting them. Successful development in turn requires effective governmental institutions which operate under the rule of law and which guarantee individual civil and political rights and freedoms.

The conference will be remembered less in terms of offering immediate answers to the explosion of ethno-nationalist conflict in different parts of Europe, Africa and Asia or to the massive violations of human rights which flow from such conflicts. However, the Conference conclusion that the promotion and protection of human rights must be treated as a priority objective of the United Nations as well as its recognition of the link between that objective and maintaining international peace and security, reflects new thinking which will prove significant in current debates over strengthening United Nations work in preventive diplomacy, peace-making and peace-keeping.

The World Conference was preceded by a negotiating process that centred on four preparatory meetings held in Geneva and a number of regional and

---

[4] The six objectives laid down for the World Conference were, (i) to review and assess progress in the field of human rights since 1948 and to identify obstacles and ways to overcome these; (ii) to evaluate the effectiveness of the UN's methods and mechanisms in the field of human rights; (iii) to formulate concrete recommendations for improving the UN human rights activities and mechanisms; (iv) to make recommendations to ensure the necessary resources for UN human rights activities; (v) to examine the relationship between development and all human rights and (vi) to examine ways and means to improve the implementation of existing human rights standards and instruments. General Assembly Resolution 45/155 of 18 December 1990.

satellite meetings.[5] In addition the preparatory process involved contributions from all the major UN agencies including the World Health Organization, UNESCO, the United Nations High Commission for Refugees, UNESCO and the ILO. The plan had been that the regional consultations would feed into the Geneva preparatory conferences and an agreed text might emerge for adoption at the Vienna Conference. In the event given a commitment to drafting by consensus, the text to be considered in Vienna was very far from a finished draft, due to disagreements between states and obstruction by some in the preparatory meetings.

Nevertheless the World Conference at the eleventh hour did manage to agree a text; the *Vienna Declaration and Programme of Action*.[6] Using the Vienna Declaration as a focus point, this paper will discuss some of the major controversies and outcomes of the World Conference, and what they tell us about the future possibilities of the human rights mission of the United Nations. Social scientists have difficulty in relating to the normative language of documents such as the Vienna Declaration. Such texts mirror the often abstract, rhetorical and coded diplomatic discourse of international gatherings. Nevertheless, declarations, communiqués, resolutions, treaties and conventions, are the end products of international diplomacy, and are a significant means of making sense of the world. They are also the building blocks of such international order as exists. In the case of the World Conference, given the unavoidable rules adopted – that the drafting of conclusions was by consensus, that no country could be named and that no reference could be made to any actual situation of violation of rights – abstractness and a degree of circumlocution in the final text were unavoidable.

It is certainly possible to read over the Declaration with glazed eyes and to put it aside as nothing other than well crafted but empty exhortation. It is however something more than that. It represents an admittedly uneasy global consensus on core human rights principles for the 1990s and at the least, an outline of priorities for action to implement that consensus. It also represents language of commitment which the third force in international human rights politics, after states and international agencies, non-governmental organizations (NGOs), can and will use to effect in all parts of the world on behalf of the victims they exist to represent. Quite the most optimistic outcome of the World Conference was the depth of common understanding on the level of values, on goals and required policies, expressed by human rights activists from both the South and the North of the world. In so far as tensions in the official conference reflected the divide between the developed and the developing world, the common cause made between local human rights advocates from

---

[5] Regional meetings were held for Africa, Latin America and the Asia Pacific Regions, which led to three regional declarations; Africa, A/conf.157/AFRM/14 Tunis 2–6 November 1992; Latin America and the Caribbean, A/CONF/.157/PC/58, San José 18–20 January 1993; Asia Pacific A/CONF.157/ASRM/4 Bangkok 29 March–2 April 1993. No European regional meeting was held, partly because of the argument that interregional meetings were to be preferred partly for cost reasons. A satellite interregional meeting was organized by the Council of Europe, see; *Human Rights at the Dawn of the 21st Century* (Strasbourg, Council of Europe, January 1993).

[6] Vienna Declaration and Programme of Action Adopted by the World Conference on Human Rights on 25 June 1993, UN Doc. A/CONF.157/23, reprinted in *Netherlands Quarterly of Human Rights*, 11 (1993), 346–68.

across the globe was a victory for the human rights idea.[7] The NGOs held their own parallel Forum in advance of the official conference and despite efforts to restrict their access to both the preparatory Geneva meetings and in Vienna, the sheer scale of their presence and particularly in the case of women's groups, their persistence and level of organization, ensured that the final conference document was less insubstantial than at least some of the diplomats might have wished.

Human Rights and International Law

'The World Conference on Human Rights reaffirms the solemn commitment of all States to fulfil their obligations to promote universal respect for, and observance and protection of, all human rights and fundamental freedoms for all in accordance with the Charter of the United Nations, other instruments relating to human rights, and international law. *'The universal nature of human rights and freedoms is beyond question.'*

This citation from the first paragraph of the Vienna Declaration brings out the core idea of international concern with human rights; that states, the principal subjects of international law, are obliged by international law to uphold them. International law suffers from problems of enforcement as is well known, but it has primacy over national law. Since 1945 the United Nations has, through its principal organ the Commission on Human Rights and its subordinate body the Sub-Commission on Prevention of Discrimination and the Protection of Minorities, developed international standards for universal application through numerous declarations, treaties and conventions.[8] The ultimate purpose is to ensure that such standards which are negotiated and agreed upon by states themselves, have effect on the lives of individuals within member states through their incorporation in national law and institutions. The international accountability for ensuring that states fulfil their treaty commitments is maintained through the operation of a variety of international human rights monitoring mechanisms and through procedures, albeit limited, for complaint by individuals to international bodies.

As part of the international system for implementing human rights the United Nations has encouraged the establishment of regional systems linked to regional international bodies. To date such regional systems exist for Africa, the Americas and Europe.[9] The need for further efforts to establish regional and sub-regional human rights systems in other parts of the world (in particular the Asia Pacific region and the Middle East), was one recommendation of the Vienna Conference.

The United Nations Commission on Human Rights began the task of elaborating standards with the Universal Declaration of Human Rights 1948,

---

[7] F. Azzam, 'Non Governmental Organizations and the UN World Conference on Human Rights', *The Review, International Commission of Jurists*, 50 (1993), 89–100.

[8] For the most comprehensive appraisal see, P. Alston (ed.), *The United Nations and Human Rights* (London, Oxford University Press, 1992).

[9] The three regional organizations which maintain permanent institutions for the protection of human rights are: The Council of Europe, The Organization of African Unity and the Organization of American States. The major conventions initiated by these bodies are The European Convention on Human Rights and Fundamental Freedoms in force since 1953, The African Charter of Human and Peoples Rights (1981) and the American Convention on Human Rights (1978).

still the most significant of all normative documents in United Nations history. While this catalogue of rights embracing civil, political, economic, social and cultural rights, was drafted and adopted by a United Nations General Assembly one third the size of the UN today, there has been a gradual process of adoption of the principles in the Declaration in most countries in the world as reflected in their constitutions and laws. The Universal Declaration was intended to set goals for all countries and for the international order itself in the recognition and protection of individual human rights. But it was not intended to be legally binding. Over the past forty years the United Nations has initiated a large number of treaties designed to commit states to uphold the principles of the Declaration as a matter of international obligation. In particular the International Covenant on Civil and Political Rights and the International Covenant on Social Economic and Cultural Rights may be mentioned here. These Covenants have now been ratified by the majority of states in the world community. A clear recommendation from the World Conference was that all states should ratify these texts, which along with the Universal Declaration are termed the International Bill of Human Rights.[10] In addition to 'standard setting' through the drafting of new agreements on human rights, the Commission on Human Rights has gradually developed a role in pressing states to implement their treaty commitments and in responding directly to the ever increasing scale of complaints about human rights violations in all parts of the world. Along with the separate bodies which monitor treaty commitments the Commission has evolved a complex system of special experts or rapporteurs and working groups, mandated to investigate a range of human rights violations, with competence to raise issues with governments and to publish reports which are then publicly discussed in the Commission's annual session. These 'thematic' rapporteurs who are unpaid, include experts working on the subjects of summary and arbitrary executions, torture, disappearances, mercenaries, and religious intolerance.[11] 'Country' rapporteurs, have also been created, for example in the case of Sudan, Iran, Iraq and the Israeli-Occupied territories.[12]

A major goal of the World Conference was to make this complex system work more effectively in the task of enforcing the agreed international standards of human rights protection. There can be no doubt that in a significant portion of the world, governments and armed opposition groups flagrantly violate these standards. At the outset of the Vienna Conference, the United Nations Human Rights Centre in Geneva, which services the work of the Commission on Human Rights, offered a sobering stock-taking of the state of human rights in the world: 'at least half of the world's people suffer from some serious violation of their economic, social, cultural, civil or political

---

[10] A large number of other human rights treaties have been initiated by the United Nations. The core treaties which states were pressed at Vienna to ratify in addition to the International Covenants are: The Convention on the Elimination of All Forms of Racial Discrimination, The Convention on the Elimination of All Forms of Discrimination Against Women, The Convention on the Rights of the Child and The Convention Against Torture. For a complete list of UN human rights treaties and declarations, see *A Compilation of International Instruments* (New York, United Nations, 1988).

[11] Following the World Conference, the latest such appointment is a special rapporteur on violence against women, see below.

[12] H. M. Cooke, 'International human rights mechanisms', *The Review, International Commission of Jurists*, 50 (1993), 31–55.

rights. These violations range from torture, execution, rape, arbitrary detention, violence and disappearances, to extreme poverty, slavery, child abuse, famine and undernourishment and lack of access to clean water, sanitation and health care'.[13]

Despite this depressing reality and despite the current failures of the United Nations and the governments which comprise it, to cope with the new challenges of peace-keeping in countries such as Bosnia, Somalia, Liberia and Rwanda, it is important not to dismiss the incremental achievements of the world body over half a century in building the foundations of a global human rights law. Those foundations were not dislodged in Vienna as some Western countries feared they might be. Rather in the unanimity of the non-governmental voice from all regions of the world in support of a stronger international commitment to eliminating violation, the obligation of states to respect human rights in international law was significantly reinforced.

Progress at Vienna on Old Disputes

As already noted, one unexpected result of the World Conference was the extent to which the fundamental concepts on which the United Nation's human rights achievements rest came under scrutiny. The initiative had come from mostly Asian countries and was inevitably viewed by Western countries as an effort to weaken the international system. But while an initiative spearheaded by countries such as China, Indonesia, North Korea, Malaysia and Iran, could hardly gain credibility as intended, the challenge in Vienna is likely to have positive results. At its heart Asian dissidence was based on a claim that the idea of human rights was not a universal one, but a Western and developed world construct. The West, it was feared, sought to use human rights as a stalking horse, to achieve global economic dominance over the developing and poorer world.

In the Vienna Declaration, the terms in which the universality of human rights was confirmed, the acceptance by Western countries of the equal validity of economic and social rights with other rights as well as the right to development, all represented positive outcomes. If the developed world regards these new commitments as existing only on paper, in particular the need to address the macro-economic causes of poverty, then the struggle against dictatorships in the South as well as gross violation of civil and political rights can only be frustrated. The challenge of promoting all human rights without distinction, left by the Vienna Declaration requires major responses from the North as well as South.

Human Rights and State Sovereignty

A measure of change in the growth of acceptance of the international law of human rights is how weakly the traditional claim of state sovereignty as an inhibition on the expression of international concern or positive action over the human rights practices of states, was directly canvassed in Vienna. The right of the international community to be concerned with human rights practices in any country was firmly restated in the Vienna Declaration.

---

[13] *World Conference on Human Rights Newsletter*, No. 2, May 1993, Geneva.

The United Nations Charter, Article 2 (7), enshrines the principle of state sovereignty in that the world body may not intervene in matters within the domestic jurisdiction of a state. That principle has been held in uneasy balance with the inevitable surrender of sovereignty implied by states' voluntary commitments to international agreements on human rights and international supervision under such agreements. In earlier times the claim of sovereignty precluded even the discussion of human rights violations in any state and led to the refusal of the UN to give any response to the complaints from victims which poured into the organization. The World Conference confirmed the competence of United Nation bodies such as the Commission on Human Rights not alone to discuss, but to subject to scrutiny and to critical study human rights violations in all countries.

During the Cold War the USSR and USA responded in different ways to the expansion of international law into areas of traditional sovereignty, their different responses contributing to the relative paralysis of the UN human rights system for half a century. In the case of the USSR, its allies and clients in Eastern Europe and world wide, the state was considered the only actor in international law and it was for the state not international agencies to supervise international commitments. The USSR ratified all treaties largely for propaganda reasons, but kept the international monitoring agencies at bay and denied the possibility of individual complaints to international bodies. A measure of change is that the international human rights standards to which the Russian Federation as successor state is committed, can be invoked directly by the individual litigant in the courts of Russia. Russian citizens may also petition international treaty bodies with complaints against their government.

The United States withdrew from the drafting of the International Covenants in 1953 and has until recently refused to accede to most human rights instruments. It argued that as its standards of human rights protection were higher than the international norm, accession to international conventions was unnecessary.[14] Whatever the merits of this argument such a policy damaged the credibility of the United Nations efforts to build universal binding norms, and denied to the fledgling international machinery the enormous contribution which US ratification of common standards would have entailed.[15] The United States has now ratified the International Civil and Political Covenant, and The Convention against Torture.[16] It has still to accede to the International Covenant on Economic, Social, and Cultural Rights.

The lowest level of ratifications of international human rights instruments is among states in Asia.[17] China in particular has stood outside the regime of the international law of human rights, and it is China which continues to claim that its human rights practices not least in the Tibet region are solely its internal

[14] F. Newman and D. Weisbrodt, *International Human Rights* (Cincinnati, Anderson, 1990), pp. 385–400.

[15] N. Rodley 'On the necessity of United States ratification of the international human rights conventions' in R. Lillich (ed.), *International Human Rights Instruments* (New York, 1985), pp. 4–13.

[16] See David P. Forsythe 'Human rights and US foreign policy: two levels, two worlds' in this volume.

[17] As of July 1992 of 45 UN member states in the Asia region, 19 only had ratified the International Covenant on Economic Social and Cultural Rights, and 18, the International Covenant on Civil and Political Rights.

affair. The exclusion of one fifth of the world's population from the international system of human rights protection is self-evidently a major continuing limitation on the ambition of universal acceptance of common human rights norms. Nevertheless in the longer term the call made in Vienna for global ratification of the main human rights treaties and the strong confirmation in the Vienna Declaration that human rights practices of all states are a legitimate concern of the international community has fundamental importance.[18]

However the acceptance of the principle of international accountability in Vienna was not matched on the part of states North or South, by a willingness to create more effective means for the securing of that accountability. One positive outcome has been the creation of a new United Nations position of Commissioner for Human Rights, discussed further below. But a proposal for the establishment of an international criminal court with jurisdiction to try those who violate human rights was not pursued.[19] Nor did the Conference take forward the debate over when it might be appropriate for international concern over massive violations of human rights to result in direct intervention by the international community even against the will of a country. No consensus is yet possible on that subject or on the need to equip the United Nations to fulfil its expanding peace-keeping role in the terms sought by the Secretary General in *Agenda for Peace*.[20]

Universalism v. Relativism

A variation on the theme of tension between state sovereignty and the evolving international human rights order, expressed itself at the World Conference in a challenge to the very possibility of universal standards. This topic caused most of the controversy in the preparatory meetings and at the plenary sessions in Vienna. Those who disputed the idea of universal rights were again Asian countries. The speech by the representative of China was typical:

> The concept of human rights is a product of historical development. It is closely associated with specific social, political and economic conditions and the specific history, culture and values of a particular country. Different historical development stages have different human rights requirements. Countries at different development stages or with different historical traditions and cultural backgrounds also have different understanding and practices of human rights. Thus one should not and cannot think the human rights standards and models of certain countries as the only proper ones and demand that all countries comply with them. It is neither realistic nor workable to make international economic assistance or even international cooperation conditional on them.[21]

---

[18] 'The promotion and protection of human rights is a legitimate concern of the international community' (para. 5).

[19] However important developments have taken place in the building of international criminal jurisdiction. The International Law Commission completed a draft statute to establish an International Criminal Tribunal, in May 1993, which has been received positively by the General Assembly. See, C. Tomuschat, 'A system of international criminal prosecution is taking place', *The Review, International Commission of Jurists*, 50 (1993), 56–70.

[20] N. Rodley (ed.), *To Loose the Bands of Wickedness, International Intervention in Defence of Human Rights* (London, Brasseys, 1992).

[21] Speech of Liu Huaqiu, head of the Chinese delegation, Vienna 15 June 1993.

The point was put more explicitly by the Iranian Deputy Foreign Minister at the Bangkok regional conference:

> To enhance the universality of human rights and relevant instruments it is imperative to be cognisant of the cultural diversity of the human family and respect the values of various cultures. This would not only contribute to the richness of human rights norms, but also provide the best guarantee for their universal observance. The political predominance of one group of countries in international relations, which is temporary by nature and history, cannot provide a licence for imposition of a set of guidelines and norms for the behaviour of the entire international community, especially since these states do not present an ideal feasible or practical model, in theory or practice, nor do they possess admirable pasts.[22]

These positions were countered by strong defences of universalism from not only the Western group of countries, but also in the declarations adopted at the Latin American and African regional conferences and by countries such as India and Japan in the Asia Group. The attack on universalism at the World Conference was considered by most participants as a rather thinly disguised objection to external criticism of the serious human rights violations in many Asian countries. The most effective counter to the proposition that the world's cultural diversity negates the possibility of common global standards of human rights, came in the Resolution adopted by Asian NGOs meeting in parallel session at the Bangkok regional human rights conference.

> *Universality.* We can learn from different cultures in a pluralistic perspective and draw lessons from the humanity of these cultures to deepen respect for human rights. There is emerging a new understanding of universalism encompassing the richness and wisdom of Asia-Pacific cultures.
>
> Universal human rights standards are rooted in many cultures. We affirm the basis of universality of human rights which affords protection to all of humanity including special groups such as women, children, minorities and indigenous peoples, workers, refugees and displaced persons, the disabled and the elderly. While advocating cultural pluralism, those cultural practices which derogate from universally accepted human rights including womens rights must not be tolerated.[23]

In the event the Vienna Declaration confirmed the principle of universality but in an important formulation that addresses all states, including those who defend universality:

> *All human rights are universal indivisible inter-dependent and inter-related. The international community must treat human rights globally in a fair and equal manner, on the same footing and with the same emphasis. While the significance of national and regional particularities and various historical cultural and religious backgrounds must be borne in mind, it is the duty of States, regardless of their political economic and cultural systems to promote*

---

[22] Statement by Dr Mohammed Javad Zarif, Asian Regional Meeting on Human Rights, Bangkok, 31 March 1993.

[23] The Bangkok NGO Declaration on Human Rights, 27 March 1993, reproduced, in *Fortnightly Review Law and Society*, 3 (1993) (Trust, Colombo), 5–21.

and protect all human rights and fundamental freedoms. (Vienna Declaration
paragraph 5.)

The injunction to treat human rights 'globally in a fair and equitable
manner', underscores the hypocrisy which surrounds the subject in almost all
states. The argument can be made that the attack on universalism by some of
the countries in Vienna represents a defensive reaction to the relativism
practised in the foreign policy of powerful states towards human rights
violators. For many countries it is still a case of ignoring violations of friends
and attacking the violations of enemies. Objectivity, impartiality and
consistency in treating human rights problems are concomitants of
universalism. As far as most Middle East and Islamic countries have been
concerned, the prime example has been at least until recently the indulgence of
the United States towards Israel and the related failure of the United Nations
to take any effective measures in response to that country's ignoring of Security
Council resolutions arising from its occupation of the West Bank and the Gaza
Strip. In other parts of the world the scepticism about human rights has been
engendered by the sorry record of the West during the Cold War of ignoring
dictatorships or even installing them with questions of human rights and
democracy forgotten. The circle of hypocrisy is completed when states, for
example in the Middle East, complain of double standards of others while
denying the same international standards of human rights to their own
populations. As already noted those states from Asia which spearheaded the
attack on universalism have consistently failed to ratify the international
human rights conventions.

The reference to 'national and regional peculiarities' which are to be borne in
mind, in implementing common international standards, need not in practice
qualify the idea of universality. The virtual abolition of the death penalty in
Western Europe in contrast to its retention in the United States, including in
some states, for minors convicted of murder, illustrates that national
peculiarities are not all expressed between the North and the South of the
world. An example of mandated discretion for states in implementing
international common standards is to be found in the Convention on the
Rights of The Child. The Convention provides that the definition of childhood
and the age of majority is a matter for national decision not international
prescription. Where conflict with the Convention would arise is if for example,
the girl child was treated in a less favourable manner as regards her rights to
the boy child, and this was justified by national, religious or cultural practices.
The rights of the girl child and adult women was the subject of special attention
in the Vienna Declaration (see below), but the Declaration's affirmation of
universality offers no warrant for gender or other discrimination contrary to
global standards.

The Indivisibility and Interdependence of Rights

The Cold War saw unresolved disputes over the priority of civil and political,
versus economic, social and cultural rights, and over the nature of the right to
development. These old controversies were again debated in Vienna and with
constructive outcomes. The United States in particular had hitherto set its face
against the recognition of an international concept of economic and social

rights. This had been a subject of sterile confrontation with the former socialist states. Indifference or ideological hostility to economic and social rights with one fifth of the world's population afflicted by poverty, disease, illiteracy and insecurity, undermined the idea of a universal understanding of rights.[24] The acceptance at Vienna by the United States and other richer countries of the validity of economic and social rights and the interdependence of these rights with civil and political freedoms, represents one small positive gain from the aftermath of the Cold War. This is true also of the Western group of states' acceptance of the right to development (discussed below). Whether the implications of these commitments will be as potentially revolutionary as they might be, in terms of addressing global causes of poverty and under-development may be doubted. One proof of the United States conversion would be the ratification of the Covenant on Economic Social and Cultural Rights, an event which, however, seems unlikely after the mid-term elections in Congress have returned a Republican majority which includes forces openly hostile to the United Nations if not the very concept of an international community.

The theoretical status of economic and social rights as rights is discussed in detail in David Beetham's contribution.[25] On the practical level the Vienna Conference endorsed the present work of the Commission on Human Rights and the Economic Social and Cultural Rights Committee in drafting a protocol to the ESCR Covenant which would make possible complaints about violations of these rights to the ESCR Committee. It also endorsed the proposal that a system of indicators to assess progress achieved in implementing economic and social rights should be developed. These initiatives are the beginnings of an overdue answer to the complaint from the developing countries that the mechanisms of the Commission have been exclusively concerned with responding to violations of civil and political rights. The greater attention to the violation of economic and social rights and the development of effective means of responding to them is among the most important challenges to the UN human rights system in the years ahead.[26]

New Human Rights Linkages

Human Rights Democracy and Development

Democracy, development and respect for human rights and fundamental freedoms are interdependent and mutually reinforcing. (Vienna Declaration, paragraph 8.)

This sentence from the Vienna Declaration reflects the progress of democratization in the world since the fall of the Berlin Wall. It also marks the end to the conceptual distance traditionally maintained in international thinking about development, rights and democracy. The debate over human rights and development has been a continuing one in the United Nations since the 1960's and the beginning of the period of decolonization. It became another

---

[24] Statement to the World Conference on Human Rights on behalf of the Committee on Economic Social and Cultural Rights, A/CONF/.157/PC/62/Add.5.

[25] See 'Introduction' in this volume.

[26] A. Eide, K. Kruase and A. Rosas, *Economic, Social and Cultural Rights: a Textbook* (Dordrecht, Martinus Nijhoff, 1994).

point of confrontation between West and East as well as with the developing world. At heart the issue was and remains one about means. How are the poorer countries to advance economically, and what is the role of the developed world in assisting their economic advancement? Debates raged over the issue of whether the goal of economic development justified one party political systems in developing countries and the sacrifice of civil and political rights.[27] The controversy at international level was reflected in the efforts of the developing countries backed by the Soviet Union to fashion a concept of the 'right to development'.[28] This met hostility and rejection by the West which denounced the idea of collective rights and the global economic reforms sought by the advocates of a right to development.

The General Assembly of the United Nations did finally adopt a Declaration on the Right to Development, after many years of preparation in 1986.[29] This Declaration states that the right to development is:

> an inalienable right by virtue of which every human person and all peoples are entitled to participate in, contribute to, and enjoy economic, social, cultural and political development, in which all human rights and fundamental freedoms can be fully realized.

The Declaration goes on to provide that 'the human person is the central subject of development and should be an active participant and beneficiary of the right to development'. The duty holders of this right are states acting at the national level 'to ensure *inter alia*, equality of opportunity for all in access to basic resources, education, health services, food, housing, employment and the fair distribution of income'. States at international level have the duty to cooperate to ensure that developing countries have the means to enable comprehensive development.

The Vienna conference document establishes convergence between the developed and developing world that development requires a democratic base. Democracy, defined as a political system which is based on the freely expressed will of the people and which involves the full participation of men and women in all aspects of their lives, provides the political framework for the guarantee of all human rights. Development in turn requires effective institutions governed by the rule of law and popular participation by men and women on equal terms.[30]

In the new post-Cold War international environment, there remains however fundamental dispute over the global economic order, over the role of the agencies linked but not controlled by the United Nations, the World Bank and International Monetary Fund, and the pursuit of free market ideology. The hostility of the South to donor countries imposing conditions on development

---

[27] R. Howard, 'The full belly thesis: should economic rights take priority over civil and political rights', *Human Rights Quarterly*, 5 (1983), 467–90.

[28] P. Alston, 'Making space for new human rights: the case of the right to development', *Harvard Human Rights Yearbook*, 1 (1988), 3–25.

[29] Declaration on the Right to Development, adopted by the General Assembly resolution 41/128 of 4 December 1986.

[30] C. J. Dias and D Gillies, *Human Rights Democracy and Development*, paper commissioned by the UN Centre for Human Rights for the World Conference, A/CONF.157/PC/20, also published by the International Centre for Human Rights and Democratic Development, Montreal, May 1993.

aid because of concern over human rights or to press for the implementation of 'good governance' policies, was also very evident in Vienna. These questions were beyond the competence of the World Conference to other than broach. The next round of global debate on North and South will take place in the World Conference on Social Development in Copenhagen in March 1995. The likelihood of fundamental agreement on such issues, as the effects on developing countries of structural adjustment policies of the World Bank and IMF, the cancellation of the debt burden, fairer import policies for the products of the poorest economies and aid conditionality will hardly be resolved there either. But the outcome of Vienna that the donor countries and the developing world are agreed on the linkage between development, democracy and human rights is an important advance over the sterile debates of the 1970s on the supposed trade-offs between these concepts. The Human Rights Commission has subsequent to the World Conference established a permanent working group on the right to development.[31]

Women and Human Rights

Under the slogan 'women's rights are human rights' women's groups made a huge impact on the Vienna Conference as reflected in the range of recommendations adopted relating to women and the girl-child. The point of the slogan was not to claim different rights for women, but to protest the treating of discrimination and violation of the rights of women as separate and marginal as compared to other kinds of human rights violations.[32] Despite the existence of a Convention on the Elimination of Discrimination against Women, which has been in force since 1979 and has been ratified by some 130 countries, it has largely been true that gender-specific violations have been invisible in international human rights debate. The fact that the Committee to monitor complaints of discrimination under the Women's Convention is located in Vienna and not at the hub of UN human rights discussion and activity, Geneva, is a concrete example of the problem. Women's groups sought and achieved a recommendation that gender issues should be integrated or 'mainstreamed' in the UN system. They achieved a recognition and condemnation of male violence against women in public and private. Following the Conference the Commission on Human Rights appointed a special rapporteur on the global problem of violence against women and the General Assembly also agreed a Declaration on the Elimination of Violence Against Women.[33]

One significant feature of these initiatives is the extension of international concern and state accountability for violence done to women by males as

---

[31] Resolution No. 1994/21. The first report of the working group is contained in document E/CN.4/1994/21.

[32] C. Bunch, 'The global campaign for women's human rights', *The Review, International Commission of Jurists*, 50 (1993), 105–9.

[33] 48/104 Declaration on the Elimination of Violence against Women, Resolution adopted by the General Assembly (on the report of the Third Committee (A/48/629); The Special Rapporteur on Violence Against Women is Mrs Radhika Coomaraswamy, Sri Lanka. For her terms of reference see E/CN.4/1994/L.8/Rev.1) The Special Rapporteur will gather information on violence against women its causes and consequences. She may name countries where abuse of the rights of women occur and make recommendations to eliminate such abuses.

individuals whether in private or public. Traditionally violation of human rights have been conceived of as resulting from actions by the state and its agencies, not by private individuals. The international accountability of the state will now be engaged in the area of domestic violence for example, where governments neglect to investigate, prosecute and punish such violence. The assumption of concern by the international community over male violence against women offers a vivid example of how the dynamic of the international human rights system continues to transform the concept of state sovereignty.

The Vienna Declaration also called for efforts to eliminate 'conflicts that may arise between the rights of women and the harmful effects of certain traditional or customary practices, cultural prejudices and religious extremism'. The target of this recommendation – widespread discrimination in the treatment of the girl-child, in the civil status of adult women, in property rights including inheritance, in access to credit, more often than not sanctioned by customary law or religious precept, in many developing countries – could hardly be clearer. The injunction in the new UN Declaration on the Elimination of Violence Against Women is equally explicit: 'States should condemn violence against women and should not invoke any custom, tradition or religious consideration to avoid their obligations with respect to its elimination'.

Scepticism over the likely effects of such statements on the status of women in the countries in question, has to be balanced by the advance made for women's equality by such specific recognition and condemnation of gender injustice in an international declaration. At least one positive function of an event such as the Vienna Conference was the opportunity it provided for practical cooperation and the expression of solidarity between women from developed and developing worlds. The global women's movement which has been built since the UN Decade for Women (1975–85) has had tangible effects on perceptions and attitudes throughout the world community towards the subordination and oppression of women. It is unlikely that the pressure for equality will be relaxed after Vienna. The Fourth World Conference on Women to be held in Beijing in September 1995, will provide another opportunity to ensure that the Vienna commitments are fulfilled by governments.

Other Human Rights Themes: Self Determination

Space does not permit a commentary on all human rights themes and issues lobbied over and debated at the Vienna Conference. The Vienna Declaration identifies and makes recommendations about many such questions including the rights of indigenous peoples, minorities, children and the disabled. The document also contains important sections on gross violation of human rights in all parts of the world, including the need to more effectively counter racism, xenophobia and ethnic cleansing. It condemned the evils of torture, arbitrary killings and disappearances, and emphasized the importance of effective remedies and properly resourced and functioning criminal justice systems. It called for greater efforts by the world community and by national governments to eradicate illiteracy and to deepen human rights education. The text speaks of including human rights, humanitarian law, democracy and the rule of law as subjects in the curriculum at all levels.

But there were issues which were neglected, most significantly that of the right to self determination and the outbreak since 1989 of ethnic conflict and disputes over territorial boundaries. Probably more victims of human rights violations today suffer from ethnic conflict or from the collapse of states as in the case of Somalia, Liberia, Rwanda or Afghanistan than from authoritarian regimes. The Vienna Declaration achieved nothing except the reiteration of the formal norms of international law on self determination issues. These acknowledge a right of peoples to self determination and permit those under 'colonial or other forms of alien domination or foreign occupation' to take any legitimate action to realize their right to self determination. At the same time, the right to self-determination must not be construed as authorizing 'action which would dismember or impair, totally or in part, the territorial integrity or political unity of sovereign States conducting themselves in compliance with the principles of equal rights and self determination of peoples and thus possessed of a Government representing the whole people belonging to the territory without distinction of any kind'.[34]

[That careful piece of drafting can be taken to mean that apart from the special cases of colonial and equivalent occupation, there is no right to secede from existing states.]That is one of the few principles on which in a world of states there is complete firmness in law and practice. But the Vienna document is regressive in that it fails to discuss the idea of 'internal self determination' including that of local or regional autonomy for ethnic minorities.[35]

The current suppression of the self-proclaimed independent republic of Chechnya by Russia, and the military suppression of the Kurdish minority in Turkey are examples from among many situations of the failure of the international order to insist upon democratic mechanisms for the internal recognition of the diversity of peoples and of the need to achieve negotiation over the often arbitrary or unjust territorial borders that states defend. The sensitivity and difficulty of the self-determination question should not on the other hand be underestimated. The brutal practices of ethnic cleansing and the rupture of the pluri-ethnic state of Bosnia Herzogovina is the clearest reminder of the abuse of possible claims to independence and self determination, as the Conference recognized in a resolution passed on Bosnia, at the behest of Moslem countries.

Strengthening the United Nations Machinery in the Field of Human Rights

In advancing the Conference objectives to reform the United Nations human rights system, the predominant and correct view is that the World Conference Action Plan was a disappointment. The Conference did call for more financial resources for the system. At present the human rights budget represents less than one per cent of the total UN budget.[36] Whether governments have the will

[34] Vienna Declaration, para. 2.

[35] The most open of the international texts on minority rights is The Document of the Copenhagen Meeting of the Conference on the Human Dimension of the CSCE. The text is to be found in R. Brett and E. Edison, 'Minorities a report on the CSCE Human Dimension Seminar on Case Studies on National Minority Issues: positive results', *Papers in the Theory and Practice of Human Rights*, 6 (1993), University of Essex, Appendix 1.

[36] See M. Vassiliou, Strengthening of the United Nations human rights programme: one of the priorities of the organization', 1993 A/CONF.157/PC/60/Add.7, pp. 45–7.

to meet the true costs of the enlarged human rights agenda they approved in Vienna remains to be seen. The one institutional reform has been the appointment following the conference of a High Commissioner for Human Rights. The idea of the High Commissioner has been debated for many years and succeeded on this occasion mainly because of NGO pressure.[37] The High Commissioner will have overall responsibility for the UN human rights programme. He will in particular add a political and diplomatic presence able to meet directly with governments at the highest level. The High Commissioner has already pledged to make follow up to the Vienna Conference a priority. Given his appointment the many important studies and proposals for coordination and integration of the complex UN human rights programme, which were prepared for the Vienna Conference, have now the possibility of gradual implementation. Reform however will prove impossible if the human and financial resources are not made available.

Conclusion

There is a saying in UN circles that the only possible outcomes of a United Nations conference is that it is successful or very successful. The World Conference in Vienna has failed to secure even these conventional plaudits. No one describes it as a failure but neither will it be the springboard for the vision of a new international commitment to human rights. The fundamental reality which the World Conference brought out behind all the tensions and disputes is the dramatic inequalities in the world often described as interdependent and a single family. The gap between North and South in life chances and prosperity may yet prove a greater challenge to an international order based on human rights than the nuclear stand off in the Cold War.

There were steps symbolic and practical taken at Vienna which give cause for hope. The detailed reforms proposed for the Human Rights Centre and not debated at the Conference can nevertheless be pushed further by the one major new advance flowing from Vienna, the appointment of the High Commissioner for Human Rights. The consensus on the interdependence of economic and social rights with civil and political rights, and the recognition equally of the links between democracy, human rights and development are positions which states cannot easily resile on even if they are reluctant to grasp their implications. International conferences such as occurred in Vienna do raise popular consciousness and concern about human rights abuses. Above all they facilitate the 'networking' of NGOs and strengthen their capacity to press governments to fulfil promises.

The scale of humanitarian catastrophe in various parts of the world reflects fundamental failings of the system of international order, and the world community seems unprepared for the radical changes necessary to prevent such tragedies, in particular by reform of the United Nations and equipping it to play an effective preventive role.[38] There is a risk that these spectacular failures of the inter-state system in ensuring peace in the post-Cold War world can lead

---

[37] The new High Commissioner appointed by resolution of the General Assembly on 20 December 1993, is Mr Jose Ayala Lasso a Peruvian diplomat.

[38] E. Childers, in *A Time Before Warning. Strengthening the United Nations System* (London, Catholic Institute of International Relations, 1993).

us to ignore the less visible and in the longer term most hopeful ways of ending such disasters, the growth of common human rights understandings expressed in the norms of international law.

The Role and Limits of Human Rights NGOs at the United Nations

RACHEL BRETT

'... *organizations that operate as an essential brake on the juggernaut of state power*'.[1]

Introduction

The United Nations (UN) is an intergovernmental body. However, in an historic precedent, article 71 of the UN Charter[2] created a formal relationship between the UN and non-governmental organizations (NGOs). The term 'non-governmental organization' with its negative phraseology is inherently unsatisfactory; it could encompass any grouping that is not a government. It can also have unfortunate connotations; apparently in Chinese it translates as '*anti*-government'.[3] It is unclear how distant from government, both in terms of political power and funding, an organization has to be to qualify as 'non-governmental'. The Charter itself having established the term makes no attempt at definition. The CSCE (Conference on Security and Co-operation in Europe), when it faced the question of NGO status in the 1990s, opted for self-definition, recognizing as NGOs 'Those who declare themselves as such according to existing national procedures' with a bar only on those using or publicly condoning violence or terrorism.[4] This singular decision has so far caused surprisingly few problems[5] but the UN shows no sign of following this example.

The relationship between NGOs and the UN is again under review, but at present the required characteristics remain those listed in Resolution 1296 of the Economic and Social Council (ECOSOC).[6] 'The organization shall be of

---

[1] L. Wiseberg, 'Protecting human rights activists and NGOs: what more can be done?', *Human Rights Quarterly*, 13 (1991) 525–44, p. 525.

[2] Charter of the United Nations, article 71: 'The Economic and Social Council may make suitable arrangements for consultation with non-governmental organizations which are concerned with matters within its competence...'.

[3] H. Tolley Jr., 'Popular sovereignty and international law: ICJ strategies for human rights standard setting', *Human Rights Quarterly*, 11 (1989), 561–85, p. 562.

[4] Document of the Moscow Meeting of the Conference on the Human Dimension of the CSCE, 1991, para. 43; CSCE Helsinki Decisions 1992, ch. I, para. 16.

[5] See R. Brett, 'NGOs and the human dimension of the CSCE', *CSCE ODIHR Bulletin*, 1 (1992/93), 1–6; R. Brett, 'Non-governmental organizations and the CSCE', *Helsinki Monitor*, 3 (1992), 19–24; and R. Brett, 'A new role for NGOs in the CSCE' in A. Bloed (ed.), *The Challenges of Change* (Dordrecht, Nijhoff, 1994), pp. 359–82.

[6] UN Economic and Social Council Resolution 1296 (XLIV) 'Arrangements for consultation with non-governmental organizations' of 23 May 1968.

representative character and of recognized international standing; it shall represent a substantial proportion, and express the views of major sections, of the population or of the organized persons within the particular field of its competence, covering, where possible, a substantial number of countries in different regions of the world.'[7] The Resolution specifies the required structure of the organization, including its policy-making procedure and members voting rights, and the question of financing: 'The basic resources ... shall be derived in the main part from contributions of the national affiliates or other components or from individual members'.[8] Provision is also made, exceptionally, for national NGOs 'after consultation with' the government concerned.[9]

Resolution 1296 qualifies human rights NGOs by specifying that they 'should have a general international concern with this matter, not restricted to the interests of a particular group of persons, a single nationality or the situation in a single State or restricted group of States'.[10] Human rights NGOs are however not simply products of the UN system. Archer[11] identifies the Anti-Slavery Society, founded in 1837, as the first human rights NGO but the creation of Amnesty International (AI) in 1961 marked the beginning of the real development of the international human rights movement, and over 1500 NGOs participated in the World Conference on Human Rights (Vienna 1993).[12]

Wiseberg suggests 'what distinguishes a human rights NGO from other political actors ... is that the latter typically are seeking to protect the rights only of their own constituents; a human rights group seeks to secure rights for all members of society. Furthermore a political group seeks to advance its own particular interests or programs; a human rights group seeks to keep the political process open to all legitimate societal forces'.[13] It is this general disinterested focus which distinguishes human rights NGOs from on the one hand 'sectional groups' such as trades unions, whose *raison d'être* is to protect the interests of their own members and on the other 'promotional groups', including humanitarian organizations and specific issue lobbies.[14] There is general agreement, too, in distinguishing them from political movements; thus Thoolen and Verstappen, 'their aim should not be to take over ... institutions or to have direct governmental responsibility'.[15]

Clearly, not all organizations fitting this definition have consultative status at the UN. Of those which do, many also work at the local, national and regional levels or have national affiliates who do, mobilizing interest groups, educating the public and representing clients in their dealings before national

---

[7] ECOSOC Resolution 1296, para. 4.

[8] ECOSOC Resolution 1296, para. 8.

[9] ECOSOC Resolution 1296, para. 9.

[10] ECOSOC Resolution 1296, para. 17.

[11] P. Archer, 'Action by unofficial organizations on human rights' in E. Luard (ed.), *The International Protection of Human Rights* (London, Thames and Hudson, 1967), pp. 160–82.

[12] M. Nowak and I. Schwarz, 'Introduction: the contribution of Non-Governmental Organizations' in M. Nowak (ed.), *World Conference on Human Rights* (Vienna, Manz, 1994), pp. 1–11, p. 3.

[13] Wiseberg, 'Protecting human rights activists and NGOs', p. 530.

[14] P. Willetts, 'Pressure groups as transnational actors' in P. Willetts (ed.), *Pressure Groups in the Global System* (London, Pinter, 1982), pp. 1–27.

[15] H. Thoolen and B. Verstappen, *Human Rights Missions: a Study of the Fact-finding Practice of Non-Governmental Organizations* (Dordrecht, Nijhoff, 1986), p. 12.

officials, courts and regional or international organs. Where the political situation allows, they may make representations to parliament or take out advertisements in the newspapers.[16] These grass-roots and national activities both inform and legitimize their international lobbying.

Conversely, by no means all the organizations which address UN human rights bodies are 'human rights NGOs' thus defined. To anyone attending such meetings, it soon becomes clear that some of the allegations of bias, political motivation and covert funding by hostile governments are credible, which unfortunately detracts from the perceived impartiality and standing of all NGOs.

In part, this is the result of the subjectivity of the ECOSOC criteria, compounded by the political nature of the decision-making on NGO status and the tendency of the governmental committee responsible not to give reasons for its decisions.[17] However there is also the problem that such status is the only access to the UN for those outside government (with the exception of observers of a rapidly diminishing number of recognized liberation movements).[18] Thus, when the UN Commission on Human Rights held a Special Session to consider the human rights situation in Rwanda, the then government was represented, but the only means available to the Rwandan Patriotic Front (not then in power) to address the Commission was under the auspices of NGOs. This is not an isolated incident; during the regular session of the Commission in 1994, the Government of Myanmar objected to an NGO speaker on the ground that he was 'the leader of the self-styled democratic opposition'. Similarly, minorities, unlike indigenous people, do not yet have a UN forum of their own, and thus seek NGO status in order to raise their voices at human rights meetings. This problem may be alleviated if a Working Group on Minorities is established as proposed by the 1994 UN Sub-Commission on Prevention of Discrimination and Protection of Minorities,[19] but some groups (for example, the East Timorese and Tibetans) are likely to resist the political implications of classification as 'minorities'.

Furthermore, organizations that are not essentially human rights NGOs may on occasion operate as such, for example, professional associations such as the medical associations that support doctors refusing to participate in torture and draw up guidelines for their members about medical ethics, and labour unions opposing repressive regimes abroad.[20] Also, organizations may over time and with changing circumstances develop into human rights NGOs in the way that the Mothers of the Plaza de Mayo, a grass-roots self-help and community organization in Argentina, led to the development of FEDEFAM (the Latin American Federation of Families of the Disappeared) whose role is not only to

---

[16] See H. Steiner, *Diverse Partners: Non-Governmental Organizations in the Human Rights Movement* (Cambridge MA, Harvard College, 1991); H. Hannum, 'Implementing human rights: an overview of strategies and procedures' in H. Hannum (ed.), *Guide to International Human Rights Practice* (Philadelphia, Pennsylvania University Press, 2nd ed., 1992), pp. 19–38; and L. Whelan, 'The challenge of lobbying for civil rights in Northern Ireland: the Committee on the Administration of Justice', *Human Rights Quarterly*, 14 (1992), 149–70.

[17] Chiang Pei-Heng, *Non-Governmental Organizations at the United Nations* (New York, Praeger, 1981), p. 96.

[18] The International Committee of the Red Cross has observer status.

[19] Sub-Commission Resolution 1994/4.

[20] D. Forsythe, 'Protecting human rights: the private sector' in D. Forsythe (ed.), *Human Rights in World Politics* (Lincoln, University of Nebraska, 1989), pp. 83–101, p. 83.

support the different local groups, but also advocacy at the regional and international level on particular situations and issues.[21]

Human Rights NGOs at the UN

[International] NGOs have become a bridge between the real world of violations, 'what happens out there', and legal–political and bureaucratic institutions in the human rights world.[22]

Although there was no formal provision for them, NGOs in practice had access to the League of Nations and this experience influenced future developments. The US delegation to the San Francisco Conference of 1946 which drafted the UN Charter, included NGO representatives but Chiang[23] disputes the traditional view that Article 71 is directly attributable to them, rather that they shifted the US position thus enabling its inclusion. Either way it was a radical development, particularly in the human rights field which is inevitably a battleground between governments and civil society (in international relations terminology), pressure groups (in British political terms) or interest groups (in American political science). The inherent tension was illustrated at the UN Commission on Human Rights in 1993, when the Indonesian Ambassador found himself chairing some Commission sessions at which representatives of NGOs from East Timor raised the human rights situation there. As Chair, he was required to give these representatives the floor and permit them to speak without interruption or comment.

A recent Report of the UN Secretary-General observes that although the NGO role does not amount to 'the statutory consultation on political questions that NGOs had aimed for',[24] NGOs nevertheless provide 'the closest approximation to direct popular participation in the intergovernmental machinery' of the UN.[25] Nor is this participation restricted to the formal structures.[26] The Secretary-General's Report concedes 'Even a cursory examination of the participation of NGOs in the decision-making systems and operational activities of the United Nations shows without any doubt that NGO involvement has not only justified the inclusion of Article 71 . . . but that it has far exceeded the original scope of these legal provisions'.[27] The formal situation[28] is that NGOs in 'consultative status with ECOSOC'[29] are entitled to attend public meetings of ECOSOC and its subsidiary bodies, to make oral

---

[21] See Wiseberg, 'Protecting human rights activists and NGOs'.

[22] Steiner, *Diverse Partners*, p. 62.

[23] Chiang, *Non-Governmental Organizations at the United Nations*, pp. 42–4.

[24] General Review of Arrangements for Consultations with Non-Governmental Organizations (Report of the Secretary-General) E/AC.70/1994/5 of 26 May 1994, para. 36.

[25] General Review of Arrangements for Consultations with Non-Governmental Organizations, para. 33.

[26] See R. Brett, 'The contribution of NGOs to the monitoring and protection of human rights in Europe: an analysis of the role and access of NGOs to the inter-governmental organizations' in A. Bloed, L. Leicht, M. Nowak and A. Rosas (eds), *Monitoring Human Rights in Europe* (Dordrecht, Nijhoff, 1993), pp. 121–44.

[27] General Review of Arrangements for Consultations with Non-Governmental Organizations, para. 40.

[28] Contained in ECOSOC Resolution 1296.

[29] Although there are three levels of NGO status, Category I, Category II and the Roster, in practice the distinctions between them are generally ignored.

statements and to submit short written statements which are translated into the UN languages and circulated as official UN documents. It would be altogether wrong, however, to measure the NGO contribution in terms of its formal volume just as it would be misleading to think that the most vocal NGOs are necessarily the most influential.[30] Much of the input is made behind the scenes in the lobbying of government delegations and experts, drafting of resolutions, working with the UN Human Rights Centre and using the implementation procedures. In fact, the entire UN human rights system would quite simply cease to function without the NGOs.

Dolgopol[31] defines the role of human rights on organizations as 'to promote knowledge of human rights, identify problems in the protection and enjoyment of human rights and seek changes in legislation and practice that would further their protection and enjoyment'. At the UN this translates into ensuring that people know of their rights and the means of claiming them, taking up the cases of individual victims (or groups) or supporting the victims in doing so, making humanitarian appeals, monitoring, investigating and reporting on the human rights situations in states, including using public and confidential procedures to raise large-scale human rights violations, lobbying to affect the foreign policy of countries in relation to states violating human rights, mobilizing interest groups and standard-setting. Which of these roles are undertaken, and whether 'passively', providing information which may or may not be used by governmental delegates or experts, or 'actively' by participating in the drafting of resolutions or standards, depends on the NGO.[32] These roles can be illustrated more specifically by dividing the UN's human rights activities into standard-setting, treaty bodies and political bodies.

Standard Setting

The easiest area in which to document the contribution of NGOs is in standard-setting because the product is a new standard or specific wording in a standard which can often be traced directly to the activities of NGOs.

Perhaps the most extensively documented[33] are the roles of the International Commission of Jurists (ICJ) and AI in relation to the Declaration and Convention against Torture, including the AI campaign of 1972/3 which initiated the whole standard-setting process in this area. Baehr notes in particular the role of these NGOs in successfully pushing the concept of universal criminal jurisdiction in relation to alleged torturers in the face of

---

[30] See 'Oral Participation by NGOs in the Fiftieth Session of the Commission on Human Rights, February–March 1994', (Geneva, Quaker UN Office, 1994).

[31] U. Dolgopol, 'Human rights activist organizations and the protection of human rights', in *Collection of Lectures* (Strasbourg, International Institute of Human Rights, 1986), p. 1.

[32] F. Ermacora, 'Non-governmental organizations as promoters of human rights' in F. Matscher and H. Petzold (eds), *Protecting Human Rights: the European Dimension*, (Cologne, Heymanns, 1990), pp. 171–80, pp. 173–4; and see D. Weissbrodt, 'The contribution of international nongovernmental organizations to the protection of human rights', in T. Meron (ed.), *Human Rights in International Law* (Oxford, Clarendon, 1984), pp. 403–38; Steiner, *Diverse Partners*; and H. Hannum, 'Implementing human rights'.

[33] See Tolley, 'Popular sovereignty and international law'; N. Rodley, *The Treatment of Prisoners under International Law* (Oxford, Clarendon, 1987); and P. Baehr, 'The General Assembly: negotiating the Torture Convention' in D. Forsythe (ed.), *The United Nations in the World Political Economy* (Basingstoke, Macmillan, 1989), pp. 36–53.

scepticism even from governments promoting the Convention. He provides an illuminating account of the interactions between national and international NGOs and Governments, showing that the Dutch approach at the UN was changed by the activities of the Dutch section of Amnesty working through their parliament, but that positions were subsequently reversed, with the (governmental) chairman–rapporteur of the drafting group visiting London in order to lobby both the UK Foreign and Commonwealth Office and AI (which had reservations about the draft), for support for the Convention in the General Assembly – an action which demonstrates a conviction about the real importance of AI support.

The role of the NGO group in the drafting of the (1989) Convention on the Rights of the Child, has been described as being 'without parallel in the history of drafting international instruments'.[34] Its imprint, claims Price Cohen 'can be found in almost every article'.[35] Even so the NGOs failed in their effort to raise the minimum age for recruitment into armed forces and participation in hostilities to 18 years. However, the NGOs (in particular Radda Barnen and the Friends World Committee for Consultation) refused to accept this failure as final and persuaded the Committee on the Rights of the Child (the expert body set up to oversee the implementation of the Convention) to take up the issue. The result is a further standard-setting exercise: the drafting of an Optional Protocol to the Convention to remedy this deficiency, in which again, the NGOs are playing a significant part: initiating ideas, co-ordinating with the intergovernmental agencies and others concerned about the issue and reminding governments of the realities of the situations in which under-age recruitment occurs.[36] Some indication of the extent to which on this working level NGOs are taken into partnership with governments is given by the fact that at the 1994 Working Group drafting the Optional Protocol, the proposal to give the Committee on the Rights of the Child greater powers appeared in draft headed 'Poland (Quakers' art. 7 amended)' and was referred to through-out as the 'Polish/Quaker proposal'. Not surprisingly, the Draft Report of the Working Group[37] shows strong evidence of NGO input.

Treaty Bodies

'Governments lie'[38] should be inscribed over the doorway of every human rights NGO and forum in which human rights issues arise. Even the most democratic and law-abiding governments do not publicize their human rights violations and most try to conceal or deny them. The greatest myth of human rights implementation – breathtaking in its naivety – is the idea that by receiving a report from the government concerned an international body could ascertain the degree of compliance of that country with its international legal human rights obligations. The treaty bodies, the committees set up by the

[34] S. Detrick, J. Doet and N. Cantwell, *The United Nations Convention on the Rights of the Child: a Guide to the* Travaux Preparatoires (Dordrecht, Nijhoff, 1992), p. 24.
[35] C. Price Cohen, 'The role of non-governmental organizations in the drafting of the Convention on the Rights of the Child', *Human Rights Quarterly*, 12 (1990), 137–47, p. 142.
[36] See FWCC Comments on the preliminary draft optional protocol in E/CN.4/1994/WG.13/2/Add.1 of 14 September 1994.
[37] Draft Report of the Working Group on its first session E/CN.4/WG.13/CRP.1
[38] The words of an international civil servant who must remain anonymous.

human rights covenants and conventions to oversee their implementations, rely extensively, therefore, on NGO information when examining these reports from States.

Although NGOs were not initially provided with an official role in the international human rights treaty-monitoring process in general, the changes in the former Soviet Union and the consequent acceptance of NGOs enabled the contribution of NGOs to be made public and official. Thus in 1993 the Vienna Statement of the International Human Rights Treaty Bodies recognized that 'the active cooperation of non-governmental organizations is essential to enable the treaty bodies to function in an informed and effective manner. They have important roles to play in: scrutinizing States party's reports at the national level; providing information to treaty-bodies; assisting in the dissemination of information; and contributing to the implementation of recommendations by the treaty bodies'.[39]

The procedure of each Committe and the extent and method of involvement of NGOs varies, but it is now not only accepted practice but a position of principle that NGOs should be involved in the process. In this context it is important to recall that the concept of the UN as a purely intergovernmental body is, at least in the human rights field, misleading since most of the human rights bodies are (in theory and to a greater or lesser extent in practice) composed not of representatives of governments but of independent experts. The confrontational element inherent in NGO-Government relations is therefore reduced, with NGOs and experts together endeavouring to bring about changes in governmental attitudes and actions.

The experience of Ireland's report under the International Covenant on Civil and Political Rights, demonstrates the kind of role and the effectiveness of such a procedure.[40] Although NGOs were not involved in the drafting of the State report the Irish Commission on Justice and Peace (ICJP) produced a guide for NGOs on the Covenant and the reporting process; the Government made their report widely available; and a number of NGOs sent information to the Human Rights Committee with a copy to the Government. The ICJP were present during the consideration of the report, which enabled them to provide additional information, to comment to Committee members on the Government replies, and to keep the other NGOs and the media in Ireland informed about what was happening in the Committee. The result was a well-informed discussion between the Committee and the high-level government delegation, and a number of changes in the law and practice in Ireland.

The role of NGOs in the reporting procedure under the Convention on the Rights of the Child is more specific and well-developed, partly because of the major contribution of NGOs to the drafting of the Convention. There is an NGO Group for the Convention on the Rights of the Child, (a successor to the NGO Group which participated so actively in the drafting), with a paid co-ordinator, part of whose assignment is to alert children's rights organizations or networks in the countries whose reports are to be considered, and to brief

---

[39] Recommendations for Enhancing the Effectiveness of United Nations Activities and Mechanisms: Vienna Statement of the International Human Rights Treaty Bodies (A/CONF.157/TBB/4) of 16 June 1993, para. 16.

[40] M. O'Flaherty, 'The reporting obligation under Article 40 of the International Covenant on Civil and Political Rights: lessons to be learned from consideration by the Human Rights Committee of Ireland's First Report', *Human Rights Quarterly*, 16, 515–38.

them on when and how to make their input. Thus NGO contributions are less random than to other treaty bodies and it is rare for there to be no input from NGOs on the ground. Where the local NGOs feel too much at risk to be identified as the authors of the information, it is channelled through one of the international NGOs.

Although NGOs themselves cannot use the individual petition procedures under the international human rights treaties, they play a major facilitating role in making known the procedures. More directly, the Committee against Torture has a unique power to investigate if it receives reliable information of systematic use of torture,[41] and this has been used by Amnesty International to raise the use of torture in Turkey, a practice further exposed by the Committee's subsequent investigation.

Political Bodies

Fact-finding is one of the distinctive contributions of human rights NGOs[42] because of their access to information directly, through networks and through field visits. It is also their greatest challenge to governments who wish to hide or ignore what is happening. LaRose-Edwards[43] notes that before the Special Session of the Commission on Rwanda 'other countries [apart from France] in view of the small size and strategic unimportance of Rwanda, would invariably have relied more on NGO and UN intelligence' than their own sources. The reliability of an NGO's information is crucial and is likely to be subject to constant challenge by accused governments. Mistakes will be thrown back at them and will rapidly erode their credibility, 'their most important asset',[44] while a reputation as purveyors of accurate information will gain 'privileged access of governments'.[45]

By publicizing situations, human rights NGOs can literally 'put them on the map'. In 1993, the situation in Bougainville was raised at the Commission on Human Rights by a number of NGOs. After the second or third reference, one ambassador enquired, 'Where *is* Bougainville?' Similarly, the politically sensitive issue of internally displaced persons (the ultimate interference in internal affairs?) did not figure in international discussions until highlighted by an unusual ecumenical alliance of the Quakers, the World Council of Churches and, later, Caritas Internationalis, drawing on their experience as humanitarian organizations working with refugees and displaced persons in the field. These NGOs persuaded a group of countries to put the issue on the agenda of the UN Commission on Human Rights and, subsequently, to ensure the appointment of a Representative of the UN Secretary-General to undertake a comprehensive study of the subject and report to the Commission (in 1995).

A high-profile initiative by AI at the World Conference on Human Rights bore fruit at the 1993 General Assembly, when the post of High Commissioner

[41] Convention against Torture and Other Cruel, Inhuman or Degrading Treatment or Punishment, (1984), article 20.

[42] See Thoolen and Verstappen, *Human Rights Missions*.

[43] P. LaRose-Edwards, *The Rwandan Crisis of April 1994: the Lessons Learned* (Ottawa, International Human Rights, Democracy and Conflict Resolution, 30 November 1994), p. 4.

[44] N. Rodley, 'The work of non-governmental organizations in the world-wide promotion and protection of human rights', *Bulletin of Human Rights* 90 (1991), 84–93, p. 86.

[45] P. Willetts, 'The impact of promotional pressure groups on global politics' in Willetts, *Pressure Groups in the Global System*, pp. 179–200, p. 187.

for Human Rights was created. Similarly, many of the mechanisms of the Commission, including the UN's first 'thematic mechanism', the Working Group on Enforced or Involuntary Disappearances (1980), resulted from NGO initiatives or consistent provision of well-documented information about widespread violations, and rely on NGO sources, as well as responding to NGO pressure for action and results.[46] Personnel and methods have been adopted from NGOs. Two of the thematic rapporteurs are former AI staff members and urgent action procedures, an AI 'invention', are part of the UN response to alleged or threatened violations of human rights.

Limits

'[R]eal changes' can be brought about only by people in a country, not by 'outsiders looking through windows'[47]

The most obvious limitation on NGO action is that 'governments are the sole agencies capable of enforcing international conventions and respect for human rights in their territories'.[48] Of course, NGOs can seek to influence or persuade governments directly or indirectly in this direction (e.g. the public criticism by AI of Kenya's harassment of its domestic critics led to governmental pressure by Norway, Sweden and the USA)[49] but in the last resort they cannot themselves improve the human rights situation nor can they force governments to change. In the UN these limitations take the form of an inability to break the gridlock of political power. As Pritchard[50] observes 'evidence . . . indicates that, while government rhetoric and policy may espouse human rights values, criticism of human rights violations in other nations depends primarily on the degree to which the foreign government is considered "friendly" or "politically important". Such states, even those with atrocious human rights records, tend to be immune from criticism . . .'. Draft resolutions on the situation of human rights in China are defeated by a procedural motion to take no action on them. Other countries, such as Colombia and Peru, do not even reach the stage of having resolutions tabled.[51] More generally, governments may simply find it more convenient not to act, either because of genuine ignorance or because of plausible deniability. It is, therefore, incumbent on NGOs not only to provide information but to ensure that it reaches, and is known to have reached, decision-makers.[52]

Governments impose further limits indirectly. As mentioned above, NGOs are excluded from direct access to almost all international treaty complaints procedures. The division of the UN, between Geneva (human rights) and New York (peace, security and peace-keeping) makes it difficult both physically and conceptually for NGOs to integrate these issues. Similarly, the UN's separation

---

[46] D. Garcia-Sayan, 'NGOs and the human rights movement in Latin America', *Bulletin of Human Rights*, 90 (1991), 31–41, p. 38.

[47] Steiner, *Diverse Partners*, p. 62.

[48] Y. Beigbeder, *The Role and Status of International Humanitarian Volunteers and Organizations* (Dordrecht, Nijhoff, 1991), p. 182.

[49] Forsythe, 'Protecting human rights: the private sector', p. 101.

[50] K. Pritchard, 'Human rights: a decent respect for public opinion?', *Human Rights Quarterly*, 13 (1991), 123–42, p. 123.

[51] See R. Brett, *Review of the 1503 Procedure* (Geneva, Quaker UN Office, 1994).

[52] LaRose-Edwards, *The Rwandan Crisis of April 1994*, p. 5.

of women's rights, based first in Vienna and then New York, contributed to their isolation from the mainstream of human rights work in Geneva and, therefore, from most of the human rights NGOs.

Some limits are the mundane ones of lack of finance and personnel, but these are frequently exacerbated by personality cults and reluctance to co-operate with other NGOs. The smallness of many NGOs renders them prone to considerable fluctuation in their fortunes depending on the quality of the individual staff members at any given time. Often, there is a perceived need for public success to enhance the reputation of the NGO and to attract funding, whether from members or external sources. This in turn encourages the 'bandwagon' approach, joining in on a popular, or media led, issue or simply responding to crises, and with it a reluctance to pursue the longer term or lower profile areas of work. Exposing violations is always more 'sexy' than prevention, which by definition if successful is not only not newsworthy but virtually unprovable. From none of these problems, of course, is the UN itself free.

International NGOs suffer the further limitation that 'it is local human rights organizing and education that is the decisive component in the protection and promotion of human rights in the national context'.[53] The irony is that the more repressive the regime, the harder it is to establish local NGOs because 'to promote human rights you need human rights: ... you have to be able to form a group, to meet and to seek and impart information, all of this within and across national frontiers'.[54] Unless there is at least a measure of the freedoms of association, expression and assembly, the ability to protect human rights is severely hampered[55] and access to information about what is happening is also restricted. The UN Draft Declaration on Human Rights Defenders[56] is meant to enhance the protection of NGOs in these and other areas, but the prolonged and difficult drafting process (itself an indication of the wish of some governments to prevent or control the development of human rights NGOs) is not yet complete and the end result is dubious. The creation of so many new NGOs in recent years is an encouraging feature. (The UN Secretary-General cites the establishment in 'a short space of time' of 10,000 NGOs in Bangladesh, 21,000 in the Philippines and 27,000 in Chile).[57] Although many of these are not human rights NGOs as defined above, as Posner points out 'the very existence of such groups can therefore be a useful indicator of a government's commitment to respect human rights principles within their own

---

[53] C. Jimenez, 'Human rights activism: a view from the south', *World Student Christian Federation Journal* (December 1993), 11–14, p. 13; and see: L. Livezey, 'US religious organizations and the International Human Rights Movement', *Human Rights Quarterly*, 11 (1989), 14–81.

[54] Rodley, 'The work of non-governmental organizations', p. 92.

[55] Beigbeder, *The Role and Status of International Humanitarian Volunteers and Organisations*, p. 80; L. Wiseberg, *Defending Human Rights Defenders: the Importance of Freedom of Association for Human Rights NGOs* (Ottawa, Centre for Human Rights and Democratic Development, 1993); and L. Wiseberg, *Shackling the Defenders: Legal Restrictions on Independent Human Rights Advocacy Worldwide* (New York, Lawyers Committee for Human Rights, 1994).

[56] The actual title is the 'Draft Declaration on the right and responsibility of individuals, groups and organs of society to promote and protect universally recognized human rights and fundamental freedoms'.

[57] Statement by the Secretary-General on the Occasion of the Forty-Seventh Conference of Non-Governmental Organizations, New York, 20 September 1994 (SG/SM/94/142).

societies'.[58] Certainly this trend reduces the Western predominance in the NGO field, which, paradoxically has most frequently been criticized by the governments which restrict the freedoms essential for NGO operation.[59]

International NGOs have tried to provide some measure of support and protection for local NGOs by affiliating them, as did the International Helsinki Federation with Eastern European human rights groups before the changes of 1989, and by bringing key individuals to testify to the UN bodies, recognizing the vulnerability of leaders of victim support groups and demonstrating that they are known and supported by the international community. However, the limits of such protection are clear. Wiseberg[60] observes that 'disturbingly, the governmental practice of "disappearance" may have emerged in response to the success achieved by the human rights movement in attaching public vilification to governments which locked up large numbers of political prisoners'. In Guatemala, the situation became so bad that in 1985 Peace Brigades International tried a new approach, 'accompaniment' of local activists by a foreigner, trained in non-violence and armed with a camera. The same technique has been used in El Salvador (1987) and Sri Lanka (1990) with some success, but it is labour intensive, and can therefore only be used for key people.

Not all the limits on NGOs are external. Many are self-imposed either deliberately or because of lack of vision. Humanitarian, refugee and development NGOs, for example, do not see themselves as human rights organizations and do not use human rights terminology, concepts or procedures. The self-imposed limited mandate of AI[61] is in itself a strength. By focussing on prisoners of conscience AI was able to build up a remarkable degree of consensus about the justice of its cause as well as providing assistance to many victims, and a sense of purpose and not infrequently achievement to its members who work on the individual cases. However, it is also a weakness, compounded by the fact that, in Alston's words[62] 'Amnesty International, whether it likes it or not, ... is the single dominant force in the entire field, more representative and more influential than most of the other groups put together'. This has certainly assisted in the bias of the UN human rights system towards civil and political rights, although there is also a tendency to forget that AI does not even cover all civil and political rights. This should be viewed not so much as the fault of AI as of the failure to create NGOs of counterbalancing prominence covering areas such as economic, social and cultural rights and the monitoring of human rights in armed conflicts.

There is a wider issue here: the question of whether 'issues of human rights violations can be adequately addressed without advocating for changes in the overall structure that begets such violations'.[63] Traditionally, human rights NGOs have followed the principle of international human rights law that the

[58] M. Posner, 'The establishment of the right of nongovernmental human rights groups to organize' in L. Henkin and J. Hargrove (eds), *Human Rights: an Agenda for the Next Century* (Washington DC, American Society of International Law, 1994), pp. 405–23, p. 407.

[59] See *Shackling the Defenders*.

[60] Wiseberg, 'Protecting human rights activists and NGOs', p. 531.

[61] P. Baehr, 'Amnesty International and its self-imposed limited mandate', *Human Rights Quarterly*, 12 (1994), 5–21.

[62] P. Alston, 'The Fiftieth Anniversary of the Universal Declaration of Human Rights: a time more for reflection than for celebration' in J. Berting *et al.* (eds), *Human Rights in a Pluralist World: Individuals and Collectivities* (Westport/London, Meckler, 1990), p. 10.

[63] Jiminez, 'Human rights activism', p. 12.

governmental system or structure *per se* is not a legitimate concern of the international community. That community's involvement is with the results; thus if the end product is violations of human rights, NGOs will address these, but not the fact that the government is a military dictatorship (or whatever). Against this, there is the beginning of a general retreat from 'the myth, so damaging to international efforts to protect human rights, that a state lacking a democratic form of government and a commitment to the rule of law can nevertheless guarantee the enjoyment of human rights'.[64] A growing acceptance that democracy is the only form of government compatible with human rights[65] has reached its most explicit form in the CSCE. The CSCE commitments in these respects are clear and unconditional,[66] and since they fall within the human dimension of the CSCE should be enforceable (to the extent that any CSCE commitments are enforceable)[67] by the CSCE human dimension mechanisms. However, it was only in December 1993 that NGOs were given the first small access to these procedures, which are otherwise purely inter-governmental, and there is as yet no evidence that NGOs have attempted to raise the democratic question by these means. Indeed it is not clear that human rights NGOs as such should be taking up this issue. There are obvious practical difficulties of persuading those in power to give it up, of defining what democracy means and assessing the degree of 'acceptability' of supposedly democratic systems. Moreover is not the role of human rights NGOs indeed to address the human rights issues, while recognizing the causes, and leave other NGOs and pressure groups to address the political, economic and other underlying factors which go far beyond even the broadest definition of human rights? The fundamental dilemma is that the sharper the focus of an NGO, 'the more distinctive will be its contributions to the larger task, and the greater its credibility and legitimacy within this defined field of activity. The more expansive the role of this sector – say, advocacy of programs of political change and active participation in political struggle – the closer the NGO movement may come to the core of the problem. But it risks its distinctive position by becoming more contentious and more assimilated to a movement for political change'.[68]

The relationship with governments is perforce a delicate one. In the last resort NGOs can achieve nothing without governmental co-operation. But, if this is sought, it requires a negotiating and balancing process between quiet diplomacy and public denunciation. This applies not only to the government which is responsible for the violations, but also to governments who may be able and willing to bring pressure to bear on the offending government. Are they more likely to act if approached privately or if there is a public campaign? On the other hand, in Rodley's [69] words 'the purpose of human rights NGOs is to stop human rights violations ... If NGOs are sometimes perceived as being

---

[64] T. Buergenthal, 'The CSCE rights system', *George Washington Journal of International Law and Economics*, 25 (1991), 333–86, p. 382.

[65] 'Democracy, development and respect for human rights and fundamental freedoms are interdependent and mutually reinforcing', Vienna Declaration and Programme of Action, June 1993, Part I, para. 8.

[66] CSCE Charter of Paris for a New Europe (1990); Helsinki Decisions ch. VI, para. 2.

[67] See R. Brett, *Is More Better?* (Essex, Human Rights Centre, 1994).

[68] Steiner, *Diverse Partners*, pp. 38–9.

[69] Rodley, 'The work of non-governmental organizations', p. 85.

nuisances to governments, it is because that is their role'. If the relationship with government, any government, becomes too close, the NGOs may in fact become part of the establishment, with a vested interest in it, preserving their status, rights and privileges, and accepting its agenda and procedures rather than being prepared to challenge the entire direction, nature and content of UN decisions, policies and programmes.[70]

Balance Sheet

Organizations can either be viewed as a threat to an existing government or system and labelled as subversive or they can be viewed as a useful watchdog and an activating and motivating force within the society.[71]

In the most sanguine assessment of NGO effectiveness, Willetts[72] refers to 'the ability to mobilize legitimacy' as an aspect of political power. 'In this domain', he continues 'it is conceivable that Amnesty International, for example, has greater power than any single government. It derives global legitimacy both from its very high status [e.g. Nobel Peace Prize 1977]...and from the high moral value that so many people attach to the policies it is pursuing'.

One of the problems in assessing the effectiveness of human rights NGOs is that there are so many different factors which may influence a change in governmental policy, or the adoption of a resolution, and rarely is the role of NGOs cited as the official reason. Steiner,[73] for example, plays down the role of NGOs in mitigating the excesses of repression in Uruguay under the military regime, suggesting that the intervention of the Canadian government, then negotiating a trade agreement with Uruguay, was more significant. This may be true, but it does not address the question of whether the Canadian government's position had itself been influenced by the active NGO campaign on Uruguay. Again, on 4 May 1994, the recently-appointed UN High Commissioner for Human Rights called on members of the Commission to consider the advisability of convening a special session on Rwanda. The reasons he gave for this suggestion did not include the fact that on the same date AI launched a public appeal for a Special Session. Was the timing, then, purely coincidence?

This problem is faced in an acute form by NGOs such as AI which focus on individual cases. Archer[74] points out that not only are governments rarely if ever prepared to admit that they are responding to NGO pressure when a prisoner is released, but that any attempt to claim credit might be counter-productive, jeopardizing the chance of future successes. A corresponding caution, however, must be exercised in the other direction in assessing public governmental endorsements of the importance of NGOs. Is this mere lip service, similar to the human rights rhetoric of those who continue to violate human rights? More subtly, NGOs tend to be praised when they support the positions which governments want to take in any case, or provide the expertise or technical skills governments lack. It is only to be expected that they attract fewer plaudits when they are critical.

[70] Chiang, *Non-Governmental Organizations at the United Nations*, p. 244.
[71] Dolgopol, 'Human rights activist organizations', p. 2.
[72] Willetts, 'Pressure groups as transnational actors', pp. 23–4.
[73] Steiner, *Diverse Partners*, p. 88.
[74] Archer, 'Action by unofficial organizations', p. 178.

Whatever their fact-finding strengths in the field or their ability to muster political legitimacy, why should NGOs be as effective as they are within the inter-governmental, diplomatic environment of the United Nations? In part this reflects the complete inadequacy of the UN's own provision. Less than one percent of the UN budget is allocated for human rights. The UN Human Rights Centre, which 'is responsible for a far wider range of mandates than Amnesty International'[75] has only about 40% of that organization's headquarters staff (and the Centre has no national sections). Of course, AI is a special case, with its membership of more than 1.1 million in over 150 countries, its international section budget of £12.75 m and staff of about 300 in its London headquarters, but it is only one of some 150 NGOs which regularly attend the annual session of the UN Commission on Human Rights. Weissbrodt[76] also refers to the limited resources of many national delegations, but to see the weight of the NGO contribution simply in terms of resources is to understate the degree of specialist knowledge and continuity of many NGOs. In contrast, governmental delegates are frequently drawn from the ranks of civil servants, and are usually generalists, liable to be assigned to work on human rights issues at the UN for a couple of years between postings as, for example, cultural attaché in Poland and trade adviser in Nigeria. Such delegates are often grateful to tap the wisdom of NGOs and although they receive instructions from their capitals, these 'are not necessarily very detailed; it is the delegates who themselves have to decide whether to ask for further instructions as the debate progresses; and instructions may be reinterpreted or even on occasions disobeyed'.[77] Less drastically, instructions may be queried in the light of new information or arguments, whether put forward by NGOs or other governments.

Price Cohen[78] suggests 'if one takes the position that the role of NGOs in an international body is to advise, to assist, and to inspire', it is hard to evaluate, but 'when governments listen to NGO group recommendations, even if they are ultimately rejected, this is a measure of their respect. When governments specifically request NGO Group assistance in resolving difficult drafting problems, this too is a measure of respect. When an NGO Group document is used by governments as an instrument for diminishing intergovernmental tension during the drafting process, surely this shows that not only is the Group's work respected, but that it also resulted in smoother, more efficient deliberations'.

One indicator of the effectiveness of human rights NGOs is to compare the large number of country specific procedures under the UN human rights programme with the negligible number of inter-state cases which have been brought under the human rights treaties; none under international treaties and effectively only two (the 'group' cases against Greece and Turkey) under the European Human Rights Convention, the others having political overtones. It is certainly not unknown for UN special rapporteurs or experts to have been appointed as a result of political pressure from a particular country or grouping (for example in the case of Cuba), but the number of occasions on

---

[75] M. Schmidt, 'Achieving much with little: the work of the United National Centre for Human Rights', *Netherlands Quarterly of Human Rights*, 8 (1990), 371–80, p. 374.
[76] Weissbrodt, 'The contribution of international nongovernmental organizations', p. 419.
[77] Willetts, 'The impact of promotional pressure groups on global politics', p. 182.
[78] Price Cohen, 'The role of non-governmental organizations', p. 144.

which such appointments are not the result of pressure and information from NGOs is very small indeed.

The case of Colombia measures perhaps most precisely the extent of NGO influence. The fact that no resolution has been passed, let alone appointment made, in regard to Colombia shows that even concerted NGO pressure has not been strong enough to overcome the resistance of influential governments. On the other hand, without the NGOs it is unlikely that Colombia would have been considered at all.

Human rights failures, like the poor, are always with us. Most spectacular in recent months has been the case of Rwanda. But just as NGOs cannot take all the credit for the many – always qualified – successes of recent years (the new South Africa, the democratization of Latin America, the dissolution of the Soviet system) so to blame them for the failures is no more reasonable as it does not take account of what they are actually trying to do: to influence attitudes, not to govern the world. It is only to be expected that the success rate for NGO action is greater where the violations are individual and 'accidental' rather than large-scale and systematic, since it is those governments who are most concerned about human rights who are most likely to respond to NGO exposure of violations.

Despite the increasing acceptance of the need for and legitimacy of human rights NGOs, ambivalence remains. Even when NGOs 'merely draw the attention of governments to the international commitments on human rights issues to which they themselves have freely subscribed, and inform people and individuals of their rights and ways and means of defending them, [they] are often a subject of controversy for governments who see them as dissident, even subversive'.[79] The Turkish Government's banning of an AI researcher illustrates the continuing hostility to effective human rights work by an influential NGO.[80]

Given the inherently political nature of human rights work, it is not surprising that many governments continue to have reservations about the role of human rights NGOs; indeed this might be seen as a measure of their success. If governments who continue deliberate violations of human rights did not wish to restrict human rights NGOs, it would be a certain indication of NGO ineffectiveness.

[79] C. Eya Nchama, 'The role of non-governmental organizations in the promotion and protection of human rights', *Bulletin of Human Rights* 90 (1991), 50–83, p. 52.
[80] See the Statement by the Delegations of the United Kingdom and the Netherlands to the CSCE Budapest Review Conference: Working Group Three, 28 October 1994.

Human Rights and US Foreign Policy: Two Levels, Two Worlds

David P. Forsythe

Any state's foreign policy is a two level game made up of domestic demands and foreign facts. For US foreign policy and human rights, any President must contend first with the domestic expectations of American exceptionalism. American political culture generates the demand, albeit inconsistently, that US foreign policy should reflect the American self-image of an exceptional people who stand for freedom around the world. Unresolved, however, is choice of grand strategy. Should the US promote its vision of human freedom through foreign activism, or through more passive domestic example?

Foreign facts (perceived, of course) are different, but no less difficult to manage. In general terms, two systemic facts collide. States exist in anarchical society; no world government obtains; states must look to themselves to protect their interests. But global governance, if not formal government, does exist; international law and organization require attention to human rights for all; state borders no longer shield the relationship between citizen and public authority.

What then is any state, but particularly the United States, to do about human rights and foreign policy when caught between these two worlds? In the first world of interstate relations, governments have long been advised to pursue a realist foreign policy of self-interest. In the second world of global governance, states are advised to pursue liberal policies focusing on the human interest rather than the national interest – or at least to redefine the national interest so as to incorporate more individual interests including those of foreigners.

The United States, precisely because of domestic demands, has had more difficulty than other Western-style democracies in adopting a traditional realist approach to foreign human rights questions. Britain, for example, found it easier than the US to focus on power relations in the former Yugoslavia, and thus to be less enthusiastic than the US about the UN criminal court from 1993. Britain focused on power and diplomacy, while the US gave greater relative attention to prosecutions of individuals for war crimes. But the changing nature of world affairs from interstate relations toward global governance may mean that the US, precisely because of American exceptionalism, is better positioned for leadership on human rights, should it choose to exercise that leadership. Various administrations from Jimmy Carter's to Bill Clinton's, however, have found human rights a most perplexing issue in foreign policy.

US Domestic Demand

There is a moral streak in US foreign policy rhetoric,[1] a tendency for Americans to view their nation as a 'city on a hill'[2] and their history as a moral lesson to the world.[3] Many Americans have difficulty seeing themselves as an ordinary nation.[4] In the new words of an old critic, 'believing itself blessed by a unique and ultimately superior dispensation, America simply did not engage itself' with the world like European states.[5]

Many if not all governments delude themselves with a self-image entailing some form of virtue.[6] Saddam Hussein, with more reason than some might like to acknowledge, saw his Iraq as righting the wrongs of British map-making and other colonial errors. Russia after the Cold War tended toward seeing itself as champion of Slavs treated unfairly by outsiders. Several Asian states like China, Singapore, and Malaysia have in recent times, including at the UN World Congress on Human Rights at Vienna in 1993, pictured themselves as repositories of ancient Asian wisdom in the face of renewed foolishness by the current manifestation of young Western barbarism. Be all that as it may, and regardless of some US violations of human rights at home[7] and lack of action on some human rights abroad,[8] American mythology embraces American moral exceptionalism. (Historical exceptionalism is a distinct but related subject, dealing with such factors as the US geographical position and related, albeit very incomplete, isolationism.)

President Nixon may have been very American in some ways.[9] But when he and Kissinger produced a foreign policy that was widely perceived at home as amoral if not immoral, they lost much of their domestic base of support. Particularly for Kissinger, moral arguments in support of his positions were not lacking (see below), but policy was widely perceived as morally deficient within the US. Of course domestic events like Watergate contributed. (The naturalized Kissinger was not un-American but was very non-American, obviously styling himself on the model of Metternich if not Bismarck).[10] Since the Nixon–Kissinger era, and goaded by Congress,[11] every US President has rhetorically endorsed human rights as part of his foreign policy agenda.

---

[1] J. Spanier, *American Foreign Policy since World War II* (Washington DC, Congressional Quarterly Press, 12th rev. ed., 1992); G. Kennan, *American Diplomacy 1900–1950* (Chicago, University of Chicago, 1951).

[2] T. Davis and S. Lynn-Jones, 'City upon a hill', *Foreign Policy*, 66 (1987), 20–38.

[3] A. Schlesinger, Jr., 'Human rights and the American tradition', *Foreign Affairs*, 57 (1978), 403–526.

[4] R. Rosecrance, *America as an Ordinary Country: US Foreign Policy and the Future* (Ithaca NY, Cornell University Press, 1976).

[5] H. Kissinger, *Diplomacy* (New York, Norton, 1994), p. 376.

[6] J. Stoessinger, *Nations in Darkness: China, Russia, and America* (New York, McGraw-Hill, 5th ed., 1990).

[7] Human Rights Watch/American Civil Liberties Union, *Human Rights Violations in the United States: a Report on US Compliance with the International Covenant on Civil and Political Rights* (New York, Human Rights Watch/ACLU, 1993).

[8] P. Lauren, *Power and Prejudice: the Politics and Diplomacy of Racial Discrimination* (Boulder CO, Westview, 1988).

[9] T. Wicker, *One of Us: Richard Nixon and the American Dream* (New York, Random House, 1991).

[10] See H. Kissinger, *Diplomacy*; and also *A World Restored: the Politics of Conservatism in a Revolutionary Age* (New York, Grosset and Dunlap, 1964).

[11] D. Forsyth, *Human Rights and US Foreign Policy: Congress Reconsidered* (Gainesville FL, University Presses of Florida, 1988).

But this tradition of American moralistic thinking and rhetorical support for human rights in world affairs offers two paths to the promised land – a world of at least democratic if not always rights-protective states. (The two are not the same, as contemporary India in particular clearly demonstrates.) One path stresses America first, is closely linked to what passes for American isolationism, and traces its intellectual heritage to John Quincy Adams, among others, who warned about 'going abroad in search of monsters to destroy'.[12] In contemporary form this view advocates perfecting American society as the preferred way to advance human rights in the world.[13] The second path stresses foreign activism, can be linked to either the liberal or conservative brand of internationalism in American public opinion, and traces its intellectual heritage, in part, to James Monroe in 1823 (protect the Western Hemisphere from evil European politics) and William McKinley in 1898, although pushed into activism by Congress and the media (liberate Cuba and the Philippines from evil Spanish control).

This bifurcated approach, among other reasons such as presidential preference or congressional mood, gives presidents, or Congress for that matter, considerable discretion in policy choice concerning human rights in foreign policy. American mythology, an informal ideology if you will,[14] informs in general but does not always determine the particulars. In fact, Congress forced US presidents to eschew direct and formal attention to international human rights from 1953 to 1973.[15] Pressured by right-wing legal and ideological circles, Congress rationalized US non-participation in international human rights regimes in terms of protecting a superior American version of freedom from pernicious international, especially communist, influences. Yet it was Congress that led the charge to put human rights back on the formal foreign policy agenda from 1974, a movement that President Carter reinforced with his human rights rhetoric during his 1976 campaign and first two years of his presidency. Few specifics of US foreign policy are predetermined.

Particularly since the mid-1970s all presidents, with general, but not always specific, congressional support have endorsed an active human rights policy in foreign affairs. When this rhetorical manifestation of American exceptionalism encounters foreign facts, however, it is a good question to outcome.

Foreign Facts

Among the few uncontested facts of international relations is that there is no world government, and certainly no approximation of world government with a monopoly over legitimate use of force to such an extent that the basic security of states is guaranteed. Historically in the state system, states were prisoners of

---

[12] N. Graebner, 'Tradition, the founding fathers, and foreign affairs' in D. Malone et al. *Rhetoric and the Founders* (Lanham MD, University Press of American, 1987), pp. 61–8.

[13] R. Tucker and D. Hendrickson, *The Imperial Temptation: the New World Order and America's Purpose* (Washington DC, Council on Foreign Relations Press, 1992); and G. Kennan, 'The failure of our success', *New York Times* (14 March 1994), p. A14.

[14] M. Hunt, *Ideology and US Foreign Policy* (New Haven CT, Yale University Press, 1987).

[15] N. Hevener Kaufman, *Human Rights Treaties and the Senate: a History of Opposition* (Chapel Hill NC, University of North Carolina Press, 1990); and L. Leblanc, *The United States and the Genocide Convention* (Durham NC, Duke University Press, 1991).

their insecurity,[16] believing that they had to adopt policies geared to protecting their existence even though in a different world they would have preferred to adopt different policies.[17] Even if traditional war among great powers were to follow formal slavery into the dustbin of history,[18] there would still remain intense competition over economic interests – which according to some realists[19] and Marxists alike constituted the fundamental foundation of power.

The classic realist prescription for coping with this situation was, in large part, to elevate pursuit of state interests to the status of ethics. Hans Morgenthau, the father of modern American realism, argued clearly that in the interstate system governmental leaders had no greater ethical duty than to pursue what was in the interest of the national group.[20] Pursuit of national power was, therefore, not just a political requirement but an ethical one as well. Especially commendable was the courage to do what was necessary to advance national interest, even if this entailed evil by ordinary ethical standards applicable to individuals within national society. To lie, even to kill, for the state became moral in interstate context, if required by the standard of national interest. It was unethical to refrain from doing what was in the national interest on grounds of traditional inter-personal ethics within orderly national society. Group ethics superseded individual ethics.

Numerous contemporary thinkers have had little difficulty in glossing over US sanctioned killings – e.g. in Guatemala from 1954 – and other violations of internationally recognized human rights when done in the name of advancing the interests of the democratic US, and larger West, in the face of challenge from totalitarian and repressive communism.[21] The realist approach to international structural anarchy does not lend itself easily to concerns for individual human rights.[22] And it is understandable that contemporary realists like Kissinger long argued that the 'domestic structure' of states, often a euphemism for repression, should not have become a subject of foreign policy during the Cold War.[23] Kissinger the diplomat opposed the early CSCE attention to human rights in the 1974 Helsinki Final Act, precisely because it made *détente* with the Soviet Union, and in his view ultimate Western security (and hence freedom), more difficult to preserve.

And yet the realist approach to management of international anarchy, which in one form regards attention to individual human rights as a luxury that rational state leaders frequently cannot afford,[24] is not very clear on a central point. Realists disdain 'sentiment'. Kissinger, referring to the US in the 1930s, writes of 'an outburst of pro-isolationist sentiment'.[25] When writing approvingly of Bismarck, Kissinger said that he 'urged a foreign policy based

---

[16] B. Russett, *The Prisoners of Insecurity: Nuclear Deterrence, the Arms Race, and Arms Control* (New York, Freeman, 1983).

[17] K. Waltz, *Theory of International Politics* (Reading MA, Addison-Wesley, 1979).

[18] J. Mueller, *Retreat from Doomsday* (New York, Basic, 1989).

[19] P. Kennedy, *The Rise and Fall of the Great Powers: Economic Change and Military Conflict from 1500 to 2000* (New York, Random House, 1987).

[20] H. Morgenthau, *Politics among Nations* (New York, Knopf, 1974).

[21] E.g. C. Nolan, *Principled Diplomacy: Security and Rights in US Foreign Policy* (Westport CT, Greenwood, 1993).

[22] S. Hoffmann, 'The hell of good intentions', *Foreign Policy*, 29 (1977–8), 3–26.

[23] H. Kissinger, *American Foreign Policy: Three Essays* (New York, Norton, 1969).

[24] J. Schlessinger, 'Quest for a post-Cold War foreign policy', *Foreign Affairs*, 72 (1992/3), 17–28.

[25] H. Kissinger, *Diplomacy*, p. 381.

on neither sentiment nor legitimacy but on the correct assessment of power'.[26]

On the other hand, Kissinger approves of some 'values'. He always stressed the role of conservative agreement in the success of the Congress of Vienna.[27] More generally Kissinger writes: 'equilibrium works best if it's buttressed by an agreement on common values. The balance of power inhibits the *capacity* to overthrow the international order; agreement on shared values inhibits the *desire* to overthrow the international order'.[28] Later he writes of the contemporary US: 'to be true to itself, America must try to forge the widest possible moral consensus around a global commitment to democracy'.[29]

An uncharitable analysis could suggest that 'sentiment' is an idea that Kissinger dislikes, whereas 'value' is one that he likes. A different analysis is that a principled idea which is shared among dominant states can reinforce their power, but the same idea, if not so shared, becomes mere sentiment and disruptive to order. Apparently in Kissinger's version of realism, attention to human rights in foreign policy would be a desirable value if shared among major states, but would be undesirable sentiment if not shared. What then for the state that seeks to lead other important states into a consensus on human rights that is not yet widely shared? Valued principle that can give legitimacy to the distribution of power? Or troublesome sentiment interfering with the ordering effect of dominant power? Or, perhaps a desirable long term goal if not confused with short term analysis of power? Would this mean that pursuit of democracy (or human rights) should be abandoned whenever it interfered with pursuit of power?

Realists, certainly as represented by Kissinger, are not very clear whether human rights comprise debilitating 'sentiment' or facilitative 'value'. Thus realism, at least as formulated by Kissinger, provides little precise guidance for the US – or other states – concerning the place of human rights in interstate politics.

Yet it is another broad fact of contemporary world affairs that while there is no world government, there is ample world governance.[30] International law and organization, combining to produce international regimes, mandate attention to a broad range of individual rights.[31] The late John Vincent analysed matters precisely: 'foreign ministers no longer have a choice about the inclusion of human rights. They cannot escape the tension between human rights and [other goals of] foreign policy simply by declaring that the former have no place in the latter'.[32]

Clearly in the United Nations many human rights norms and many supportive diplomatic practices have been institutionalized.[33] Accelerated

[26] H. Kissinger, *Diplomacy*, p. 129.

[27] H. Kissinger, *A World Restored: the Politics of Conservatism in a Revolutionary Age*.

[28] H. Kissinger, *Diplomacy*, p. 77 (emphasis in the original).

[29] H. Kissinger, *Diplomacy*, p. 166.

[30] J. Rosenau and E. Czempiel (eds), *Governance without Government: Order and Change in World Politics* (Cambridge, Cambridge University Press, 1992).

[31] J. Donnelly, *Universal Human Rights in Theory and Practice* (Ithaca NY, Cornell University Press, 1989), ch. 11.

[32] R. Vincent, *Human Rights and International Relations* (Cambridge, Cambridge University Press, 1986), p. 130.

[33] D. Forsythe, 'Human rights and the United Nations at 50: an incremental but incomplete revolution', *Global Governance*, 1 (1995), forthcoming.

attention to human rights in the UN occurred in the late 1960s and 1970s, but for reasons different from renewed attention to rights in US foreign policy.[34] The same increased attention is true in many regional international organizations as well. In the Council of Europe a supranational human rights court regularly ruled against states, and its judgements were always implemented.[35] In the European Union a supranational court had done much to protect individual rights while advancing regional economic community.[36] By 1993 the point was reached that even in the Organization of American States, where traditional notions of state sovereignty had long held sway, every state member present and voting regarded the overthrow of democracy in Haiti as an international rather than internal matter. (The regional use of force to restore democracy was a different question.) Other regions lagged behind these developments, but the global trend, while mixed, was clearly in favour of more attention to human rights than in the past.[37]

Whereas most realists warn vaguely of the dangers of 'sentiment' in anarchical interstate politics, states themselves have created a normative and organizational framework that mandates attention to human rights.[38] Some states, as an empirical matter, have defined their conception of the national interest to include attention to individual human rights.[39] Realists urge attention to power; advocates of principled world order urge attention to ideas (values?) like human rights.[40] The US and other states function in these two worlds of interstate relations and global governance, in which trends sometimes point in contradictory directions, and in which the overall condition is one of turbulence,[41] derived from unclear patterns.

How has US foreign policy on human rights responded to domestic demands, in the context of these two external worlds? With both inconsistency and constancy.

---

[34] V. Van Dyke, *Human Rights, the United States, and World Community* (New York, Oxford University Press, 1970); P. Alston (ed.), *The United Nations and Human Rights* (New York, Oxford University Press, 1992); and T. Farer and F. Gaer, 'The UN and human rights: at the end of the beginning' in A. Roberts and B. Kingsbury (eds), *United Nations, Divided World* (New York, Oxford University Press, 1992), pp. 241–96.

[35] R. Beddard, *Human Rights and Europe* (Cambridge, Cambridge University Press, 3rd ed., 1993).

[36] G. Mancini, 'The making of a constitution for Europe' in R. Keohane and S. Hoffmann (eds), *The New European Community: Decisionmaking and Institutional Change* (Boulder CO, Westview, 1991), pp. 177–94.

[37] D. Forsythe, 'Human rights in a post-Cold War world' in S. Spiegel and D. Pervin (eds), *At Issue: Politics in the World Arena* (New York, St. Martin's Press, 7th ed., 1994), pp. 417–30; compare J. Donnelly, 'Human rights in a new world order', in D. Forsythe (ed.), *Human Rights in the New Europe* (Lincoln NE, University of Nebraska Press, 1994), pp. 7–34.

[38] D. Forsythe, *The Internationalization of Human Rights* (Lexington MA, Lexington Books, 1991).

[39] H. Shue, 'Morality, politics, and humanitarian assistance' in B. Nichols and G. Loescher (eds), *The Moral Nation: Humanitarianism and US Foreign Policy Today* (Notre Dame IN, University of Notre Dame Press, 1989), pp. 12–40.

[40] K. Sinkink, 'The power of principled ideas: human rights policies in the United States and Western Europe' in J. Goldstein and R. Keohane (eds), *Ideas and Foreign Policy: Beliefs, Institutions and Political Change* (Ithaca NY, Cornell University Press, 1993), pp. 139–72.

[41] J. Rosenau, *Turbulence in World Politics: a Theory of Change and Community* (Princeton NJ, Princeton University Press, 1990).

Five Administrations

It was not until 1945 and the UN era that states dealt extensively with human rights issues *per se* in their foreign policies.[42] One study argues that the Truman administration took the lead on human rights issues at the UN and that even the Eisenhower administration, despite congressional pressures otherwise, tried to continue that leadership role.[43] Most scholars agree that because of McCarthyite and Brickerite pressure in Congress, combined with agreement on giving priority to containment of communism, human rights did not receive broad and specific consideration in US foreign policy until the mid-1970s. Paradoxically during much of the Cold War, containment of communism in the name of defending freedom reduced attention to specific human rights abroad. We start, therefore, given constraints of space in this essay, with the Carter administration.

In so doing, it is well to recall that the US is not seriously restricted in its foreign policy on human rights by regional and global human rights treaties. The US position is quite different from the West European democracies who are subject to authoritative review by the European Court of Human Rights and European Court of Justice, and who have accepted the review mechanisms of various UN human rights conventions. The US, by comparison, is either not a party to the human rights treaty in question, or has freed itself from most monitoring mechanisms in one way or another. The US is not subject to the jurisdiction of any human rights tribunal. Thus any US President has considerable leeway to initiate human rights measures in foreign policy. Whether he can obtain congressional, public, and allied support is another matter.

Carter

The conventional wisdom is that Jimmy Carter's personal disposition toward rights rhetoric was reinforced by its emergence as an effective campaign theme in 1976.[44] American exceptionalism was alive and well in the body politic, especially in the wake of Vietnam and Watergate, Nixon and Kissinger. Domestic demands reinforced personal disposition; Carter won much applause on the campaign trail by asking for 'a government as good as the American people'. The Democratic majority in the Congress, especially the House, had already used the rhetoric of rights – and legislation – to try to force changes in Republican foreign policy.[45] Carter used the bully pulpit of first a presidential campaign, then the White House, to accelerate that orientation.

Carter entered office with a vague and naive view of the place of human rights in foreign policy. He wrote in his memoirs: 'I did not fully grasp all the ramifications of our [human rights] policy'.[46] He never developed a strategic vision in this regard, much less an awareness of the negative consequences of

[42] J. Burgers, 'The road to San Francisco: the revival of the human rights idea in the Twentieth Century', *Human Rights Quarterly*, 14 (1992), 447–77.
[43] C. Nolan, *Principled Diplomacy: Security and Rights in US Foreign Policy.*
[44] E. Drew, 'Reporter at large: human rights', *The New Yorker* (18 July 1977), 36.
[45] D. Forsythe, *Human Rights and US Foreign Policy: Congress Reconsidered.*
[46] J. Carter, *Keeping Faith* (New York, Bantam, 1982), p. 44.

good intentions.[47] How did human rights relate to state security? Should human rights pre-empt transnational pursuit of private profit?

His Assistant Secretary of State for Human Rights and Humanitarian Affairs, Patricia Derian, although committed and dynamic was without foreign policy experience. His Secretary of State, Cyrus Vance, was genuinely interested in rights but did not turn out to be as effective a bureaucratic infighter as some anticipated. His principal deputy on human rights, Warren Christopher, was a case-by-case lawyer without much interest in conceptual or strategic thinking. The 'Christopher Committee' interjected some rights considerations into some foreign assistance decisions but lost control over much security assistance.[48] Continuation of most economic assistance was rationalized as being for the most needy in developing countries. Carter's National Security Advisor, Zbigniew Brzezinski, seemed content to see human rights directed mostly at the Soviets, the historical oppressors of his native Poland.

Carter, having proclaimed human rights to be the cornerstone and soul of his foreign policy, wound up doing business as usual with, *inter alia*, communist Poland, the dictatorial Philippines, and reactionary Saudi Arabia. Carter was apparently genuinely surprised when the Soviets reacted strongly to his human rights rhetoric, and after their invasion of Afghanistan and the militants' takeover of the US embassy in Iran he shifted both rhetoric and policy so as to emphasize more traditional security concerns. It was Carter who first increased assistance to the El Salvadoran government, despite its connection to murderous elements. If Carter's human rights policy amounted to a crusade,[49] it was a very weak and inconsistent one. In places like Iran, careful research failed to discern much human rights pressure on the Shah during the Carter years.[50] It may still be true that the Shah felt pressured by congressional debate on the subject and feared what might happen in the future. It was Congress, not Carter, that imposed economic sanctions on the tyrant, Idi Amin, in Uganda.

Carter did, to be sure, exert some gentle diplomatic pressure on various authoritarians in Zaire and South Korea, *inter alia*. He successfully fought to restore pressure on Ian Smith and his white minority government in Zimbabwe, *née* Rhodesia. He helped institute a United Nations arms embargo against racist South Africa. He particularly pressured Latin authoritarians to liberalize, an orientation that won him plaudits with hemispheric democrats but scorn from many domestic conservatives who charged him with selling out friendly if repressive allies in the Cold War. Lives were saved in places like Argentina and Chile because of Carter, Derian, Vance, and company. Typical of his hemispheric policy was his orientation toward Anastasio Somoza Debayle in Nicaragua. Carter would not intervene directly, but he worked for

---

[47] B. Kaufman, *The Presidency of James Earl Carter, Jr* (Lawrence KS, University of Kansas Press, 1991); S. Hoffmann, 'The hell of good intentions'.

[48] S. Cohen, 'Conditioning US security assistance on human rights practices', *American Journal of International Law*, 76 (1982), 246–79.

[49] E. Haas, 'Global evangelism rides again', *Paper in International Affairs #5* (Institute of International Studies, Berkeley, CA, University of California, 1978); J. Muravchik, *The Uncertain Crusade: Jimmy Carter and the Dilemmas of Human Rights Policy* (Lanham MD, Hamilton, 1986).

[50] J. Bill, *The Eagle and the Lion: the Tragedy of American–Iranian Relations* (New Haven, Yale University Press, 1988).

Somoza's removal, which infuriated his domestic critics when the leftist Sandinista-dominated coalition took over.[51] Carter signed three human rights treaties and submitted them to the Senate for advice and consent, although he allowed lawyers from the State and Justice Departments to load the treaties with reservations.

It proved important that the Carter team began serious implementation of congressional mandates calling for human rights reporting on countries receiving US security assistance. Kissinger had stalled the reports, finally allowing superficial ones to be written and published. Carter's Administration broadened the reports and made them more serious. Over time this was to cause human rights to be taken more seriously by the Foreign Service Officers and others that had to report, write, edit, and then defend the annual country reports before congressional and NGO critics. The annual country human rights reports became eventually a valuable source of information about rights conditions around the world. They helped sensitize sceptical foreign policy professionals to rights concerns, even if there remained a sizable gap between reports of human rights violations and US policy initiatives to deal with those violations.[52]

Overall the Carter Administration is historically associated with international human rights largely because of presidential rhetoric, even if congressional initiatives had already laid a legislative foundation. That Administration did satisfy certain domestic demands linked to American exceptionalism, and did confront – on the basis of rights principles – certain foreign facts like racism in southern Africa and brutal authoritarianism in Latin America. Yet American exceptionalism is only one part of American political culture and public opinion. Many Americans also want to be wealthy and secure, not just high minded. And some of the American right, as will be made clear, thought that Carter's focus on rights interfered with a more considered defence of freedom, namely a more vigorous containment, if not rollback, of communism.

Domestic demands unrelated to international human rights, namely an end to stagflation, and important foreign facts, namely an expanding Soviet Union and militant Islamic revolution in Iran, overshadowed many of Carter's rights initiatives, making him a one-term President. The President and his Secretary of State accepted the broad international definition of human rights, including economic rights, but found them difficult to advance in concrete diplomacy. Carter started out being a postmaterialistic, post-Cold War President stressing global community. Unfortunately for him, America was still materialistic, and interstate relations was still dominated by the Cold War and other security clashes.

Having entered office with the expressed desire to move beyond the Cold War, Carter wound up being trapped by it – and by related difficulties in places like Iran, El Salvador, and the Philippines. Part of his initial vision was that of

---

[51] A. Lake, *Somoza Falling: a Case Study of Washington at Work* (Amherst MA, University of Massachusetts Press, 1989); R. Pastor, 'George Bush and Latin America' in R. Oye, *et al.*, *Eagle in a New World: American Grand Strategy in the Post-Cold War Era* (New York, Harper Collins, 1992), pp 361–88.

[52] J. Innes De Neufville, 'Human rights reporting as a policy tool', *Human Rights Quarterly*, 8 (1986), 681–99.

global politics on behalf of world community,[53] in which human rights would occupy centre stage, but interstate politics and its security dilemma refused to go away.

Reagan I

One observer who was genuinely concerned about human rights and US foreign policy wrote that the main problem with Jimmy Carter was that he did not do what he said he was going to do, while the problem with Ronald Reagan was that he did exactly what he said he would do.[54] Reagan said he was going to direct human rights concerns toward the Soviet Union and other communists, and he started out doing precisely that. Reagan did indeed identify with the published views of Jean Kirkpartrick, namely that friendly authoritarians should not bear the brunt of US rights policies abroad, but rather communist totalitarians.[55] Communist violations were seen as greater, and these states intended no good for the Western democracies. Carter was criticized for not recognizing this truth. The first Reagan Administration collectively personified an assertive American exceptionalism.[56]

The view that permeated the first Reagan Administration, although highly moralistic, was at least partially compatible with standard realism – namely, that nothing was more important than defending the US and its allies from the Soviet challenge. This view, in its initial and crude form in the human rights domain, resulted in the nomination of Ernest Lefever to be Assistant Secretary of State for Human Rights and Humanitarian Affairs. But since Lefever had earlier advocated repeal of congressional legislation on human rights, on grounds that it interfered with the struggle against communism, and since his think tank had taken money from South Africa to circulate views favourable to that anti-communist but racist state, his name was withdrawn despite Republican control of the Senate. But this same guiding view within the Reagan Administration was to reappear consistently during 1980–4. The first Secretary of State, Alexander Haig, said that fighting terrorism, which was often supported by communism, would replace human rights as the cornerstone of foreign policy. Reagan officials made clear that nothing could be worse in El Salvador than a rebel victory;[57] therefore human rights violations by the government side were to be discounted or played down.[58]

Reagan, or whoever calculated these things for a President who was distant from many policy details, was able to establish this orientation through two primary means. First, there was attention to the image of balance. After the Lefever debacle, Elliott Abrams was moved from another State Department position to the Human Rights Bureau, from where he wrote memos about the importance of an even-handed approach to human rights. Abrams also

---

[53] J. Rosati, *The Carter Administration's Question for Global Community: Beliefs and their Impact on Behavior* (Columbia SC, University of South Carolina Press, 1987).

[54] D. Heaps, *Human Rights and US Foreign Policy: the First Decade 1973–1983* (American Association for the International Commission of Jurists, 1984).

[55] J. Kirkpatrick, 'Dictatorships and double standards', *Commentary*, 68 (1979), 34–45.

[56] T. Davis and S. Lynn-Jones, 'City upon a hill'.

[57] E. Abrams, *Human Rights Conditions in El Salvador* (Department of State, 29 July 1982).

[58] M. Danner, *The Massacre at El Mozote* (New York, Vintage, 1994); A. Lewis, 'Rights and wrongs', *New York Times* (20 January 1986), p. A19.

oversaw the annual US human rights country reports, and they remained about as accurate as during the Carter period. More importantly in 1982 Reagan gave a speech to the British House of Commons in which he endorsed a global crusade for democracy. While Margaret Thatcher made clear that the speech was part of an ideological offensive against communism,[59] 'spin doctors' at home put out the interpretation that Reagan intended to pursue democratic rights with an even hand. These symbolic gestures in the name of balance helped pacify Congress somewhat, even if Abrams was clearly a neo-conservative interested in focusing on communist violations of rights, and even if there was little direct follow-up to Reagan's democracy speech in the Commons. (Later, for different reasons, the US Agency for International Development started a focus on democracy, and the National Endowment for Democracy was created.)

Secondly, those at the top of the first Reagan Administration made sure that loyalists were sprinkled throughout the bureaucracy to ensure faithful execution of the President's foreign policy – including their activist version of American exceptionalism applied to human rights. Abrams headed the Human Rights Bureau, Kirkpatrick was ambassador at the UN, Gregory Newell headed the International Organization Bureau in the State Department, Robert Allen was the first National Security Advisor. The best known example of this general trend was the nomination of Judge William Clark to high State Department position despite his evident lack of knowledge of foreign affairs. His real role was to keep an eye on Haig.

In the first Reagan Administration human rights policy consisted largely of double standards through which communists were criticized if not punished, and friendly authoritarians were courted.[60] Administration officials argued that friendly authoritarians were the targets of quiet diplomacy directed at persuasion toward progressive change. This was the South African policy of constructive engagement writ large. But in fact friendly authoritarians were courted for strategic reasons and their human rights violations were discounted. Anti-communist authoritarian leaders from South Korea, Zaire, Liberia, and elsewhere were brought to the Reagan White House and prominently displayed in Washington political and social circles. All had been given the diplomatic cold shoulder by the Carter Administration. At the UN the Reagan team focused almost exclusively on Cuban and other communist violations of rights. A Cuban who did not speak English, Armando Valladares, was eventually named head of the US delegation to the UN Human Rights Commission. The US was aligned with the Argentine junta in an effort to block attention to gross violations of rights in the southern cone.[61]

Indicative of Reagan's human rights policies was the fact that US security assistance in various forms was increased dramatically around the world, without attention to human rights records. Congress was unable to oversee effectively the legislation it had previously adopted, in order to guarantee

[59] M. Thatcher, *The Downing Street Years* (New York, Harper Collins, 1993), p. 258.
[60] C. Maechling, Jr., 'Human rights dehumanized', *Foreign Policy*, 52 (1983), 96–117; A. Tonelson, 'Human rights: the bias we need', *Foreign Policy*, 49 (1982–83), 52–74; T. Jacoby, 'Reagan's turnaround on human rights', *Foreign Affairs*, 64 (1986), 1066–86.
[61] I. Guest, *Behind the Disappearances: Argentina's Dirty War against Human Rights and the United Nations* (Philadelphia PA, University of Pennsylvania Press, 1990).

presidential application in keeping with apparent congressional intent. The Reagan team supported anti-communist rebels in places like Angola and Afghanistan, and largely created them in Nicaragua, regardless of their attacks on civilians or other violations of human rights. What counted was alignment in the renewed Cold War, not human rights performance.

Symptomatic of attitudes in Washington during the time was that the National Endowment for Democracy, a quasi-private organization but headed by neo-conservatives supportive of Reagan, provided secret money to a right wing political movement in democratic France, and to a movement in Panama whose democratic credentials were not obvious.[62] Overall the first Reagan Administration achieved the clarity and consistency lacking in the Carter Administration concerning human rights. But a good part of Congress and public opinion was not content, primarily because Reagan so skewed rights policies to fit with his anti-communist fixation. On issues like Central America and South Africa, Congress fought a running battle with the Reagan team over balance. In so far as one can generalize about a faction-plagued Congress, that branch was less inclined to see human rights policy simply as an appendage to the Cold War. Domestic demand for a different version of American exceptionalism was at least periodically important.

The second world of global governance was anathema to Reagan. He saw the world in terms of competing states: free versus enslaved. The UN was an arena for that conflict, and one symbolizing waste and inefficiency.[63] Did the World Health Organization want restrictions on the marketing of infant formula to better protect babies? The Reagan team was the only vote against. Did most states want a new law of the sea? The Reagan team refused to renegotiate the comprehensive draft treaty and blocked its evolution.[64] Had UNESCO made beneficial changes? The Reaganites were uninterested. Even in the World Bank and IMF, where the US had enormous influence and voting power, the initial Reagan approach was critical.[65] The most unilateralist Administration since 1945 was uninterested in the international definition of human rights, believing that the more limited US version was better. The early Reagan nativist version of American exceptionalism was mostly unrestrained by global governance.

Reagan II

About the second Reagan Administration it has been written that there was a 'turn around' on human rights.[66] This was both true and not true, but in any event US policy shifted regarding human rights in a number of countries. The exact nature of this shift, and its reasons, are complex. First, a number of idealogues left the Reagan team, to be replaced by more pragmatic persons. Haig had been replaced by George Shultz, Kirkpatrick by foreign service officers, Abrams changed bureaus again and Richard Schifter took over at HA, William Casey died of a brain tumour, *inter alia*. Eventually Howard Baker

---

[62] T. Carothers, 'The NED at 10', *Foreign Policy*, 95 (1994), 123–38.

[63] R. Gregg, *About Face? The United States and the United Nations* (Boulder CO, Lynne Rienner, 1993).

[64] R. Frank, 'Jumping ship', *Foreign Policy*, 43 (1981), 121–38.

[65] R. Ayres, 'Breaking the bank', *Foreign Policy*, 43 (1981), 104–20.

[66] T. Jacoby, 'Reagan's turnaround on human rights'.

and Colin Powell brought more pragmatism to the White House staff and National Security Council. With a frequently disengaged President, the presence of more pragmatists in the Administration made a difference. The President himself was eventually distracted and weakened by the Iran–Contra affair.

Second, these pragmatists, especially Shultz and a number of foreign service officers reporting to him, decided that in several countries an anti-communist authoritarian was actually inimical to US long-range security interests. In the Philippines they feared another Iran, in which a corrupt, repressive, and oppressive Marcos government linked to the US would be swept away – and US influence with it. Thus Shultz and others struggled to get Reagan to jettison an anti-communist ally, which the President was decidedly reluctant to do.[67] In Chile, the US feared that if Augusto Pinochet stayed as President too long, there would be a resurgence of the radical left. Thus Shultz and others like Ambassador Harry Barnes worked to get Pinochet to leave the presidency. At the UN, whereas the first Reagan team had defended Pinochet, the second Reagan team helped draft and co-sponsor a resolution critical of the Chilean human rights record. These changes did not stem from an elevation of purely human rights policy over other concerns. The changes stemmed from a new evaluation of long-term US security interests; human rights was still secondary to that strategic policy.

In other places like Zaire US policy did not shift but rather continued to reinforce gross violations of human rights. In still other places like Liberia the US embraced more warmly the incompetent and repressive Samuel Doe, doing nothing to prevent the slide of that American-oriented country into genuine anarchy.[68] In South Africa, US policy shifted away from constructive engagement and toward economic sanctions because Congress overrode a Reagan veto. By the end of the second Reagan Administration, some increase in balanced attention to human rights had been purchased at the cost of over-all clarity and consistency. To the extent that the Shultz memoirs capture reality, the struggle to make foreign policy during 1985–8 was so intense and confusing as to make one long for the good old days of the Carter Administration. The changing nature of Soviet leadership, and accelerating winds of change in Eastern Europe, only added to the lack of clear policy lines in that Administration.

By 1988 there were important similarities (and some continuing differences) between Reagan and Carter on human rights.[69] Each sought to advance human rights inconsistently, where major security and economic interests did not interfere. Each largely ignored some major human rights problems. Congress had forced Carter's hand on Idi Amin's Uganda, and Reagan's hand on South Africa, both via economic sanctions. Congress pushed Carter further than he wanted to go regarding introducing human rights considerations into World Bank proceedings, and it pushed Reagan further than he wanted to go regarding human rights violations by friendly forces in Central America.

---

[67] G. Shultz, *Turmoil and Triumph: My Years as Secretary of State* (New York, Scribners, 1993); R. Bonner, *Waltzing with a Dictator: the Marcoses and the Making of American Policy* (New York, Vintage, 1988).
[68] D. Forsythe, *Human Rights and Peace* (Lincoln NE, University of Nebraska Press, 1993), ch. 5.
[69] G. Mower, Jr., *Human Rights and American Foreign Policy: the Carter and Reagan Experiences* (Westport CT, Greenwood, 1987).

Domestic demand was still periodically unmanageable for the President, and evaluations of some foreign facts shifted.

Reagan moderated somewhat his view toward the UN, as Congress took 'UN bashing' further than the executive branch now wanted to go.[70] But in general, international governance through international law and organization still did not matter much. When the Reagan Doctrine of covert overthrow of pro-Soviet governments ran into predictable trouble under the international law principle of non-intervention, Reagan ignored the World Court's critical judgment in *Nicaragua v. the US* and launched a series of debilitating diplomatic attacks on the court for being 'political' and anti-American. As in the first Reagan Administration, it was not respect for international standards on human rights that impacted executive decision-making. Rather, it was changing views of the national interest in interstate politics, plus congressional pressures.

Reagan's foreign policy, both in general and on human rights, started out as a mixture of rampant American exceptionalism of the activist sort and militarized realism. The US was 'the' city on a hill, and the way to advance 'good' was to build up the military power of the US and its allies – including repressive ones – relative to the Soviet Union. Over time more pragmatic elements at home moderated this orientation. Foreign facts – including the rise of Gorbachev and the Iran–Contra scandal – made their contribution to the same evolution. Reagan had not started where Carter did – with a desire to replace Cold War politics in the state system with human rights in global governance. And Reagan had never moderated his American exceptionalism the way Carter had by acknowledging American human rights deficiencies at home, especially regarding economic and social rights (which Reagan did not accept as rights). But each wound up failing to convince a large number of Americans, in and out of Congress, that he had fashioned a sound human rights policy.

Bush

Most Presidents are complex. Jimmy Carter the Sunday School teacher and rhetorical champion of human rights ran a racist campaign at one point for the governorship of Georgia.[71] Ronald Reagan manifested both pragmatic and ideological dimensions.[72] George Bush's overall foreign policy has been analysed in terms of mastery combined with incompetence.[73] His record on human rights in foreign policy defies easy labelling. He, or his lieutenants, protested Bulgarian discrimination of its Turkish minority. He increased the pressure on the Salvadoran government to bring death squads and other human rights violators under control.[74] But he also down-graded gross violations of human rights in places like Iraq prior to August, 1990, and China during and after June, 1989.

Bush on international human rights was much less moralistic than either Carter or Reagan. His version of American exceptionalism was more

[70] D. Forsythe, 'Human rights in US foreign policy', *Political Science Quarterly*, 105 (1990), 435–54; R. Gregg, *About Face? The United States and the United Nations*.

[71] B. Kaufman, *The Presidency of James Earl Carter, Jr.*

[72] R. Tucker and D. Hendrickson, *The Imperial Temptation: the New World Order and America's Purpose*.

[73] T. Deibel, 'Bush's foreign policy: mastery and inaction', *Foreign Policy*, 84 (1991), 3–23.

[74] R. Pastor, 'George Bush and Latin America'.

perfunctory, using the standard appeals to American greatness in public speeches, but perhaps believing the words somewhat less as befitting one with extensive experience in foreign affairs. Pragmatism characterized his core foreign policy team of National Security Advisor Brent Scowcroft, Secretary of Defense Dick Cheney, and Secretary of State James Baker.

The neo-conservative Schifter, a Democrat but with overriding interests in the evils of European communism, was kept on at HA, which turned out to be an ironic choice. Schifter was to eventually resign and campaign for Bill Clinton on the rather surprising grounds that Bush showed much less interest in human rights than his predecessors in the White House. In fact, in places like Israeli-controlled territory, Baker and Bush showed more interest in human rights, not less, than Reagan and Carter. Bush showed more interest in human rights in El Salvador, not less, than Reagan and Carter. Of course by the time of the Bush Administration the US did not need states like Israel and El Salvador as strategic allies in the Cold War. So the realist reason for down-grading human rights was no longer relevant.

The situation in the Persian Gulf was illustrative of Bush's approach to human rights. Prior to August, 1990 Saddam Hussein was seen as a useful ally in containing Iranian influence. When Congress wanted to curtail trade with Iraq on human rights grounds during the spring and summer of 1990, the Bush Administration was strongly opposed. Realism guided policy. After the Iraqi invasion of Kuwait that August, Bush led the charge in picturing Saddam Hussein as not just a threat to oil lines in the Western coalition but an incarnation of Hitler, thoroughly evil to the core. The most lurid charges about Saddam Hussein's policies in both Kuwait and Iraq were used to mobilize American support for Desert Storm. As a result, some observers viewed Bush as highly moralistic and legalistic.[75] But the Bush Administration did not pressure Saudi Arabia to democratize after Desert Storm; after all, Saudi Arabia had served as the main base of military operations and was still important to Western economies. So the overall record on US attention to human rights in the Persian Gulf was shifting, dependent as it was on Washington's perceptions of short term interests – particularly access to oil and containment of Iran.

As was true for other modern Presidents, where countervailing interests were absent, Bush could be forceful for human rights. It was his decision in the fall of 1992 that placed some 30,000 US troops in Somalia to provide a secure environment for the delivery of humanitarian relief in a situation of widespread starvation and break-down in order. (The UN Security Council authorized the operation, but key decisions were made in the White House.) It was Bush's decision in the spring of 1991 that led to military involvement inside Iraq and the eventual creation of a zone of Kurdish autonomy where, with the help of the UN, Kurdish rights were better protected than before. But in China, where the US had important economic and security interests, Bush postured in public over the 1989 crackdown in Tiananmen Square, while sending envoys in private to tell Chinese leaders that important relations would continue.

There was not much of a pattern to Bush policy on internationally recognized human rights. It was not driven by a frequently articulated belief in American exceptionalism, as was the case for Carter and Reagan. Nor was it

[75] J. Smith, *George Bush's War* (New York, Henry Holt, 1992).

driven by attention to global governance. Bush signed and sent to the Senate the UN Convention Against Torture, where advice and consent was obtained. Bush also obtained advice and consent for the UN Covenant on Civil and Political Rights, signed by Carter long before. But Bush did not push for US ratification of other international agreements, including a globally popular treaty protecting the rights of the child. And even Reagan had achieved US agreement to the UN Convention Against Genocide. As before, there was a gap between symbolic adherence to human rights treaties and using those treaties to seriously inform foreign policy.

Without a clear strategy on rights, the Bush Administration was buffeted by 'the CNN factor'. On Iraq in 1991 and Somalia in 1992, media coverage combined with European and UN pressures, respectively, explained at least partially why Bush committed military force. The lack of Western media coverage in places like Mozambique, where disorder and starvation were also remarkable, helps explain the lack of US concern.

Bush seemed a classic American politician, with moral impulses as long as they did not prove inconvenient to expediential concerns, but with a lack of conceptual thinking and strategic vision. Sometimes Congress pressed him to go further on rights, as regarding Iraq, but not very often. His record on international human rights was similar to his predecessors in terms of its inconsistency (the first Reagan Adminstration excepted), but different in terms of lack of lofty rhetoric. Bush did speak of a 'New World Order', in which human rights would figure prominently. But like Reagan's democracy speech in Britain, Bush's new world order speech at the UN was devoid of specific follow-up and had no lasting importance. It did not prove to be a real guideline for either foreign policy or human rights, and nothing was later substituted for it.

Clinton

After observing President Clinton's foreign policy for about 18 months, one wag said that he was George Bush with angst.

Clinton campaigned in the Carter tradition, criticizing the Republican incumbent for having abandoned the high moral ground in world affairs. In 1992 Clinton repeatedly criticized Bush for his inattention to rights in places like China and Haiti. Clinton promised to make at least democracy, if not the broader concept of human rights, a main issue in foreign policy. He named Warren Christopher as Secretary of State on the basis of his experience in the Carter Administration, and John Shattuck as Assistant Secretary of State for Human Rights, partially on the basis of his work for the American Civil Liberties Union. Secretary of Defense Les Aspin supported more attention to democracy and humanitarian affairs in the Pentagon. A number of Clinton appointees had experience with private human rights groups.

Upon assuming office, however, Clinton continued a number of Bush policies, while agonizing over the choice. This was most prominent regarding Haitian policy during 1993, when Clinton continued the very policy he had lambasted during the campaign – namely, the interception of fleeing Haitians outside US territorial waters and their forced return to Haiti without a full hearing of their claims to refugee status meriting temporary asylum. In early 1994, under intense domestic pressure from the Black Caucus and cooperating private groups, and with a politically prominent Black activist engaging in a hunger strike in protest, Clinton altered policy slightly, so at least to grant an asylum hearing on board ship, with a representative of the office of the UN High Commissioner for Refugees present. Clinton was personally distraught about his policy, and changed it several more times during 1994. In September of that year, Clinton was on the eve of a military invasion, when former President Carter was authorized to negotiate the peaceful entry of US troops in order to guarantee the return of the elected Father Aristide. Thus Clinton's policy on Haiti evolved in fits and starts, without clear strategy, but with persistent and growing attention to human rights. Clinton's Haitian policy tended to disprove the assumption that after Somalia the notion of humanitarian intervention had peaked. Clinton was prepared, finally, to remove the Haitian military rulers by force if necessary.

Similar was Clinton's dilemma in China. He had made China the centrepiece of his rights rhetoric, and in his first year as President had delayed a tough decision by issuing an Executive Order linking Most Favoured Nation status in trade to Chinese improvement in specified human rights matters. But in June, 1994, Clinton abandoned that linkage. China had not made significant progress in a number of human rights areas, so clearly so that no amount of rhetorical gymnastics could obfuscate that fact. Yet the US had continuing economic interests in China of sizeable proportions. And the US wanted Chinese cooperation on a range of political issues involving North Korea, Cambodia, Iran, the UN Security Council, etc. So Clinton essentially reverted to the Bush policy of mixing human rights into a broad foreign policy dialogue, while giving Beijing a mild slap on the wrist in the form of limited sanctions – a ban on US importation of certain Chinese weapons. Factions in Congress, in cooperation with private human rights groups, repeatedly tried to compel more attention to rights in China.

It might appear that Clinton had learned little from Carter's experience. A typical American tendency toward American exceptionalism of the activist variety had not been combined with careful anticipation of how human rights abroad could be blended with economic and other self-interests in the anarchical state system. Carter and Clinton had both been governors of southern states and were without foreign policy experience (although both had experienced foreign policy advisors). Like Carter, Clinton showed an inclination toward international standards on human rights, promising to advance a number of human rights treaties pertaining to children, economic and social rights, and rights in the Western hemisphere under the American Convention on Human Rights. With Clinton's support, in the fall of 1994 the Senate Foreign Relations Committee recommended US ratification of the UN treaty on discrimination against women. At the 1993 UN Congress on Human Rights in Vienna, the Clinton Administration accepted the notion of a human right to development – long favoured by the poorer states but long rejected by American conservatives fearing socialism and an obligatory transnational transfer of wealth from the rich to the poor.

In general Clinton's foreign policy team started out talking about 'assertive multilateralism' in which great weight would be given to international norms and institutions.[76] While Clinton agonized over how to respond to the war in

[76] T. Weiss, D. Forsythe and R. Coate, *The United Nations and Changing World Politics* (Boulder CO, Westview, 1994).

the former Yugoslavia, he did provide relatively large diplomatic and financial support to the associated war crimes tribunal created by the UN. Like Carter, Clinton seemed to want to tilt toward a liberal foreign policy geared toward the global politics of transnational governance. He sought UN approval for military action in Haiti.

Yet what counted in the last analysis (in so far as an intermediate judgment can be made) was different domestic demand, in Clinton's case a domestic demand for economic benefits and low costs to foreign involvements. Big business lobbied hard to avoid interruption of Chinese trade, and even some congressional Democrats and assorted labour groups argued in the same direction. (The AFL–CIO lobbied unsuccessfully for denial of MFN status, in part because of foreign competition based on cheap if not slave labour.) When 18 American military personnel were killed in Somalia during October 1993, many Members of Congress and much of public opinion thought the effort to end starvation in Somalia was not worth the price of American lives. There was little domestic pressure on Clinton to get involved in Rwanda when in 1994 genocide and civil war took the lives of perhaps 500,000 people. The aspect of American political culture oriented toward America first and American isolationism was a domestic force after 40 years of Cold War. Clinton had boxed himself in by rhetorically stressing the importance of economics (then why interrupt Chinese trade over human rights?) and the importance of domestic issues like the plight of cities, crime, and schools (then why expend blood and treasure in places like Somalia?).

It was said by some close observers of human rights debates in Washington that while neither Bush nor Clinton had much vision about policy, at least Clinton had interest. This is not altogether a useful comparison, for as shown above Bush had interest in human rights at least from time to time. It is to say that neither Bush nor Clinton, or for that matter Carter and Reagan, found a way to clearly, persuasively, and consistently find a place for human rights in foreign policy. It may be that Clinton anguished about this more than the others. And it might prove to be the case that Clinton would eventually show more determination to advance rights in places like China over time; Haitian events suggest this possibility. Anguish, however, is neither a policy nor a strategy. American exceptionalism does not implement itself in the anarchic state system, nor does the good intention to pay attention to international norms on human rights bring automatic reward, as Carter discovered.

Conclusion

From the late 1960s the foreign policy élite in the US searched for a new cornerstone to replace global containment of communism.[77] Because of American exceptionalism, that cornerstone had to have moral appeal at home. First the Congress, from 1973–4, then Carter from 1976 through 1978, tried to substitute international human rights. Reagan returned to the Cold War theme of struggle against an 'evil empire', with a nativist version of human rights as *leitmotif*. Both Bush and Clinton were post-Cold War presidents who could not easily avail themselves of the freedom-versus-communism theme. Bush spoke

[77] R. Melanson, *Reconstructing Consensus: American Foreign Policy since the Vietnam War* (New York, St. Martin's, 1991).

vaguely of a new world order, with human rights. Clinton rhetorically endorsed democracy as one of two or three major themes of foreign policy.

But no President, and certainly not the 535-member Congress, was able to find a new cornerstone comparable to global containment that had anchored US foreign policy during 1947–67. To human rights specialists it was not surprising that a focus on rights had failed to supplant containment. Human rights was such an elastic and contentious term that few specialists held much hope for broad consensus.[78]

American exceptionalism naturally fed into rights rhetoric. At home the US displayed a rights culture. But American exceptionalism itself could be used, and had been used, to justify either activism or aloofness on foreign rights questions. Rights for Americans was one thing. US action on behalf of the human rights for foreigners was another. While a few criticized Clinton for not doing more to stop genocide in Rwanda during 1994, most were content to avoid an uncertain commitment where US 'vital interests' were not at stake. Despite deference to Clinton on Haiti as long as the US military occupation went well, there was a strong undercurrent of reservation that could erupt *à la* Somalia if the venture turned sour. The Vietnam syndrome was still present in the background. That fear of nasty entanglement could still force a change in presidential policy, as Reagan had discovered in Lebanon in the 1980s.

American exceptionalism was only one aspect of American political culture. Pragmatism rather than moralism, materialism rather than high-mindedness, security rather than ethics, even racism rather than equal rights, had all been part of the American heritage from time to time. Calculation of power had rarely been absent; the US might invade Haiti but Cuba was a different issue. Some scholars saw a variety of political cultures competing for dominance in American politics.[79]

America's external world was in transition, but transition to what? The Cold War was over, the Soviet Union gone. But a modified state system remained, with elements of global governance falling short of full international government. The US faced no traditional external security threat to its existence, but its relative economic position was not guaranteed. Just when the US had overwhelming putative power as perhaps no other state in world history, its people and parliament and president saw little reason to justify use of that power in places like Bosnia and Rwanda. Attention to human rights in places like Iraqi Kurdistan and Somalia were relatively successful as long as costs were negligible. But even small costs, as in Somalia, braked activism for human rights. Confronting massive genocide in Rwanda, which the US was legally obligated to oppose under the Genocide Treaty, the Clinton Administration opposed major UN involvement as recommended by the Secretary-General (although the US did later vote for a small French military expedition and did later play a central role in the relief effort).

Human rights will remain on the US foreign policy agenda. Vincent was correct: the US, like other states, has no choice in the matter. But after years of debate and reflection, it was still not clear how a consensus for action could be formed given splits between liberals and conservatives, those on Capitol Hill and those in the White House, activists and isolationalists. Some had hoped for

---

[78] D. Forsythe, 'Human rights in US foreign policy'.

[79] M. Thompson, R. Ellis and A. Wildavsky, *Cultural Theory* (Boulder CO, Westview, 1990).

an elementary, partial consensus on US action to help guarantee at least the right to life in the form of no mass starvation and no mass murder. Events in the 1990s in both Bosnia and Rwanda indicate much remains to be done to achieve even this minimal objective.

Human Rights and the New Europe: Experience and Experiment

HUGO STOREY

We live in the Age of Human Rights. Yet neither political theory nor political science has ever been at ease with the concept of human rights. They have made some forays into the subject, mostly but not always critical.[1] For its part the human rights movement has carried on untroubled by unease from these quarters. The international law of human rights, in particular, continues to develop at a phenomenal pace. Far from exercising a restraining influence, events such as those in the former Yugoslavia and Rwanda seem simply to intensify efforts to construct more and more international treaties or other types of international instruments, increasing more and more the multiplicity of international legal ties that bind. What is remarkable is not simply the sheer volume and array of 'treaties', 'conventions', 'charters', 'declarations' etc. which now exist,[2] but the growing effectiveness of their implementation machineries, at least in terms of the recognition by more states than ever before of the validity of such agreements and their ability to give rise to legal consequences both at the level of international law and within their own internal legal systems.[3] Aware that there remains much room for improvement, the recent 'Vienna Declaration' of the World Conference on Human Rights (1993) has proposed further reforms of human rights 'control machineries'.[4]

Not only has there been fast growth but the enterprise continues to be conducted in grandiose style, as if oblivious to the strong philosophical objections this incites. The texts of this Conference ring unashamedly with a Jeffersonian tone. Again and again they reiterate that human rights are 'universal', 'inalienable', 'indivisible', etc. Even the 'Declaration of Bangkok'

[1] D. Raphael (ed.), *Political Theory and the Rights of Man* (London, Macmillan, 1977); E. Kamenka and Tay (eds), *Human Rights* (London, Edward Arnold, 1978); J. Pennock and J. Chapman (eds), *Human Rights*, Nomos XXIII (New York, New York University Press, 1981). For further useful background see R. J. Vincent, *Human Rights and International Relations* (Cambridge, Cambridge University Press, 1986), pp. 7–36 and the contribution by S. Mendus, 'Human rights in political theory' in this volume.

[2] J.-B. Marie, 'International instruments relating to human rights: classification and status of ratifications as of 1 Jan. 1994, *Human Rights Law Journal (HRLJ)*, 15 (1994), pp. 54–67, lists over 70 instruments; M. Bersmo, 'The establishment of the international tribunal on war crimes', *HRLJ*, 14 (1993), p. 371; *HRLJ*, 14 (1993), p. 211; *HRLJ*, 15 (1994), p. 38.

[3] E. A. Alkema *et al.*, 'The domestic implementation of the European Convention on Human Rights in Eastern and Western Europe, *European Human Rights Year Book (EHRYB)*, 2 (1992); *Developing Human Rights Jurisprudence: the Domestic Application of International Human Rights Norms*, Judicial Colloquium in Bangalore, 24–6 Feb. 1988 (London, Commonwealth Secretariat).

[4] United Nations World Conference on Human Rights, Vienna 14–25 June 1993: Vienna Declaration and Programme of Action, *HRLJ*, 14 (1993), p. 352; see also the contribution by Kevin Boyle, 'Stock-taking on human rights: The World Conference on Human Rights' in this volume.

laid before the Conference by nations from the Asia region, finds no difficulty in asserting the 'universality, objectivity and non-selectivity' of all human rights and in expressing a conviction that 'economic and social progress facilitates the growing trend towards democracy and the promotion and protection of human rights'. If such terms often carry special connotations and sub-messages (e.g. 'non-selectivity') they do stand nevertheless as attributable statements freely made by participant states.[5]

This special issue of *Political Studies* is one of a number of signs of a fresh wave of interest in human rights, one other being the recent Oxford Amnesty Lectures in 1993, which include a lengthy article by John Rawls.[6] Whether it proves more sustained remains to be seen. But there is at least one good reason why it should be. As part of the growing global interdependence, modern states now transfer more key economic and political decisions to supranational levels, thus creating an identifiable 'international public domain'. Inasmuch as political theory and political science reflect the 'world of political practice', that 'world' and this 'domain' now overlap more than ever before.

Another reason is the increasing number of highly influential decisions now being made by international human rights judicial (or quasi-judicial) bodies about matters that fall squarely within the sphere of political studies, such as the meaning and scope of major political concepts like 'democracy' and the existence or non-existence of changes in political, social and moral values. Often, however, such decisions are made without much sign of any depth of analysis or systematic analysis of relevant data.[7] Certainly there would seem to be fruitful scope for students of politics to bring to bear their special competences on these materials. Indeed, when one studies the preparatory works (*travaux préparatoires*) of the major modern human rights treaties and the various case laws of the modern judicial or quasi-judicial bodies set up to supervise them, it is hard not to think that if a Rousseau or Hume were alive today he – or as likely nowadays a she – would be found working there.

Given how much of modern human rights law has been developed within the field of public international law, it would be easy to assume that giving it greater attention entails focussing primarily on the global (UN) machineries. That would be a mistake. Globalization of political and economic systems is advancing. But it is still limited, not least by the fact that modern international law has largely been built around the premise of the territorial integrity of the sovereign nation state. But *regionalization* has been far more marked, with very significant political and economic transactions now conducted at a regional level. This is increasingly true not just in Europe and the Americas, but even in regions such as Africa, the Middle East, Asia and the Pacific rim where geopolitical boundaries may sometimes be less established.[8] If one takes

[5] 'Declaration of Bangkok', *HRLJ*, 14 (1993), p. 370.

[6] J. Rawls, 'The law of peoples' in S. Shute and G. Hurley (eds), *On Human Rights: the Oxford Amnesty Lectures* (New York, Basic, 1993), reprinted *Critical Inquiry*, 20 (Autumn, 1993), 36–68.

[7] See e.g. analysis of democracy and human rights by Inter-American Court of Human Rights in Advisory Opinion OC – 13/93 of 16 July: 'Certain attributes of the Inter-American Court HR, para. 31', *HRLJ*, 14 (1993) p. 252. On 'social welfare' see judgment of the European Court of Human Rights in *Schuler-Graggen v. Switzerland* Series A No. 263, *Human Rights Case Digest*, 4 (May–June, 1993), pp. 107–110 (Sweet and Maxwell and The British Institute of Human Rights, 1993).

[8] For useful analysis of the main economic institutions at the European level see D. McGoldrick, 'A new international economic order for Europe', *Yearbook of European Law* 12 (1992), 431–64; for a recent initiative in Asia and the Pacific rim see the Bogor Declaration: APEC Informal Leaders'

seriously the idea that the study of politics should follow the changing *locus* within which major political relations are conducted – be it the Greek *polis*, the medieval city-state or the 20th century nation state – then contemporary reality calls not so much for a focus on the 'global village' as on the evolving regional power-blocs. Much of the gaze, therefore, needs to be cast upon this 'middle distance'.

It may be equally tempting for the political theorist anxious to grapple with the claims made for human rights that they are *universal* norms to again see this as requiring concentration primarily on the body of international law drawn up and operated from a global level, within the UN organization. That too would be a mistake. Even the *international* law of human rights has to be understood as a complex interplay between national, regional and international systems. It is one of the main contentions of this article that specific features of the present European experience may help elucidate some of the current problems posed by these claims to universality.

Yet just at the juncture when the attainments of the human rights movement seem to require fuller attention from the humanities and social science disciplines, the number of critics from within its own ranks have increased. Indeed we are fast approaching the point at which there may arise official declarations of a state of crisis within human rights law. This crisis is formed by the interplay of a number of conflicts. Some of these closely mirror those reflected in political theory and related disciplines, concerning the absence of any sure justificatory basis, the lack of any coherent response to relativist criticisms, etc. But each has its own distinct character and sphere of concern. The focus in this article is on two which have come particularly to the fore.

At the risk of some oversimplification, the first can be described as a clash between *minimalists* and *maximalists*. Typically the minimalist sees the viability of human rights as universal norms to lie in their ability to present an inner core of fundamental principles which can meet with the consensus of all (reasonable) people across all boundaries of culture, politics, religion and levels of economic and social development. Much of the work associated with this approach has centred around the efforts of Philip Alston and others working within UN frameworks on articulating basic subsistence rights such as the 'right to food'.[9] But most 'minimalists' do not conceive their work as aiming at a 'lowest common denominator'. They start from the assumption that within every actual culture or society there will be variable ways of perceiving what must lie within the scope of basic needs that can be endowed with the status of a human right; they contend that unless human rights are recognized as having a dynamic quality, and human rights treaties as forming 'living instruments', they cannot function as truly universal legal norms.[10]

Meeting (Bogor, Indonesia, 15 Nov. 1994); see also A. H. Robertson, revised J. Merrills, *Human Rights in the World* (Manchester, Manchester University Press, 3rd ed., 1989).

[9] Henry Shue, *Basic Rights: Subsistence, Affluence and US Foreign Policy* (Princeton, Princeton University Press, 1980); P. Alston and Quinn, *Human Rights Quarterly (HRQ)*, 9 (1987) 332–81; P. Alston, 'The International Covenant on Economic, Social and Cultural Rights' in *Manual on Human Rights Reporting* (HR/PUB/91/1, UN, New York, 1991), pp. 39–78. P. Alston (ed.), *The UN and Human Rights* (Oxford, Clarendon, 1992).

[10] See contributions by Andreassen and others, in Eide and Hagtvet (eds), *Human Rights in Perspective* (Oxford, Blackwell, 1992).

The typical 'maximalist', on the other hand, whilst agreeing that a dynamic quality is integral to the concept of a human right, believes that human rights law can only function as a truly universal system of legal norms if it progressively expands and reshapes itself to take account of every new level of social and technological innovation. Each occasion upon which human history attains a new level of understanding about freedom, e.g. as to the master-slave, serf-free labourer, man-woman relationship, or as to discrimination on the basis of race, nationality etc., requires an appropriate adjustment to the living body of human rights law. Failure to do this represents a betrayal of the human spirit.[11]

The conflict between minimalists and maximalists has been made more fraught by the advent of a distinct but interrelated conflict between human rights *conditionalists* and *anti-conditionalists*. The concept of human rights conditionality closely but not fully overlaps with that of 'democratic conditionality'[12] (for the purposes of this article, however, the two can be treated as interchangeable).

Building as it does on modern notions which see human rights and the rule of law as indispensable components of the modern conception of democracy, the phenomenon of human rights conditionality may loosely be defined as making the grant of some perceived benefit(s) to a state – e.g. receipt of aid or trade concessions or membership of key regional or international systems – conditional upon its achievement of satisfactory levels of performance in the sphere of human rights and democratic practices.[13] Much of the shaping of the mechanics of this process has occurred within various UN bodies that have powers under human rights treaties to require and monitor 'state reports' in which states have to furnish information and explanations in relation to specific questions about the extent to which they have complied with the various provisions on those treaties.[14] NGOs have also played a vital role.[15] But it has also been utilized with increasing effect by individual states or blocs of states and international organizations in their external and foreign relations

---

[11] E.g. A. Cassesse, *International Law in a Divided World* (Oxford, Clarendon, 1986).

[12] In 1991 the Council of Europe deemed Poland to possess adequate human rights norms but to lack adequate democratic features until it conducted free elections. For argument in favour of the convergence of both concepts, see Inter-American Court of Human Rights: *Habeas Corpus in Emergency Situations* (Arts 29(2), 25(1) and 7(6)), American Convention on Human Rights, para. 24 and 26, *HRLJ*, 9 (1988): '... there exists an inseparable bond between the principle of legality, democratic institutions and the rule of law' and '(i)n a democratic society, the rights and freedoms inherent in the human person, the guarantees applicable to them and the rule of law form a triad', and '(e)ach component thereof defines itself, complements and depends on the others for its meaning'; O. Jacot-Guillarmod, 'The relationship between democracy and human rights' in *Democracy and Human Rights* (Proceedings of 1987 Colloquy) (Strasbourg, Council of Europe, 1990); D. Beetham, *Democratic Audit of the UK: Key Principles and Indices of Democracy* (London, Charter 88 Trust, 1993); A. Rosas, J. Helgesen and D. Goodman, *The Strength of Diversity – Human Rights and Pluralist Democracy* (Dordrecht, Kluwer, 1992); D. Beetham and K. Boyle, *Introducing Democracy: 80 Questions and Answers* (Oxford, Polity and Unesco, forthcoming).

[13] For a useful résumé of current debates about conditionality, see Hans de Jonge, 'Democracy and economic development in the Asia-Pacific region: the role of parliamentary institutions', *HRLJ*, 14 (1993), p. 301.

[14] See *Manual on Human Rights Reporting*, 1991.

[15] See e.g. Amnesty International-inspired survey by C. Humana, World Human Rights Guide (Open University Press, 3rd ed., 1992); Freedom House's latest (1994) annual survey rates 'freedom' in 191 countries, *Los Angeles Times* (16/12/1994); and the contribution by Rachael Brett, 'The role and limits of human rights NGOs at the United Nations', in this volume.

generally. US foreign policy and its well-known peregrinations over Pakistan and China afford one well-known Western example.[16] The extent to which this phenomenon has come to be recognized as a distinct process in international relations was recently made very clear in the course of the 1993 Vienna World Conference. For example, in the text of the Bangkok Declaration already mentioned there is a clause urging discouragement of 'any attempt to use human rights as a conditionality for extending development assistance'. This hostile stance is closely tied to other criticisms of external human rights review bodies for endorsing and/or imposing double standards and applying human rights standards selectively.[17]

Undoubtedly the loudest voice in favour of human rights conditionality is currently that of Western Europe, with the EU even having made it an integral part of its *external* relations development policy as set forth most recently in the Maastricht Treaty (Treaty of European Union).[18] But in fact one of the major theatres on which the conflicts between minimalists and maximalists and conditionalists and anti-conditionalists are currently being played out is inside Europe itself.

That conflicts should emerge – and in such volatile form – inside the classical home of liberal democratic theory from which so much of the modern human rights enterprise has sprung will no doubt strike many as a fine irony, not least the sceptical political theorist. The twin aims of this paper are to examine the European dimension to the two conflicts just identified and to attempt an assessment of the extent to which modern political theory might draw lessons from it. As with any case-study this necessitates some degree of narrative; but it is hoped that this will not submerge its dual role as theoretical fable.

Europe and the European Community (EC)

Within Europe the main actor is, of course, the EC (European Community) in its new guise of the EU (European Union). It is at once the economic powerhouse and political epicentre of the architecture of the new Europe. Its commitments to the principles of human rights were already present in incipient form in the original text of the 1957 Treaty of Rome and have gradually been developed since, not without some tribulations. Interestingly, one of the main turning points in this process of development came as a result of the famous *Internationale Handelsgesellschaft* case in 1974 in which the German constitutional court gave notice that it would not necessarily accept the supremacy of EC law over its own internal law unless it could be satisfied that the former guaranteed human rights to at least the same level as did the German constitution to which German judges owed their allegiance. The response of the main judicial body of the EC – the European Court of Justice at

---

[16] For further background on US foreign policy see the contribution by David Forsythe, 'Human rights and US foreign policy: two levels, two worlds' in this volume.

[17] For further background, see R. J. Vincent, *Human Rights and International Relations*.

[18] See e.g. 1993 report of European Parliament on human rights in the world and the Community human rights policy, *HRLJ*, 14 (1993), p. 284; See further C. Duparc, *The European Community and Human Rights* (Luxembourg Office for Official Publications of the European Communities, 1993); Treaty of European Union, Article 130u(2); for text see N. Foster, *Blackstone's EC Legislation* (London, Blackstone, 5th ed., 1994).

Luxembourg – was to rule that human rights principles formed part of the fundamental law of the Community.[19]

The continuing advance of this process is reflected in the texts of the 1992 ('Maastricht') Treaty of European Unity (TEU) which embody an express commitment to fundamental human rights as well as a clause that requires Community policy in the sphere of development cooperation to, *inter alia*, 'contribute to the general objective of developing and consolidating democracy and the rule of law, and to that of respecting human rights and fundamental freedoms' (Art 130u(2)). Further steps are in train to create a 'Constitution of the Union', which would contain, among other things, a comprehensive catalogue of human rights. The EU is currently deliberating upon whether to join the European Convention on Human Rights (ECHR) as an additional party in its own right.[20]

With a view to ensuring that its own house is in order, the EC has become more and more insistent upon viewing adequate human rights performance as an essential prerequisite for its own membership. This would probably have continued to develop at a moderate pace had it not been for the collapse of the communist bloc and the urgent desire of many of its component parts to join the EC and thus benefit from it economically and politically. These dramatic events led many of the new states to embrace with an initial enthusiasm the classic liberal-democratic principle that progress in respect of human rights, the rule of law and democracy is linked integrally to free market principles.[21]

In the light of this conception, other European states lacking human rights credentials were to be seen as economic undesirables to be kept at arms length. A keynote speech setting out this new EC approach in plain terms was made in 1990 by the British Foreign Minister, Douglas Hurd, who stated:

> Membership of the Community requires an applicant to be a fully-fledged democracy in political and economic terms. A country which relies on a high level of state subsidy and state aid is simply not qualified to enter the Community. Therefore, it will be a number of years before the newly-fledged democracies of Central and Eastern Europe will be eligible.[22]

In making human rights such a policy centrepiece the EC has not been alone among other major European bodies or international organizations. The European Bank for Reconstruction and Development (BERD), NATO and others have revised their own criteria to take account of human rights dimensions to a greater or lesser degree.[23]

---

[19] *Internationale Handelsgesellschaft v. Einfur und Vorratsstelle Getreide*, Case 11/70 (1970) European Court Reports 1125, (1972) Common Market Law Reports 255; for further analysis of the development of human rights and principles within ECJ case law, see A. Cassesse (ed.), *Human Rights and the European Community* (Baden-Baden, Nomos, 1991); F. G. Jacobs, 'The protection of human rights in the member states of the European Community: the impact of the case law of the Court of Justice' in J. O'Reilly (ed.), *Human Rights & Constitutional Law* (Dublin, Round Hall, 1992), pp. 243–50.

[20] See D. McGoldrick, 'A new international economic order for Europe'.

[21] Negotiation of association agreements are seen as a half-way stage: see Foreign Affairs Committee, House of Commons, Session 1991–2, 2: D. McGoldrick, 'A new international economic order for Europe', para. 119 ff.

[22] D. Hurd, H. C. Deb., 11 June 1990, cols. 21–22.

[23] D. McGoldrick, 'A new international economic order for Europe', pp. 440–56.

But the EC has never lost sight of the fact that it is primarily an economic system. Given its constant awareness of a *separate* and older European system – the Council of Europe – in which human rights has been a primary concern, it is not surprising that the EC chose, soon after the collapse of the Berlin Wall, to largely leave the administration of human rights conditionality to that body. From the EC point of view, Council of Europe membership is an essential 'antechamber' through which all potential new EC members must pass.[24]

The Council of Europe and the European Convention on Human Rights (ECHR)

To understand how it is that the Council of Europe has come to play the role of principal democratic auditor (or human rights 'Bundesbank') of European states requires some brief explanation. Even if the historical background is well-known it is not without interest to political theorists and political scientists to re-narrate some of it at this point, especially its origins in a 1948 Hague Congress attended by representatives of the world of politics, law and the arts from nineteen countries. The horrors of the Second World War were still fresh memories. Possibly no event in human history quite so nearly approximated to Hobbes' scenario of a 'war of all against all' and the subsequent need of its surviving combatants to achieve a 'covenant' designed primarily to ensure its non-recurrence. This Congress perceived an urgent need to prevent fresh conflicts that might arise from new forms of totalitarianism. But being at an international level where the main protagonists were states, not individuals, its deliberation led on, not to a new Leviathan but to the signing by 10 states of a Statute of the Council of Europe. The inclusion within this Statute of objectives covering, *inter alia*, '... the maintenance and further realization of human rights and fundamental freedoms', the consolidation of democracy and realization of the rule of law represented a radical and unique development. These moreover were made actual requirements for membership of the Council of Europe. The new Council did not give itself law-making powers, but it did vest itself with powers to draft and assist its member states in ratifying treaties among themselves.[25] The body of European treaties that have subsequently been made under its auspices is formidable and covers a broad range of subjects, ranging from data protection, suppression of terrorism, a common code on social security.[26] However, its 'jewel in the crown' and its most famous achievement has been the conclusion in 1950 of the European Convention on Human Rights (ECHR).

The European Convention on Human Rights (ECHR)[27]

Whilst closely modelled on the 1948 UN Universal Declaration on Human Rights and closely resembling the subsequent 1966 UN International Covenant

---

[24] Andrew Drzemszewski, 'The Council of Europe's co-operation and assistance programmes with Central and Eastern European countries in the human rights field, 1990 to September 1993', *HRLJ*, 14 (1993) p. 229.

[25] A. H. Robertson, *Human Rights in Europe* (Manchester, Manchester University Press, 1963), pp. 3–4.

[26] Treaties are compiled within a European Treaty Series (ETS) (Strasbourg, Council of Europe).

[27] For further background, see R. Beddard, *Human Rights in Europe* (Cambridge, Grotius, 3rd

on Civil and Political Rights (ICCPR), the ECHR was the first international treaty under which respect for fundamental rights was collectively guaranteed by all the States who became its 'High Contracting Parties'. For the first time a number of states were prepared not only to undertake obligations to secure human rights but also to establish a supervisory body empowered to give judgements against contracting States in cases brought before it either by one of their number or by individuals. By and large rights were couched in the form of guarantees available to individuals as persons, irrespective of nationality, economic status, or any other status.

But the greatest achievement of this treaty lay not in those parts of its text that set forth a catalogue of civil and political rights. Such catalogues were already common features of the constitutions of many modern states. Paradoxically it lay in the Convention's *restriction* clauses, viz. clauses designed to qualify and counterbalance the rights guaranteed to individuals. If they had been framed in too broad terms they would have subverted the protection of the guaranteed rights; if framed too narrowly the State parties would not have found them a practical, manageable set of international duties.

Having to transpose these restriction clauses into the standard format of a multilateral treaty marked the point at which there occurred a major change of paradigm, establishing as it were, a new logical calculus for the modern international law of human rights. Creative adaptation was required because this format offered more than one possible mechanism for limiting the extent of a State's treaty obligations, the three main mechanisms being 'reservations', 'derogations' and 'permissible restriction clauses'. Whilst earlier human rights texts, in particular the 1948 Universal Declaration of Human Rights (UDHR), had grappled with these transposition problems earlier, this Declaration was not enacted as a legally binding treaty. Sharpened by the knowledge that the ECHR text was to become legally binding, the ECHR drafters had to refine the contents of the restriction clauses, with closer awareness that subsequent case law was likely to treat them as a definitive set. It owes much to the adroit mixing and matching eventually achieved by its drafters that the Convention was to prove so successful. Some elaboration is in order here. At Art 64 each state was given the right to make '**reservations**' at the time of signature or ratification as to any of the Convention articles in respect of which it felt unable to comply, so long as their terms did not subvert the object and purpose of the Convention. At Article 15 a right to make ongoing '**derogations**' from the Convention was recognized in certain defined circumstances (covering war and public emergencies threatening the life of the nation). However this right was not given in respect of a core of 'nonderogable rights' covering the right to life, prohibition of inhuman and degrading treatment, retroactive criminal penalties and protection from forced labour and slavery. (Additionally there was a provision allowing '**denunciations**' by states, albeit its requirement of six months' prior notification operated equally as a control on any state that might seek to cast off its Convention obligations overnight.)

ed., 1993); P. van Dijk and G. van Hoof, *Theory and Practice of the European Convention on Human Rights* (Netherlands, Kluwer Law and Taxation, 2nd ed., 1990); A. H. Robertson, *Human Rights in Europe*, for text see I. Brownlie (ed.), *Basic Documents on Human Rights* (Oxford, Clarendon, 3rd ed., 1994), p. 326.

These specific 'opt out' clauses co-existed with various fixed clauses attached to most of the guaranteed rights specifying the '**permissible restrictions**' which States could place on them and on what grounds. Article 8(1) for example, which guaranteed the rights to respect for family life, private life, the home and correspondence had attached at Art 8(2) a paragraph listing six grounds, justifying restriction of these rights wherever this was 'necessary in a democratic society'. Subsequent case law established not only that such clauses formed an exclusive list but they were to be interpreted narrowly, lest States take undue advantage of them to the detriment of the objective of protecting the guaranteed rights.

Amongst other clauses designed to delimit the extent of their Convention duties, the contracting States included one which made very clear their refusal to allow the Convention to be exploited by individuals or groups or even states intent on subverting Convention ideals. At Article 17 it was stated:

> Nothing in this Convention may be interpreted as implying for any State, group of person any right to engage in any activity or perform any act aimed at the destruction of any of the rights and freedoms set forth herein or at their limitation to a greater extent than is provided for in the Convention.

The Convention also chose to leave optional the extent to which each state party may subject itself to the implementation machinery. In order to become subject to Article 25, which granted to individuals the right to take a case to Strasbourg against it (the '*right of individual petition*') each state had first to make an Article 25 'declaration'. If it also chose to let this case be ruled upon by the European Court of Human Rights, it had first to make an Article 46 'declaration' granting that Court 'compulsory jurisdiction'.

These specific 'opt-in' clauses, each capable of being time-limited and requiring periodic renewal, were in addition to a ratification process which carefully permitted states the choice of simply signing the Convention or ratifying it. Only the latter step brought the Convention into force in relation to that state.

The above survey completes the description of the main mechanisms helping make manageable for States the obligations they thus undertook. A final notable feature was the express recognition within the Preamble to the Convention of its *European identity*, distinct from but linked to global human rights standards:

> Being resolved, as the Governments of European countries which are likeminded and have a common heritage of political traditions, ideals, freedom and the rule of law to take the first steps for the collective enforcement of certain of the Rights stated in the Universal Declaration [viz. the 1948 UN Universal Declaration of Human Rights (UDHR)].

The traditional approach to Council of Europe and ECHR membership

In order to complete the relevant narrative it is essential to review how the first and second-generation 'joiners' of this Convention made use of these mechanisms of manageability. Only thus is it possible to assess the character and extent of the present conflicts and challenges thrown up by the Council of

Europe's efforts to respond to the perceived needs of the new generation of 'joiners' from the countries of Central and Eastern Europe.

In the 1950s and 1960s when the Council of Europe machinery first had to consider applications from those wishing to join the original group of 10 states, it appears that the approach taken to the conditions of Council membership relating to human rights was unexacting. The gravamen of the traditional approach was flexibility. Prior to a final decision being made there were no mechanisms that ensured close critical scrutiny. Nor were applicant states expected to state specific time-frames within which they aimed to accept the full panoply of ECHR (or 'Convention') obligations. Whilst it was expected that members would go on to become parties to the ECHR this was nowhere stipulated as a definite requirement.

Both for the original and subsequent members no difficulty was seen with them approaching acquisition of Convention responsibilities by stages. To sign it but then to defer ratification was seen as the normal course. No great pressure was applied to ensure simultaneous or rapid ratification. It is true there were clear efforts on all sides to keep **reservations** to a minimum, but this was facilitated by the knowledge that there was no haste expected as regards making 'opt-in' declarations under Articles 25 and 46, without which no state had truly to expose itself to legal supervision by the new machinery based at Strasbourg in France. Even in relation to the Federal Republic of Germany, where one might have expected the greatest behind-the-scene pressures to tie its new Government to a full set of ECHR guarantees, the period between ratification and the making of these declarations was four years and eight months. In some states whose existing democratic credentials might have seemed to warrant immediate transition, the time-gaps were large: the UK did not make its Article 25 and 46 declarations until 1966 and it was not until October 1981, under President Mitterand, that France accepted Article 25! (Ireland, for the record, achieved the shortest transition, taking two years and three months).[28]

If to some extent the delay shown by members during this early period reflected the seriousness with which they took their Convention responsibilities, it has to be recalled that during this period the number of rights which the Convention granted to individuals was fewer than now: apart from the ECHR and Protocol No. 1, no other Protocol adding to this number came into force until 1970. Furthermore the Convention's implementation machinery was undeveloped and showed few signs of wishing to impose stringent standards. The first-stage Strasbourg organ of supervision, the European Commission of Human Rights (hereafter the 'Commission'), which was responsible for receiving and filtering applications, did not start doing so until 1955. It was not until 1966, in *Alam v. UK*, a case brought against the UK by a migrant worker from Pakistan whose son had been denied entry to join him, that this body made its first finding of admissibility against a contracting State. The main judicial body, the European Court of Human Rights (hereafter the 'Court'), did not come into being until 1960 and remained virtually inactive during the 1960s and 1970s. Furthermore, the Commission in its early case law

[28] A. H. Robertson, *Human Rights in Europe* (Manchester, Manchester University Press, 1963). G. Weil, *The ECHR – Background Developments and Prospects* (European Aspects, Series C, Politics, No. 12 Leyden, 1963).

adopted a deliberately cautious and conservative approach; its early decisions were quick to exclude many applications on the basis that they fell outside of the material scope of the guaranteed rights. By and large the message conveyed was that the Convention was, with one or two exceptions, a catalogue limited to selected *civil and political rights*.

Animating this type of gradualist approach was a belief that it would inspire greater confidence amongst the State parties that they could indeed 'live with' the new self-imposed limits on their sovereignty. Both bodies were also markedly respectful in their stance towards judgments and opinion of the national courts before whom Strasbourg applicants had often sought previously to exhaust their domestic remedies to no avail. It is true that, as 'low-key' as was the approach taken by both the Commission and the Court, both bodies did gradually adopt a more dynamic and innovative approach. One of the results of this process was to increase the effective number of rights which the Convention guaranteed: two major examples were the right to legal aid and an individual's right to vote. But gradualism was the order of the day.[29]

Even after ratifying Articles 25 and 46, not all states incorporated the Convention into their domestic law. (A few, the UK included, still do not.) Even in those countries that did incorporate the Convention, most took a considerable amount of time to give its norms significant direct effect within their own legal orders. In almost every state the national judiciary exhibited resistance to applying Convention norms. In short, the state parties generally took a far more dualist approach to international law treaties, and were far readier to see the Strasbourg judges as an actual or potential threat to their national sovereignty.[30]

Two aspects of post-war statehood in the European context were also significant. In the immediate aftermath of the Second World War all Western states took a more interventionist approach towards management of their own economies. Welfare-state building was seen to require individual citizens to make way if need be for slum clearances, road-building, factory developments, etc.[31]

Insofar as their role as *nations* were concerned, the state parties saw the fixing of territorial boundaries by the Allied powers as giving them the authority and the duty to oppose any further efforts by national minorities to secede or claim self-determination. Only in respect of former colonial

---

[29] *Alam v. UK*. Application 2991/66, 10 YB 478. A. H. Robertson, *Human Rights in Europe*; R. Beddard, *Human Rights in Europe*.

[30] Two of the most detailed analyses are: A. Drzemczewski, *European Human Rights Convention in Domestic Law* (Oxford, Clarendon, 1983); J. Polakiewicz and V. Jacob-Foltzer, 'The ECHR in domestic law...', *HRLJ*, 12 (1991), 65ff, 125ff. See also E. A. Alkema *et al.*, 'The domestic implementation of the European Convention on Human Rights in Eastern and Western Europe'; F. Jacobs and S. Roberts (eds), *The Effect of Treaties in Domestic Law* (London, Sweet and Maxwell, 1987).

[31] In 1950 the British Chancellor of the Exchequer, Sir Stafford Cripps, expressed concern about various articles in the draft Convention that might restrict powers of entry into private premises and would be inconsistent with the powers of economic control which were essential to the operation of a planned economy. The Lord Chancellor (Lord Jowitt) observed: 'It is quite obvious to me that the draftsman ... starts with the standpoint of a laissez-faire economy and has never realized that we are now living in the age of a planned economy...' (Cabinet minutes (CAB 128/18 107)). Letter by Jowitt of Aug. 3, 1950, LCO 2/5570 (cited from A. Lester, 'Fundamental rights: the United Kingdom isolated?', *Public Law*, 1984, 46–72 at pp. 50–1).

territories was self-determination seen as a viable right. Significantly the ECHR, unlike the 1948 Universal Declaration on Human Rights and the two 1966 UN Covenants, was not even prepared to grant either the right to self-determination by peoples, or any cultural rights to minorities.[32]

The traditional approach maintained

During the 1970s and 1980s the Council of Europe maintained the same flexible approach. In the case of Greece, which under its military dictators had earlier resigned from the Council of Europe and denounced the Convention, the new Government pledged to restore democracy was allowed ample time between renewal of ratification and acceptance of the two key 'opt-in' clauses (articles 25 and 46). A similar Council benevolence was shown to Spain and Portugal, where applications for membership followed swiftly upon the ending of their military dictatorships. In the case of Portugal, after its 'carnation revolution', the Council was content for it to enter reservations to six different Convention articles, all of which continued until 1987 – some nine years later. Clearly in these cases the dominant objective was to nurse these states back to democratic health, in full awareness by this time that the Convention implementation machinery and the by-now extensive case-law had made conformity with Convention guarantees a much more daunting prospect than had been the case in the 1950s and 1960s.[33]

The Modern Approach to Council of Europe and ECHR Membership: the Post-Communist Context

Particularly in view of the sensitive approach taken in relation to Greece, Spain and Portugal, it might have been expected that the Council of Europe's approach to the 'fledgling democracies' of the Central and Eastern European countries (hereafter referred to as CEECs) would follow suit. Yet such has so far not proved to be the case and even though roughly half of the potential applicants have now been processed, the signs are if anything that the Council's conditionality requirements will become even more exacting.[34] The evidence for this contention is overwhelming.

Firstly, in respect of membership of the Council of Europe itself, CEEC's have to jump more and higher hurdles than faced either the original members or earlier 'joiners'. There are now several extra requirements. Two were added in 1983, since when every applicant has had to show not simply that it is a 'European' country that maintains the rule of law, democracy and human rights. It must demonstrate that it is a *pluralist parliamentary* democracy' in

[32] For texts, see I. Brownlie (ed.), *Basic Documents on Human Rights* (Oxford, Clarendon, 1994).

[33] J. Polakiewicz and V. Jacob-Foltzer, 'The ECHR in Domestic Law'. For further background on Council of Europe decision-machinery on membership, see H. Klebes, 'Human rights and parliamentary democracy in the Parliamentary Assembly' in F. Matscher and H. Petzold (eds), *Protecting Human Rights: the European Dimension* (Köln, Heymann, 1988), pp. 307, 309, 316.

[34] K. Drzwicki, 'The future relations between Eastern Europe and the Council of Europe', in A. Bloed and W. de Jonge (eds), *Legal Aspects of a New European Infrastructure* (Utrecht, Asser Institute, 1992), pp. 41–60; A. Drzemczewski, 'The Council of Europe's co-operation and assistance programmes with Central and Eastern European Countries in the human rights field: 1990 to Sept. 1993', *HRLJ*, 14 (1993), p. 229.

which there is a holding of free elections at regular intervals and that it will accede to the ECHR promptly. By 1993 several further requirements were listed as ones which 'may well in the future' need to be taken into account. The five most important are: readiness to subscribe to a larger proportion of the Council's other legal instruments (which now total over 100) and to do so over a 'pre-determined time-span'; affording minorities additional rights; recognition of the inviolability of territorial borders; a sufficient degree of political stability; and acceptance, before accession, of 'the interim mechanisms for the protection of human rights in non-member States provided by the Council of Europe'.

Furthermore more flesh has been added to several of the compulsory requirements. These significantly increase the pressure on applicants not only to take on full ECHR responsibilities but to ensure their internal legal orders are structured so as to ensure fuller direct effect and better and faster compliance. They have to undertake to ratify the Convention 'with only a minimal number of reservations (including acceptance of the optional clauses, Articles 25 and 26), within a reasonable time'[35] (this particular clause was echoed in the Final Declaration of the Vienna World Conference).[36] Thus it would seem that in the new-style membership procedure, accession to the Convention, far from being simply seen as a goal to which new members must aspire, has become an integral part of the induction process.

Whilst the evidence as to how these enlarged criteria have been applied in practice suggests that the 'auditors' have been ready to relax some where they are satisfied that applicants meet their spirit if not their letter, it is equally evident that scrutiny has been close and some definite lines have been drawn. Thus in 1993, Latvia's application was refused pending better undertakings being given to remedy its too exclusionary laws on acquisition of citizenship. Earlier, in 1991, Estonia had to give an undertaking to remedy its denial of the right to vote to non-citizens. In the case of Poland the Council issued an invitation to join but made it conditional upon that country holding free elections to its Parliament, even though on the human rights side, it was agreed to have an 'advanced' legislative programme ahead even of (the then) Czechoslovakia. The course of 1994 saw six new states become new members: Estonia, Lithuania, Slovenia, the Czech Republic, Slovakia and Romania. That has brought the total of State members from Central and Eastern Europe to fifteen.[37]

In the case of Russia, even before the events of 1994/95 in Chechenya, the degree and level of scrutiny has become so careful that it has to be asked whether some of the new applicants accepted earlier would have been able to succeed under its criteria. Prior to 1994 it seemed that the main stumbling block was maintenance of the presence of its troops in the Baltic states. But in a 1994 report drawn up for the Council's Parliamentary Assembly by four eminent legal experts, a variety of deficiencies were identified, all on the basis of a very methodical evaluation of available evidence. (It must be doubted,

[35] For text see A. Drzemczewski, *HRLJ*, 14 (1993), p. 229 at 352.

[36] *HRLJ*, 14 (1993), p. 352.

[37] For relevant Council of Europe reports see (on Latvia, Estonia and Lithuania) *HRLJ*, 14 (1993), 216–23; (on Poland) A. Drzemczewski, *HRLJ*, 12 (1991), 335–44; (on Slovakia and Hungary) *HRLJ*, 12 (1991), 224–5; (on Slovenia, Czeck Republic, Slovakia) *HRLJ*, 12 (1991), 437–53.

however, that the group did not stray somewhat from their brief in expressing 'alarm' at Russian interest in a Euro-Asian convention on human rights 'as far as it might introduce its own mechanism of implementation': could not the same objections have been brought against all other regional human rights conventions?)[38]

ECHR responsibilities

Once membership has been conferred on applicant CEECs, the Council has proceeded to require – and obtain – from them rapid acceptance of full ECHR responsibilities.

Time-periods in respect of signature, ratification, and declarations under Articles 25 and 46 have been significantly shorter than under the traditional approach. In the case of Bulgaria, a bare four months separated all four processes. Reservations have been very few. Hungary made one in relation to right of access to courts and Bulgaria's two cover the right to education and the right to property (on the right to education the UK maintains a reservation to this day). The Council's policy of requiring nil or minimal reservations seems to be acting as a constraint on new 'joiners' looking at this mechanism in terms of the traditional approach, in accordance with which a state could both pause longer to take fuller stock of its real capacity to conform to Convention norms at the outset and feel justified in making a reservation if it felt itself wanting.

Having moved swiftly to ensure they adopt a full range of Convention responsibilities, the new CEEC parties find themselves inside a system which has become extremely sophisticated. By virtue of additional protocols adding extra guaranteed rights, there are more individual human rights which they are bound to protect. By virtue of the far greater volume of cases taken to Strasbourg against 'respondent' States they face a Commission and a Court that have now evolved a sizeable body of 'established case-law'. Much of this has imposed more detailed limits on each State's 'margin of appreciation' to apply national laws at its own discretion. There have been no signs of the Strasbourg judges resiling from a strong conception of their role as interpreters and 'guardians' of the Convention, a role which has highlighted the Convention as a 'living instrument' with a progressive rationale.[39] This has meant further that the new 'joiners' no longer face a treaty binding them merely to a confined list of civil and political rights. Judicial activism has led to what might be called the 'discovery' of several new human rights (or at least new extensions of the meaning and scope of existing ones). In recent case law, for example, the judges have seen changing social standards in contracting States to require redefining the scope of the Article 6 protection of 'civil rights' so as to embrace 'social welfare benefits'[40] and (most recently) environmental

---

[38] Report prepared for Parliamentary Assembly of the Council of Europe: Report on the conformity of the legal order of the Russian Federation with Council of Europe standards, *HRLJ*, 15 (1994), 249–295. See A. Drzemczewski, *HRLJ*, 14 (1993), p. 229; updating document to 1 July 1994 from Council of Europe Secretariat: H(94) 8, Strasbourg, Council of Europe 1994 for account of recent joinings.

[39] *Tyrer v. UK*, 1978, Series A, No. 26 and *European Human Rights Reports* (EHRR), 2.1.

[40] On social welfare benefits see: Judgement of European Court of Human Rights in *Schuler-Graggen v. Switzerland* Series A No. 263: *Human Rights Case Digest*, 4 (May–June, 1993), pp. 107–10 (Sweet and Maxwell and The British Institute of Human Rights, 1993).

benefits.[41] It is now possible to discern in virtually every subject area of public law an identifiable body of norms limiting State party freedom of action. In the criminal justice sphere, for example, the period of detention allowable before a court hearing has been set at four days.[42] In the sphere of corporal punishment strict limits have been set upon its use in schools and in relation to juvenile offenders.[43] Even sensitive areas of morality, which earlier case law was content to treat as matters for church and state customs, have increasingly come under Convention coverage. The Court has censured national systems which prohibit the publishing of information about abortion facilities;[44] or deny transexuals the ability to achieve a new civil identity as a person of a different sex;[45] or impose punitive laws on freely consenting adult homosexuals.[46] With increasing authority the Strasbourg system sees itself as having attained the status of 'a constitutional instrument of European public order in the field of human rights'.[47]

New 'joiners' also confront a system which has come to expect and obtain relatively high levels of compliance from States found by the Court to be in breach of one or more Convention norms. And in any event, the broader Council of Europe programme to facilitate aspiring and new members has increased the extent to which they have had to make their internal legal orders more permeable to Convention norms. Thus most have revised or introduced new national constitutions which give clear precedence to international law obligations generally, and have armed their judiciaries with domestic jurisdiction to apply Convention principles as part of their own laws.[48]

The precise economic cost to new 'joiners' of the rapid restructuring of their legal systems and other human rights reforms is hard to assess, but such reforms must certainly appear to some of them to limit the range of options more narrowly than was allowed in the early days of the Council of Europe, when state interventionism and command economies were more in fashion. But partly because of the present ascendancy of free market values and partly because of concern to prevent any reversion to communist patterns, new members are only permitted to operate within the parameters of the modern European conception of the state as manager and regulator of its economy.[49]

The extent to which the ECHR imposes greater constraints on each state's sovereign ability to deal with ethnic conflict as it sees fit has become a matter of great uncertainty, especially in the wake of events in the former Yugoslavia. But certainly every new CEEC now knows that any such conflicts which arise within its territory may cause greater repercussions in terms of international human rights monitoring and supervision than otherwise, and that the stance

---

[41] By same Court: *Zander v. Sweden, EHRR*, 18 (1993), p. 175.

[42] *Brogan v. UK*, Series A 145-B *HRLJ*, 9 (1988), p. 293.

[43] *Tyrer v. UK* 1978, Series A 1976 No. 26 and *EHRR*, 2.1; *Campbell and Cosans* Series A 48 *HRLJ*, 3 (1982), p. 221.

[44] *Open Door and Dublin Well Woman* Series A, 246-A, *HRLJ*, 13 (1992), p. 378.

[45] *X v. France*, Series A 243-C, *HRLJ*, 13 (1992), p. 269.

[46] *Norris v. Ireland*, Series A, No. 142, *EHRR*, 13 (1988), p. 186.

[47] *Chrysostomos* et al. *v. Turkey, HRLJ*, 12 (1991), p. 113.

[48] See A. Drzemczewski, *HRLJ*, 14 (1993), p. 229; S. I. Pogany, 'Human rights in Hungary', *International and Comparative Law Quarterly (ICLQ)*, 41 (July, 1992), p. 676.

[49] D. McGoldrick, 'A new international economic order for new Europe', pp. 252–464.

taken by the Council of Europe unambiguously favours more, not less intrusion by investigative committees.[50]

In regard to both these aspects of the Convention's constraints upon the exercise of each state's powers, each of them has also to bear in mind the principal reason why it has subjected itself to Council of Europe norms. In this broader context the *Council of Europe* features only as the '*antechamber*' to the main room of the European 'home' – *the EC (now EU)*. For the latter, the daily priorities hinge much more on economic priorities, e.g. around trade and commerce and, in particular, the formation of belief that CEECs can offer secure climates for EC investors, businesses and companies.

Far from the Council of Europe viewing the changing composition of its membership to call for a slowing down or softening of the process of 'furthering' the realization of human rights, it has seen the actual or anticipated entry of CEECs as one of the – although certainly not the only – reasons calling for a radical overhaul of the Convention's control system. The treaty groundwork for this has now been completed, with the signing in 1994 of a Protocol No. 11, combining its two judicial organs into a *unified European Court of Human Rights* and making the right of individual petition an *automatic* rather than an optional obligation. Even if entry into force of this Protocol takes some time, it is already beginning to work its effects on existing European legal cultures.[51]

In addition both the Council of Europe and the EU are actively rethinking the role of *economic and social rights*: the Council of Europe has taken steps to strengthen the implementation machinery of the 1961 European Social Charter. The Council is also actively encouraging CEECs to ratify this convention. The EU, in response to the efforts by all Members to curb soaring welfare state expenditures, has expressed its determination not to condone regression or dismantling. To this end it increasingly identifies the need for protection of economic and social rights to be put on a more *constitutional* footing, whereby they can become justiciable before national courts, as well as its own European Court of Justice. This new thinking is working to erode the classic distinction between civil and political rights on the one hand and economic and social rights on the other. (Some of the new democracies, finding as they have that to date democratic transition has gone hand-in-hand with reduction in social and economic standards, may rue that the latter set of guarantees were not available sooner.)

Consequences and Implications

Given the stark contrast between the traditional and contemporary approaches to Council of Europe membership and Convention compliance, it is surprising how muted criticism has been. Understandably those involved in the Council of Europe programmes designed to facilitate the democratic restructuring of

---

[50] The 'Final Declaration' of the Third Strasbourg Conference on Parliamentary Democracy Compendium of Documents, Council of Europe, Strasbourg, 1992 states *inter alia* that 'human rights are no longer the exclusive province of States. The infringement of human rights entails an actual international duty of intervention'.

[51] The first country to ratify Protocol No. 11 was Slovenia, 28 June 1994, see further A. Drzemeczewski and J. Meyer-Ladewig, 'Principal characteristics of the new ECHR control mechanism, as established by Protocol No. 11', signed on 11 May 1994, *HRLJ*, 15 (1994), 81–6 (text etc. is given in same issue, pp. 86–111 at 103ff).

CEECs have been driven by practical priorities. Possibly the lack of critique is testimony to the relative success and effectiveness of those involved in easing the transition. Another factor has certainly been the relatively positive response of CEECs themselves, who so far have by and large not chosen to portray this conditionality process as 'neo-colonialist', 'imperialist' or 'superimpositive'.[52]

But among more detached observers, including historians and political scientists, there are an increasing number of studies that identify economic, social, political and legal factors which must give cause for serious doubt as to whether the new CEECs can in fact 'live with' such exacting human rights norms. All highlight factors which distinguish their situation from that of the Western democracies in the immediate post-war period or the more recent experience of other European states–e.g. Spain and Portugal–where democratic traditions had been interrupted by military dictatorships. These factors include: the previous history of failure of most CEECs as agrarian economies; their relative lack of industrialization; their high degrees of social stratification; the high incidence of significant minority problems; the lack of a common democratic heritage ('*Rechtstaaten*'); their weak democratic traditions which make their new democratic 'topsoils' appear ominously thin; the deep damage done to political and legal cultures by roughly 50 years of communist rule; the extra pressures that stem from the fact that a number of the CEECs are new states and thus face extra problems in establishing new financial systems and properly administered border controls (e.g. to control influxes of economic or political refugees); the fact that the relative bloodlessness of most of the post-1989 revolutions has left previous communist power élites in an ambiguous position, sometimes seen to be culpable collaborators, sometimes adaptable entrepreneurs, sometimes legitimate power blocs within new political party formations, sometimes repackaged saviours from the new economic and social hardships.

Yet these factors have to be counterbalanced against the fact that the CEECs themselves have begun to devise–with a relative degree of success so far–a number of strategies to enable them to adjust more easily to the Council of Europe (and EC) demands made on their capacity to meet with exacting human rights norms. Notably they have shifted from overreliance on Western experts to exchanging expertise based on their own national constitutional experiences and the different approaches taken by CEEC members who have now been accepted as meeting the Council of Europe and ECHR conditions. Reference is made to different possible 'roads'–the Hungarian, the Romanian road etc.[53] Further developments on the human rights side continue to be made in the CSCE (now OSCE) process, which served such a crucial role in the 1975–1989 period as a 'half-way house'. If the Council of Europe experiment fails, it is likely these developments might enable that system to instigate a regional human rights machinery more attuned to a specifically CEEC heritage.[54]

---

[52] For awareness of strains, see however R. Sadurska 'Reshaping Europe–or how to keep poor cousins in (their) home', *Yale Law Journal*, 100 (1991), 2501–10.

[53] I. Pogany, Constitutional reform in Central and Eastern Europe: Hungary's transition to democracy, *ICLQ*, 42 (1993), p. 332. P. Paczolay, 'The new Hungarian constitutional state: challenges and perspectives', in Howard, (ed.), *Constitution Making in Eastern Europe*, 1993.

[54] On CSCE generally, see D. McGoldrick *ICLQ*, 14 (1993), 411–32; D. McGoldrick, 'Human rights developments in the Helsinki process', *ICLQ*, 39 (1990), 923–40; A. Bloed and van Dijk (eds), *The Human Dimension of the Helsinki Process* (Dordrecht, Nijhoff, 1991); the OSCE's Office for

Can one draw definite conclusions from this analysis? Whilst Council of Europe policy might seem to run a high risk of long-term failure, from having set too onerous prerequisites for CEECs struggling with serious problems of transition, there are too many contingent variables and the experiment is a bold one. If despite commonly identified adverse factors the CEECs do achieve a democratic transition, it will certainly owe a great deal to the co-operation and assistance programmes devised by the Council of Europe and indeed most of the major European institutions, including the EC itself. Their assiduous, 'hands-on' approach has done much to prevent the ECHR legal order being perceived as a too-tight corset. Having said that, it remains that it has *not* made a good job of explaining why the 'new order' of the new Europe justifies so striking a departure from the traditional approach as described above.

Conclusion

The purpose of the above analysis of old and new-style approaches to the adaptation of European states to human rights norms is not to hazard predictions or pronounce on European contingencies. But this case-study does offer several clues to a possible resolution of some of the main sources of conflict within human rights law, which were identified earlier.

The Minimalist-Maximalist Conflict

The efforts of the Western European states to create a common legal space based on human rights and democratic principles appear to offer an example of a regional bloc of states pursuing a maximalist strategy, designed not so much to ensure a minimum floor of basic guarantees as to achieve a highly refined and comprehensive catalogue of human rights guarantees within the framework of a distinctly European model based on a (redefined) 'common European heritage'. Despite the existence of valid grounds for pursuing a more cautious and gradualist approach, such as was applied to its original Western membership in the immediate post-war period, the contemporary Western European institutions have gambled on the CEECs proving capable of gearing up to their own high standards. By choosing to do so through the conceptual framework of human rights, however, they have committed themselves to the view that there exist realizable *universal human* rights to certain individual needs and goods that appear to extend well beyond the economic or social capacity or resources of many of the states of the global 'South', if not indeed of the Central and Eastern European region.

At first sight this case study might appear as a vindication of the criticisms raised by minimalists (not all) to the effect that the concept of 'universalism' has clearly been abused within this system, since to an increasing degree the body of human rights guaranteed within the European legal order contains norms which are unrealizable outside of the global 'North'.

My own perception, however, is that the CEECs case study warrants a quite different conclusion. The fact that their democratization programmes have

Democratic Institutions and Human Rights based in Warsaw now produces a regular Bulletin (00-522, Warsaw, Poland).

been able to advance thus far, notwithstanding so many adverse preconditions, suggests that a real and effective realization of human rights depends upon the world of political practice constantly setting higher goals. The minimalist conception of human rights may be correct as a description of what human beings anywhere in the present world can accept as a set of basic needs forming valid moral claims. But it is only by constantly seeking to consolidate and further the realization of a comprehensive catalogue of human rights that the concept of humanity itself can be enlarged.

What is primarily objectionable about the maximalist enterprise in the form it currently takes is that it tends too easily to lose sight of the criterion of universality. This problem is beginning to be addressed in various ways, including at the global UN level where 'proliferation of human rights' is now accepted as a serious malady.[55] But in many ways, it is at the *regional* level that there now seems the greatest need for better clarification. Certainly this seems so in Europe, where the established case law and the degree of dynamic interpretation of human rights norms have been most extensive. Indeed, if in fact one of the main abiding objectives of a regional human rights system is to '*integrate* the regional and the universal systems of human rights protections'[56] then it would seem incumbent upon that system to distinguish more clearly, for example, between (i) regionally 'discovered' human rights which depend upon regional modalities and (ii) those which do not. The right to a fair hearing by an impartial and independent body of a judicial character might seem to be a clear example of the latter, being one that can now be seen, on the basis of human historical experience, as integral to a fair hearing of any kind. But would the European Court of Human Rights consider the right to social welfare as also belonging in this category, given that it has only just recognized it as a 'civil right' in view of changes in political and economic perceptions of 'civil rights' within the countries that are current parties to the ECHR?[57] Would it consider, to take another example, that a ban on the use of corporal punishment in schools is something which can function as a universal norm?[58] In relation to such complex problems the broadened landscape opened up by the newly enlarged group of ECHR parties, including most of the CEECs, has been seen to carry the danger that it might cause a 'dilution' of high European standards. That may be true. But by the same token it should afford better opportunities for testing whether previously 'discovered' human rights are truly capable of serving as free-standing universal norms.

It is unlikely, however, that a more rigorous adherence to the criterion of universality, would remove the need for fresh steps to ensure that talk of 'indivisibility' and 'interdependence' of human rights does not lead to a weakening of the effectiveness of guarantees of 'core' rights such as the rights to life, subsistence and to prohibition of torture and inhuman and degrading treatment. Separate treaty action at both the UN and regional levels may prove the only practical way of handling the problem of proliferation.

[55] T. Meron, 'On a hierarchy of international human rights', *American Journal of International Law*, 80 (1986), 1–23; P. Alston, 'Conjuring up new human rights: a proposal for quality control'. *American Journal of International Law*, 78 (1984), 607 ff.

[56] *Other Treaties* case, American Court of Human Rights, *HRLJ*, 13 (1992), p. 140.

[57] *Schuler-Graggen v. Switzerland, Human Rights Case Digest*, 4 (May–June 1993), pp. 107–10 (Sweet and Maxwell and The British Institute of Human Rights, 1993).

[58] As per *Campbell v. Cosans*, Series A 48, *HRLJ*, 3 (1982), p. 221.

Conditionality v. Anticonditionality

Again the fact that the exacting human rights conditionality regime presently imposed on the CEECs has *not* broken down, despite such an unpromising set of objective preconditions, suggests that conditionality in this field of international standard-setting is not intrinsically invalid. Even though there are strong reasons for doubting whether the process of transition can be sustained, the new participation by CEEC judges more attuned to human rights and the contribution of their own national rights case laws offer the prospect of European human rights case law achieving more broadly-based redefinitions of human rights, capable for example of reworking the right of property so that it achieves a more coherent balance between free market and social market principles.[59] This may prove of particular value in the emerging areas of economic and social rights, dealt with at present within a companion treaty to the ECHR – the 1961 European Social Charter.[60] Some of the CEEC states possess rich and useful legislative and legal experience in the conceptualization of economic and social guarantees as effective human rights. Given the growing fears in Western Europe of the demise of the Welfare State, such experiences and perceptions may contain some useful guidelines, as the European Union and other European bodies attempt to fashion a viable social policy for the next century.[61] At the same time it seems very clear that the inter-European conditionality regime would not have got as far as it has without the consent and positive response of CEECs themselves. That consent may of course be driven by reasons of self-interest – in becoming fuller participants in European economic markets, in obtaining a type of 'insurance cover' against the risk that their governments might fail to secure human rights guarantees at the national levels, for example. But if these are the type of reasons that sustain them, that would seem to show that legal consensus about human rights guarantees can be achieved across national borders, despite the lack, in some cases at least, of any common legal culture or heritage. That in turn would seem to suggest that countries of the global 'South' are wrong to object to conditionality on the basis of distinct and unique legal cultures, different conceptions and approaches etc.

Nevertheless it would appear that *in practice* viable conditionality regimes are likely to operate better at intra-regional levels, simply because at such levels there will be, usually, common bases of mutual self-interest between those involved on both sides of the conditionality process: economic, political, legal, historical, cultural etc. That is certainly true in the contemporary era. This in itself is not an argument against an active, even an increased, role being taken by bodies at a global level such as the UN; but the practical and technical

---

[59] This is not to say, however, that greater UN-level activity in the setting up and running of technical assistance and co-operation (especially legal cooperation) programmes does not also have a valid role. The need for such schemes, at both UN and regional levels, is clearly identified in the Vienna Declaration and Programme of Action of the 1993 World Conference on Human Rights (paras. 66–71, 76), *HRLJ*, 14 (1993), pp. 361–2. For further background see E.-R. Mbaya, 'The compatibility of regional human rights systems with international standards' in Eide and Hagtvet (eds), *Human Rights in Perspective*, pp. 66–89.

[60] On European Social Charter 1961, see D. Harris, *European Social Charter* (University of Virginia, 1984); D. Harris, 'A fresh impetus for the European social charter', *ICLQ*, 41 (1992), 659–76.

[61] See H. H. Storey, 'Some social security and social welfare aspects' in *The Future of the European Social Policy: Options for the Union* (Louvain University Press, UCL, 1994), pp. 237–46.

assistance programmes (e.g. for training up new administrators and judges) are likely to be more effective if regionally co-ordinated.

But both at a global and regional level the fuller development of international norms will require considerable reworking of concepts and criteria. Only thus can human rights operate as genuinely universal norms freed of the historical legacy of possessive individualism and ethical egoism as well as of cultural bias. In this enterprise political theorists and political scientists seem well-placed to play far more of a prominent role than they have hitherto. Some of their criticisms might help resolve some of the current crises within human rights law. One way or another, if these are not resolved, the human rights movement may not survive. Elaborating Ronald Dworkin's 'rights as trumps' metaphor, the late R. J. Vincent wrote: 'Among trumps, it may be said, human rights are the coloured cards'.[62] All too well, we know, however, that even law's empire can collapse like a pack of cards.

[62] R. J. Vincent, *Human Rights and International Relations*, p. 10.

Relativism and Universalism in Human Rights: the Case of the Islamic Middle East

FRED HALLIDAY

Introduction

'Islam approaches life and its problems in their totality. Being a complete and perfect code of life, it holds no brief for partial reforms or compromise solutions. It starts by making man conscious of his unique position in the universe, not as a self-sufficient being but as a part, a very important part, of Allah's creation. It is only by becoming conscious of their true relationship with Allah and His creation that men and women can function successfully in this world'. *Universal Islamic Declaration of Human Rights*, 1981, p. 9.

'For a Muslim country, as for all complex state societies, the most pressing human rights issue is not local cultural preferences or religious-cultural authenticity; it is the protection of individuals from a state that violates human rights, regardless of its cultural-ideological facade'. Reza Afshari, *Human Rights Quarterly*, 16 (1994) p. 249.

Within the international debate on human rights that has evolved over the past two decades, the Islamic countries of the Middle East have occupied a position both common and specific – articulating, on the one hand, views that are shared with other third world and non-Western countries, and, on the other, defining a specific position on human rights derived from the particular religious, in this case Islamic, character of their societies and beliefs. Thus, at the June 1993 Vienna UN Conference on Human Rights, and in the regional conferences which preceded it, Islamic states, including those of the Middle East, joined with Asian states in criticizing UN and Western policy for its double standards, its violation of sovereignty, its neglect of economic rights, its imposition of 'Western' values. Yet if Islamic states and movements have expressed views on issues common to other developing societies – on economic rights, global equity, decolonization, nationalization and the like – they have also marked out a particular position on certain questions pertaining to the field of human rights: thus at Vienna Islamic countries submitted the 'Cairo Declaration on Human Rights in Islam', originally propounded at the 19th Conference of Islamic Foreign Ministers in August 1990.[1] This specific, Islamic, position on the international human rights debate pertains both to the position of what constitutes a 'right', and its derivation from divine, rather

[1] Entered as in Vienna conference documents as A\CONF\57\PC\35.

than human or natural law bases, and to a number of more specific issues within the rights field.

This dual relationship to the international debate has also been reflected in the international, state and non-governmental, reporting on the human rights position within the Middle East Islamic states: while many of the practices of which these states have been accused have been shared with other countries (denial of political rights across a wide spectrum), some pertain to specific aspects of the ideologies and laws of these countries, which are, at least formally, phrased in terms of Muslim law and practice. Four of the latter have been of particular prominence – the rights of women, the rights of non-believers, the rights of people deemed to be apostates, and the question of punishments.[2] Recent examples of apparent conflict with international norms include the treatment of non-Muslim minorities in Islamic states, the use to which a law against apostasy has been put in Pakistan, and the persecution, through judicial and extra-judicial means, of writers whose views are said to offend Islam.[3] In addition, the place of these states and societies within the international debate has, beyond its intrinsic importance, achieved greater resonance because of other factors, be it the wealth derived from oil which these states have deployed to defend their position, or the particular international attention which the Islamic revolution of Iran, and its imitators elsewhere, have drawn to their programme. An examination of the claims, and practices, of these states may therefore throw light both on the general, global, debate on human rights and on the particular ideologies and political structures of these states.

Many commentators, Islamic and other, have fallen into the habit of presenting this question as part of a broader, historical and enduring, conflict between two determinate 'civilizations', the Western, or Judaeo-Christian and the Muslim. Convenient, and attractively polemical, as such an argument from transhistorical conflict may be, it has little relevance to the matter in hand. Whatever the philosophical foundations for a theory of human rights, or the historical roots of our modern conception thereof, the discourse of human rights as we express and formulate it today is a recent, post-1945, phenomenon.[4] Hence in explaining how and why particular attitudes to human rights are articulated we are looking above all at influences that have operated since that time, whatever anterior religious or ethical principles they may invoke. While there are some elements in the Islamic tradition and literature that can be drawn on to discuss the issue of human rights, what we are dealing with here is, as in other states, a relatively recent set of arguments, the result of contemporary trends in the international system and within Islamic states.[5]

[2] Ann Mayer, *Islam and Human Rights* (London, Westview, 1991) provides the most thorough survey of these. A fifth issue, the rights of ethnic minorities, is also pertinent here, since Islamic states have tended to deny the need for any specific recognition of these, on the grounds that all Muslims share a common identity. Nationalist regimes in Muslim, as in other countries, have said the same thing of their own peoples – Turkey being, until very recently, a clear example of this.

[3] On the Pakistani apostasy law see 'Islamic vigilante justice', *International Herald Tribune* (18–19 June 1994).

[4] For background see John Vincent, *Human Rights and International Relations* (Cambridge, Cambridge University Press, 1986) and Jack Donnelly, *Universal Human Rights in Theory and Practice* (Ithaca, Cornell University Press, 1989).

[5] For one exploration see James Piscatori, 'Human rights in Islamic political culture' in Kenneth Thompson (ed.), *The Moral Imperatives of Human Rights: a World Survey* (Washington, University Press of America, 1980).

As such, the debate on human rights in the Islamic context reflects the convergence of at least five distinct processes. First, it is part of, and a response to, the development of the international debate, arising with the Universal Declaration of Human Rights of 1948 and leading on to subsequent, more specific codes, particularly in the 1970s and 1980s. Secondly, the Islamic debate reflects the way in which, partly influenced by the UN-centred debates, a broader set of *political* questions affecting the Muslim world has come to be phrased in human rights terms – the Palestinian, Kashmir and Bosnian issues, and the treatment of Muslims in Western European society being cases in point. Thirdly, these discourses are a response to the particular use made of human rights as an issue for criticizing abuses by governments, be this on the part of non-governmental organizations, such as Amnesty, or, as with the Carter and subsequent US administrations, and with the UN Human Rights Commission, by governments. Fourthly, the debate reflects the pressure from within Islamic states for greater democratization and respect for human rights, in the direction of an increased compliance with international codes. Finally, and quite separately, it is affected by the current of what one can broadly term 'Islamization', both from above, by governments, and from below, by mass Islamist movements, that has been growing from the 1970s onwards: this tendency seeks to alter legal codes, and state practice, so that they conform more to what is deemed to be 'traditional' or correct Islamic practice.[6]

As this, rather bald, list of trends should suggest, the debate on human rights in the Islamic world has been one that reflects a range of political concerns, and ones that are often in rather marked conflict with each other. The result has been a variety of responses, as to the possible relationship of Islam as a religion to the issue of human rights. Indeed at least four distinct responses or themes from within an Islamic discourse may be identified, classifiable as, respectively, *(i) assimilation*: the argument that there is no problem about reconciling Islam with theories of human rights;[7] *(ii) appropriation*: the claim that, far from Islam and human rights being incompatible, it is only under Islam that they can be fully realized;[8] *(iii) confrontation*, i.e. the argument that international

---

[6] 'Islamization' refers to policies of governments designed to alter law and social life in accordance with Islamic doctrine, 'Islamism' refers to political movements, of a mass populist kind, that challenge established, more secular, states.

[7] Kevin Dwyer, *Arab Voices. The Human Rights Debate in the Middle East* (London, Routledge, 1991) and his 'Universal visions, communal visions: human rights and traditions', *Peuples Méditerranéens*, 58–59 (January–July 1992), 205–20, provide rich studies of the varying interpretations of Islamic tradition within the Arab debate. One of the most far-reaching attempts to produce such a liberal interpretation is to be found in the work of Abdullahi Ahmed An-Na'im, *Towards an Islamic Reformation: Civil Liberties, Human Rights, and International Law* (Syracuse NY, Syracuse University Press, 1990). Muslim feminists, such as Naawal al-Saadawi and Fatima Mernissi, have often adopted this position, whether out of conviction or tactical calculation, and have sought to show that a specific interpretation, or *tafsir*, of the relevant texts can produce a case of gender equality.

[8] One striking example, analysed in Mayer, *Islam and Human Rights*, pp. 86–9, is the 'Universal Islamic declaration of human rights', propounded by the Islamic Council in London in 1981. Thus at a German-Iranian colloquium in 1992 the Iranian ambassador to Britain replied to criticism of non-Muslims in Iran by attacking the record of Western European states towards Muslims and other immigrants, while other Iranian participants pointed to treatment of political refugees and the supply of arms to third world dictators [Heiner Bielefeldt (ed.), 'Die Menschenrechte zwischen Universalitätsanspruch und kulturelle Bedingtheit', *Tagung des Deutsch-Iranischen Gesprächskreises* (21–4 September 1992, Orient-Institute, Hamburg)]. This kind of counter-offensive has also been a stock in trade of the Chinese response to US criticism.

human rights doctrines are to be rejected as part of some imperialist or ethnocentric project, and replaced by *shari'a*; *(iv) incompatibility*, the claim that somehow 'Islam' itself is irreconcilable with human rights, or democratic, principles – a theme present within Islamic societies in the plea for particularism, but also found as well in the non-Muslim world, but outside an Islamic discourse. Given the nature of the discussion, on both sides, these themes are often combined in a particular discourse rather than mutually exclusive positions. However, it is important to note here that whether we are looking at the statements of governments or those of other Muslim entities, it is the first and second arguments that are by far the most frequent.

An Alternative Universalism

The argument that follows is one attempt to disentangle this debate, and to cast some light both on the claims of Islamists with regard to human rights, and on the broader issue of relativism in the field of human rights. It will, in the first place, look at the argument that, in some way or another, the Islamic response to the human rights debate is a form of cultural relativism, and show that, in many ways, this is a simplification. It will then proceed to look at some substantive issues underlying this apparent polarization between 'traditions' and at what it is that leads to the conflict between Islamic and universal codes. It will conclude with some reflections on the critique of universalism, based on the Middle Eastern experience.

In writing on the question of Middle Eastern and Islamic responses to the human rights issue it is certainly tempting to contrast a Western, universalistic, approach to the Middle Eastern, particularist, one. Much writing on the subject, be it by Muslims or non-Muslims, operates with such a set of generalities, implying that, in some way, the Islamic approach is comparable to the historicist or communitarian one found in Western thinking.[9] Yet, on closer examination, this is itself a simplification and can serve to confuse rather than illumine the issues at stake. In the first place, if current statements and policies are anything to go by, there is no *one* 'Middle Eastern' or 'Islamic' body of thought on this question. Attempts, declamatory or benign, to identify an 'Islamic' position are as misguided as those seeking to produce an 'African' or an 'Asian' stance. There are over fifty Muslim states in the world, with a variety of legal and political systems, and there is no single body, political or religious, that speaks for the Muslim world as a whole. The Muslim religion itself is not only highly fragmented, but is, in contrast to Christianity, one that operates without even a purported theological and legal central authority: what we have is a range of bodies, some political, some juridical, some academic, such as the al-Azhar University in Cairo, which interpret law and tradition as they see fit and which appeal to all Muslims to follow them.

While many aspire, or claim, to speak in the name of all Muslims, none do, and there are many cases of the factional, the self-appointed, and the political, who speak 'for' the Muslim world. There is, for example, a world of difference between the positions of the government of Saudi Arabia, on the one hand, with its promotion of a conservative 'Islamic' code of rights, and that of Tunisia, which has been in the forefront of the battle *for* universal rights, and

[9] Vincent, *Human Rights and International Relations*, pp. 28–30.

which even proposed to the pre-Vienna 'African' conference a denunciation of the threat to human rights posed by religious fundamentalism. In confronting what is said by governments, individual writers or organizations, one has to take them in their specific context and not assume that they speak for an Islamic world, or tradition, or that theirs is the only possible, or legitimate, interpretation of the religion. We are dealing with a diversity of views and interpretations not a single body of thought.

This variety is all the more evident if one takes not just those who claim to speak *for* the Islamic world, or in the name of 'Islam', but the full range of those who live, work and express themselves in Muslim countries. Throughout the Muslim world there are many who reject, to a greater or lesser extent, the formulation of legal, political and human rights issues in Qoranic or *shari'a* terms at all. For over a century, there have been those in the Islamic world, variously classified as liberals, modernizers and secularizers, who have sought to develop legal and political bodies of thought based on secular values, or who have inflected and interpreted the religious tradition to give maximum expression, in the given political context, to such values. The claim that those invoking Qoran and *shari'a* in some way represent, or speak for, the Islamic world as a whole is simply false. Turkey has gone the furthest in secularizing its law, but for much of the twentieth century, the majority of states in the Islamic world have sought to develop legal codes and political systems based wholly or largely on secular principles. The rise of Islamization and of Islamism over the past two decades has put such states on the defensive, but it remains quite inaccurate to present all opinion on such issues currently being aired in the Middle East as part of some common 'Islamic' or 'Middle Eastern' position: this, of course, is the aspiration of states who wish to claim a monopoly of opinion on these questions, but it has never been, and is not, the common position of all within these countries.

On the issue of human rights itself, those who are the victims of regimes speaking in the name of a legitimating 'Islam', be this in Iran, Saudi Arabia or the Sudan, have often invoked universalistic principles precisely because they contest the very legitimacy of the regimes that are repressing them.[10] In other cases, opposition to Islamization has come from those who want a more moderate, liberal, interpretation of Islam.[11] The debate on the Islamic character of law and the constitution in revolutionary Iran pitted clerical and other Islamist forces against those, many of them involved in years of opposition to the Shah's regime, who wanted a secular approach to these issues: the latter were, in time, silenced by repression, justified in the name of Islam. Indeed, as those concerned with human rights in these states so often

[10] Thus in Iran, such opposition groups as the Kurdish Democratic Party of Iran, the Liberation Movement of Iran of former premier Mehdi Bazargan, and the range of monarchist and left-wing groups all speak in a secular, universalistic, language. Even the supposedly 'Islamic' opposition of the *Mujahidin-i Khalq* formulates its critique, beyond a few token quotations from the Qoran, in secular terms. This is also true for the large body of Iranian writers and poets, let alone lawyers, who have opposed the dictatorship of the Islamic Republic. Opposition groups in Saudi Arabia have ranged from the secular left to Islamic organizations. A recently created, hybrid, group, now based in London is the Committee for the Defence of Legitimate Human Rights, where the word 'Legitimate' is *shari'i*.

[11] For one example see the study of Khomeini's first prime minister, later committed opponent, Saeed Barzin, 'Constitutionalism and democracy in the religious ideology of Mehdi Bazargan', *British Journal of Middle Eastern Studies*, 21.1 (1994).

point out, what the victims of Islamic states and societies repeatedly ask for is not a different, better or more authentic interpretation of Islamic law, but the consistent application of international, universalistic, principles.

Moreover, if one examines what self-proclaimed Islamic states actually argue then much of it can be said to avoid a culturally relativist position at all. Indeed what is striking about so much of the rhetoric emerging from such regimes, and from writers in the Islamic tradition, is that, with varying shades of explicitness, they are articulating arguments in universal terms. In regard to the overall foreign policy confrontations of the Islamic and non-Islamic worlds, the arguments most frequently heard have little to do with religion or culture. Some pertain to the arguments, heard throughout the third world, on redistribution of wealth, equity in international trade and so forth: on this the Iranians joined hands with the Singaporeans and Chinese at Vienna. Some arguments pertain to the Islamic world, and the Middle East in particular, but for reasons of substance, not formulation: thus the most frequent argument used against Western, particularly US, policy in the region has been that of 'double standards' – expounding the principle of self-determination of peoples, but denying it to Palestinians and Kashmiris, condemning Muslims for violations of international law, while permitting continued Israeli occupation of the Palestinian lands taken in 1967, calling for democracy in communist states, but denying it in such countries as Algeria or Saudi Arabia, condemning one group of nationalist militants as 'terrorists' while encouraging others as 'freedom fighters', and, most recently, upholding the sovereignty of states while denying a Muslim state, Bosnia, the right to self-defence. The underlying principles have not been relativistic at all, and are not comparable to the historicist or communitarian principles articulated elsewhere:[12] here, on the issue of double standards and historical responsibility, the critique emanating from the Muslim world has considerable validity – but this validity is a function of the force of arguments based on universalistic principles.[13]

This is also the case for the very terms in which the critiques of the Western position are articulated. In the first place, many of the rebuttals of Western human rights criticisms start by arguing that states with an imperialistic record, past and continuing, have themselves no right to criticize third world states: in other words, the argument is one that invokes a principle, implicit or explicit, that those who voice human rights criticisms should be themselves countries with a morally defensible record in the field of relations between states. This argument may or may not be valid, or properly applied, but like many of the other views expressed by Muslim states it has nothing particularly to do with

[12] A striking example of the use of universalistic arguments in an attack on Western positions was that of Saddam Hussein's Iraq and the occupation of Kuwait in 1990. While much of the international comment on this event, in the Arab world and elsewhere, looked at the differing cultural and religious perceptions of Iraqis and Westerners, Saddam himself framed his position in straightforward universalistic terms: Kuwait as a state had no historical legitimacy, Kuwait had damaged Iraq's economic interests, a popular uprising inside Kuwait had invited Iraqi forces into the country, the divisions of the Arab world were artificial, creations of colonialism. These arguments may, individually, have been debatable and, taken together, have appeared somewhat inconsistent, but culturally specific, or particular or unintelligible to non-Arabs or non-Muslims they were not.

[13] It may also be noted that much of the criticism of the West in this regard is based on the alleged denial of *collective* or *group* rights, namely those of national or religious groups, rather than on the denial of *individual* rights.

Islam. Secondly, in rebutting external criticism, Islamic states, like other objects of such criticism, frequently resort to counter-attack, on the violations by Western states of human rights and indeed on the general moral decline of Western society, be it in regard to crime, relations between sexes, treatment of the aged or whatever. Beneath what appears to be a plea for difference lies a moral critique of the West expressed, with lesser or greater degrees of explicitness, in universalistic terms. Thus the Iranian foreign minister Ali Akbar Velayati, speaking at the UN in 1993, attacked the West for seeking to impose its values on the Islamic and third worlds, but then linked this to the moral crisis in the West, arising from unlimited freedom: '... some Western countries intended to impose on other societies their own social ethical decline, to which they themselves confess, within the attractive package of human rights'.[14]

In responding to a report of the UN Human Rights Commission that was highly critical of Iran, Iranian officials and press did not reject the UN principles: rather they claimed that the West was manipulating the UN's human rights process for political ends, and that those who were criticizing Iran in the name of human rights were busy violating them in such places as Bosnia and Palestine. Iran's Foreign Ministry reply was a defence of its commitment: 'based on the supreme teachings of Islam, the Islamic Republic of Iran considers respect for human rights and the lofty character of mankind in all material and spiritual dimensions as a fundamental duty for all governments. According to this belief, the Islamic Republic of Iran, without paying attention to any propaganda hue and cry, will continue its efforts to strengthen the principles which guarantee support for the rights of all citizens. ... As the majority of the countries of the world stressed in the course of the international conference on human rights [i.e. Vienna], the only way to lend real support to human rights and promote such principles throughout the world is to end the practices of having double standards and exploiting human rights issues for political objectives. This process should be accomplished by open, independent and impartial international mechanisms'.[15] The Iranians, and Chinese, have made much of issues of selectivity and violation of sovereignty in their rebuttal of UN Human Rights Commission reports: again, whatever the rights and wrongs of this position, it has little to do with religion or specificity.

Most importantly, however, even where the critique is phrased in terms of Islamic tradition or *shari'a*, and where it is claimed that a different set of moral and legal principles should be applied, this does not take a relativistic form: indeed the claim that a particular principle is derived from Islam contains within it, explicitly or implicitly, its own universalism. Islam is a religion without overt ethnic or regional particularism, one that aspires to encompass all of humanity within its compass, and which regards other religions and traditions as, comparatively, inferior. The *da'wa* or call to submit to God, the basis of Islamic faith, is made to all of mankind. Hence, given that the truths of Islam must be applicable to all humans, be they believers or not, any position articulated in Islamic terms is itself universalistic. To imply otherwise, i.e. that

---

[14] *BBC Summary of World Broadcasts Part 4 The Middle East*, 16 (October 1993), ME/1821 MED/5-6.
[15] *BBC Summary of World Broadcasts Part 4 The Middle East*, 19 (November 1993), ME/1850 MED/1.

in a culturally relativist vein what Muslims believe is no better or worse than what non-Muslims believe, would be a violation of the faith, and of its core doctrine.[16] A consistent Islamic position is *the opposite* of that contained within communitarian Western thinking, since the latter implies that, as between different communities, values can be held to be equal. By contrast, if there is a conflict between 'Western' and internationally established codes of conduct and those of Islamic states it is not one between universalism and particularism, but between two, apparently divergent and contradictory, forms of universalism.

Myths of 'Tradition'

So far, the argument has accepted, or implied, that there is a separate 'tradition', a body of thought, unitary or diverse, which can be termed 'Islamic' and which does constitute an alternative for those states and bodies opposed to Western principles and codes. Such indeed is the argument both of Islamists themselves and of many outside the Islamic world, for whom 'Islam', 'Muslims' and indeed *shari'a* provide identifiable objects in terms of which to explain social and political behaviour, and in terms of which to conduct the debate on human rights.[17] Here is not the place to go extensively into the argument on how and why such terms are abstractions, reifications that obscure more than they illumine, and that they often reflect considerations of power be they by self-proclaimed Islamic authorities or those they oppose. Suffice it to say that, while on some questions the weight of Islamic tradition is identifiable and distinct, much of what passes for 'Islam' and its associated codes and traditions is a particular, contemporary and arbitrarily formulated, set of views, or local tradition dressed up as authoritatively 'Islamic'. Good examples of the latter are traditions of 'tribal' honour in Afghanistan and Pakistan, and the practice of clitoridectomy or female circumcision, found in parts of Africa and Arabia – neither have anything to do with Islamic doctrine and the term 'Islamic' is applied to them merely to denote that they are part of the established (male-dominated) way of life. Equally, the policy implemented in a number of Muslim countries that bans women from being judges has no Koranic basis. What we are dealing with is not an established, perennial, tradition, legal or otherwise, but a set of discourses and interpretations that are created by contemporary forces and for contemporary needs: we have to look behind the assertion of a transhistorical body of thought, supposedly both legitimate and explanatory, and examine how, in the conditions of the modern world, a specific tradition has been codified and implemented. Over the past two decades diplomacy and liberal goodwill alike have allowed the discussion of human rights to work with such categories as 'Islamic', 'African' and 'Asian' codes of human rights, but in each case this involves a simplification, naive when not manipulative.[18] To reach this conclusion in the Islamic case we shall

---

[16] Of the five *arkan* or 'pillars' of Islam, the first and pre-eminent, *shahada* or 'witness', involves the believer in uttering the words: 'There is no God but Allah, and Muhammad is his Prophet'. This brooks no contradiction or relativization.

[17] Vincent, *Human Rights and International Relations*, pp. 42–4, is an example of this.

[18] A front runner for the claim to be the *most* confected of such 'traditions' is that of 'Confucianism' now the state ideology in Singapore, Korea and Taiwan. Beyond vague injunctions to obey parents and subordinate women there is nothing in the 'tradition' at all.

examine first the issue of *shari'a* law itself, the supposed code to which Islamists would have their societies return, then the broader issue of Islamism's relationship to the contemporary world and its supposed opposition to modern and secular forms of thinking, and then the origins and purposes of Islamic political movements themselves. What we discover is not so much a clash of cultures, or civilizations, so much as the pursuit of power, political and social, in the conditions of the late twentieth century. Whatever else, we are not dealing with incommensurable values, or activities that preclude moral, and legal, judgement.

The starting point for much discussion of 'Islam' and Western concepts of human rights is *shari'a* law and the argument that it is a sufficient basis for the legal and constitutional framework of Muslim societies. This claim is itself based on the argument that *shari'a* is a divinely given code which is both, by dint of its sacredness, wholly sufficient for Muslims and which brooks no emendation or contradiction by other, subsequent and secular, legal or philosophic considerations. However, the claim that *shari'a* is such a basis for law is, even in the terms in which this claim is made by Islamists and other Muslims, contestable. The only parts of the Islamic traditional texts that are sacred are, first, the Qoran itself which is said to be the word of Allah and, secondly, the *hadith* or sayings of the Prophet Muhammad, as subsequently codified.[19] In the Qoran, of the 6,000 verses only around 80 are concerned with legal matters, in large part concerning marriage, inheritance and punishment. The term *shari'a*, literally 'path' or 'way' (the root is the same as for the conventional Arabic term for a street, *shari'*) did not initially denote a legal code at all. The interpretation of this divinely sanctioned material, and its elaboration into a set of comprehensive legal codes, is known as *fiq'* (literally 'understanding', hence jurisprudence), and it is this, humanly evolved and variously codified, body of legal material that has come to prevail in Muslim society under the, misapplied, term *shari'a*.[20]

Thus what is today invoked as an unchangeable, and sacred, body of text is, even in Islamic terms, nothing of the sort. As the Syrian writer Aziz al-Azmeh has written: 'Islamic law is not a code. This is why the frequently heard call for its "application" is meaningless, most particularly when calls are made for the application of *shari'a* – this last term does not designate law, but is a general term designating good order, much like *nomos* or *dharma*.... Calls for the "application of Islamic law" have no connection with the Muslim legal tradition built upon multivocality, technical competence and the existence of an executive political authority which controls the legal system. It is a political slogan, not a return to a past reality'.[21] This corrective can, equally, be applied to Islamic discourses on human rights: great effort has been put into finding the foundations of a theory of rights in Islam, and in claiming that such a theory

---

[19] It is important to remind Christian audiences that, in contrast to Jesus Christ, Muhammad was a human being, without divine nature.

[20] Azmi Bishara, 'Religion und Politik im Nahen und Mittleren Osten', in Hippler and Lueg, *Feinbild Islam* (Hamburg, Konkret), pp. 111–2. See also Norman Anderson, *Law Reform in the Muslim World* (London, Athlone, 1976), pp. 3–10, where *shari'a* is described as 'an amorphous volume of partly contradictory doctrine, to which lip-service, at least, was invariably given and which came to stand, like a sentinel, to bar the path of progress' (p. 10). Thus did 'road', like many other official ideologies, become the road-bloc.

[21] Aziz al-Azmeh, *Islams and Modernities* (London, Verso, 1993), pp. 12–4.

can be derived, indeed only derived, from divine revelation. But this claim is quite bogus: the core, sacred, texts of Islam have no doctrine of rights, and the imposition onto odd quotes from the Qoran and the *hadith* of a modern human rights discourse is an ahistorical and artificial, if politically attractive, venture. The majority of the relevant Islamic tradition has been concerned with obligation, to Allah and to the ruler. Those elements that indicate a different direction, such as the Qoranic line that 'there is no compulsion in religion' are quite inadequate to found a human rights doctrine – flimsy at best, and easily overridden by other, more authoritarian, elements.

This critique of the established, univocal, given character of Islamic law may be applied more generally to the concepts of 'Islam' and Islamic tradition in general. In common with all movements invoking tradition and various forms of essence, Islamic states and Islamist movements claim that there is one, true, body of thought that legitimates and guides their thought; from this, as we have seen, they, with varying degrees of emphasis, contrast their tradition and its derived legitimations with those of the West.

These discourses on human rights are, on closer inspection, variants of this kind of contemporary political project. On the one hand, the texts themselves are responses not to 'tradition' but to an international, largely Western, set of developments and mix elements plucked out of Islamic tradition with the concerns of these international discussions. As Ann Mayer has written: '... the authors [of Islamic human rights schemes] lack any clear theory of what rights should mean in an Islamic context or how to derive their content from the Islamic sources in a consistent and principled fashion. Instead, they merely assemble pastiches of ideas and terminology drawn from two very different cultures without determining a rationale for these combinations or a way to reconcile the conflicting premises underlying them.[22] On the other hand, while text and policy can never be reduced to each other, it is legitimate to enquire as to the political purposes, and records, of those advancing particular human rights interpretations. This applies, not least, to the areas onto which ideas of human rights abut, namely the construction and maintenance of Islamic political systems: for what we have, behind claims to transhistorical and divinely sanctioned legitimacy, are projects for the acquisition and main- tenance of political power in the late twentieth century. These may vary, as between tribal oligarchies (Saudi Arabia and other Gulf states), military regimes (Pakistan, Sudan, Libya), and clerical dictatorships (Iran) but the mechanisms and goals of their project are eminently comprehensible in secular terms and comparable to those of other contemporary political systems.[23]

The response of such states to the human rights pressures identified above can be seen not as, disembodied or theological, interpretations of a holy text, but as *political* responses, in a context of the promotion of power domestically and internationally. States have embraced Islamist discourses above all where this has served to consolidate power or helped to promote the state's interests vis-à-vis other Muslim states or the West. The history of human rights in all societies, Muslim and Western, is one that reflects such pressures and interests.

---

[22] Mayer, *Islam and Human Rights*, pp. 53–4.
[23] Ervand Abarahamian, *Khomeinism* (London, Tauris, 1993); Sami Zubaida, *Islam, the People and the State* (London, Routledge, 1989); Fred Halliday and Hamza Alavi (eds), *State and Ideology in the Middle East and Pakistan* (London, Macmillan, 1988).

The rise of human rights is not a result of an abstracted process in thought, even if much thought has gone into it, but of determinate social and political conflicts within societies, of some gaining and some losing power.[24] As noted earlier, the growth of human rights discourses in the post-1945 era reflects a parallel set of constraints and pressures at the international level. What we see in the response of Islamic states, and of non-governmental groups within these societies, is, similarly, a discourse reflecting considerations of power as well as of principle. These considerations of power must deny to any regime, or religious body, a claim that its policies simply reflect moral or cultural particularism: other, more instrumental, factors play their role. It is here, moreover, that it becomes relevant to look at the record of these states and to match the claims of human rights against the reality. The philosophical and legal assessment of Islamic texts on human rights, which show the limits of such interpretations, is more than compounded by the actual record, which shows that Islamic states, and not least those which invoke Islam, have been systematic violators of human rights, even on their own restricted criteria. Projects to 'Islamize' law, such as in Pakistan and Sudan, are calculated and instrumental initiatives by regimes to consolidate their own power, both by silencing critics and social groups targeted by these laws, and by mobilizing support from sections of the population who may be sympathetic to such changes. The arguments advanced in international fora to repel external criticisms may be seen as, similarly, instrumental and manipulative attempts to mobilize domestic support and ward off independent criticism.

Cultural Relativism: Clarifications and Policies

It is now possible to turn to the underlying issue, that of 'cultural relativism' itself – i.e. the claim that there are distinct, historically constituted, cultures, of equal ethical and political worth. This invites, and requires, much closer examination than it is often given. Certain objections are of a general character: a moral objection, that even if something is indisputably 'traditional', this is hardly a sufficient reason for accepting it as desirable or ethically valid; a historical objection, that what passes for 'tradition' is highly selective, when not recently created;[25] and a social objection, that the

---

[24] Sami Zubaida, 'Human rights and culture difference: Middle Eastern perspectives' in *New Perspectives on Turkey*, 10 (Fall 1994), 1–12.

[25] Even if it can be proved that some particular practice or vaue or legal prescription is indeed 'traditional' in the sense of having been upheld over a long period of time by a particular community, this need not necessarily entail that it is beyond reform, criticism or outright rejection: some of the practices, at least, that have been classified with some foundation as traditional would surely revolt even the most hardened relativist. The argument, on moral grounds, should at least be open here. Equally, such invocations of tradition are open to a critique on the basis of history, in that they deny what all studies of 'tradition' contemporarily received show, namely that traditions are themselves modern creations – selections, interested reproductions, often inventions concealing contemporary purposes behind the invocation of a time-honoured, and incontestable, continuity. In practical terms there are many examples of this from the Muslim world – the various forms of 'modest' dress now prescribed for Muslim women are one obvious example of this. So too are many of the ideological components of Islamism: these are neither traditional nor so contrasted with the 'West' as is often supposed, but reflect rather a combination of modern political themes with elements, themselves selectively identified and interpreted, of religious tradition. As many students of the rhetoric and political practice of Islamism have shown, these are, as much as anything, variants of third world populism grafted onto elements of Islam, mass mobilizations aiming for

definition, reproduction and use of tradition is as often as not a form of ideology in that it is in the hands of those with power within a society. Beyond this is the question of the meaning of the term 'culture' itself. In the context of this debate, at least three different issues have become intertwined. In origin, the concept of cultural relativism referred to the indisputable reality that, as between societies, social practices and values, including ones pertaining to law, have varied. This is, in itself, an observation without ethical import, leaving open the judgement that one culture is better than another, or that they are of equal worth. Even when ethical judgement is introduced, this leaves open the question as to whether *all* differences between societies are of equal value, or only some. It would be perfectly consistent to argue that on many issues the variation between societies is of no ethical significance (e.g. of languages, eating utensils, traffic regulations, physical gestures, cooking practices) but that on others, pertaining to the treatment and equality of human beings, some transcultural ethical standards were applicable: in other words, cultural relativism, of the ethical kind, applies in some situations and not in others. How far this can go in the legal field I am not competent to judge, but there are, self-evidently, great variations in legal culture and practice between countries with broadly similar human rights conditions, suggesting that a degree of legal relativism is also possible. Moreover, most people, of all cultures, accept some validity for universal criteria: very few people would argue that torture, starvation, infanticide, slavery are to be treated at the same level as greeting customs or festival arrangements. The question about cultural relativism is where to draw the line and where not to, rather than whether a line is to be drawn at all.[26] By dint of the international system, and the criss-crossing of moral and indeed cultural discourses, we are to some degree in a common ethical universe, in which an absolute 'cultural relativist' position is untenable and unheld. If, as is often argued, attempts to produce moral codes on the basis of an irreducible internationally recognized minimum have not yet succeeded this does not gainsay the principle that some such elements are so acknowledged.

Behind this issue lies, however, another and more intractable issue, and one that goes to the heart of the debate on human rights in Islamic states, namely that of the role of culture not in defining, but in supporting and maintaining human rights. In accounts of the rise of human rights in Western society there are, broadly, two positions on this: one a particularist one, that only in Western, generically Christian, society could human rights and democracy arise, the other, a specific but potentially universalizable one, that for human rights to be respected, indeed for democracy and the rule of law to be maintained, there are certain cultural prerequisites, involving individualism, tolerance and a general respect for legality. These two positions are not exact alternatives, since, among other things, the term 'culture' is used in different senses. There would, however, seem to be much evidence, historical and circumstantial, for this latter position: if this is so, the question to be asked of Islamic societies is whether, and how far, such cultural preconditions exist.

---

political power, with the goals, instruments and much of the rhetoric of other, more secular, late twentieth century movements.

[26] The argument advanced by John Rawls, on the tolerance of societies that are illiberal, but 'well-ordered', raises as many questions as it resolves ('The law of peoples' in Stephen Shute and Susan Hurley (eds), *On Human Rights* (New York, Basic, 1993), pp. 41–82).

Moreover, if they do not, the reasons for this absence must be addressed. The least that this suggests is that there can be no examination of the discourses of human rights in Islamic countries without a broader, concomitant, examination of the 'cultural' context in which these discourses are elaborated.

Here, of course, we encounter the argument, advanced by some Islamists as much as by many of those hostile to Muslims, that there can be no human rights, no democracy, no rule of law in Muslim societies because of 'Islam' itself. This is an extreme version of what I have above termed the 'incompatibility' theory. Such a claim is, in the terms in which it is phrased, namely by invoking a timeless and all-pervasive Islam, untenable, both because 'Islam' is itself such a varied, multivocal, system, and because the actual record of Islamic societies, contemporary and historical, shows a greater variety in the degree to which the state has, by universal standards, violated the rights of its subjects. But, unfortunately, this is not the end of the story, for, as identified earlier, there are several other variants of the 'incompatibility' thesis, based on, respectively, text, culture, instrumentality and the absence of secularism. It can be argued the difficulties which Islamic societies have with the concept of human rights reflect not any one of these, but their combination and reinforcement, and that any longer-term solution will involve addressing each in turn.

The issue of text has received greatest attention, vast amounts of effort being devoted to promulgating 'Islamic' codes, or to providing different interpretations of Qoranic and prophetic sentences. A great deal can be done to produce a more liberal, modern, humanistic interpretation of these texts and this is the great hope of the liberal interpreters of Islam, and their non-Muslim supporters. The fact remains, however, that with all the reinterpretative energy in the world some of the texts, pertaining to women, non-Muslims, apostates cannot be fudged away and remain.[27] The text is not, however, the main reason for the difficulties with human rights: in this sense 'Islam' is not the issue. What is far more intractable is the *political and social context of interpretation*, the manner in which these texts are conventionally interpreted, in the contemporary social and political conditions of the Islamic world: it is, therefore, not wholly, but largely, a contingent matter. The option of simply rejecting texts is not open, given the claim to divine origin, but that of neglect sometimes is – as certainly applies to Qoranic injunctions on, say, slavery.[28] However, to assume that this can take place and that a liberal, modern, interpretation will be put on these texts is to assume a very different political and social climate in the Islamic world than prevails to-day: here authoritarian, patriarchal, obscurantist interpretations prevail, ones inimical, in terms of broad political and legal culture, to any liberal interpretation.[29] The hopes of

[27] On this see Mayer, *Islam and Human Rights*.

[28] I am grateful to Deniz Kandiyoti for this point.

[29] For three cogent versions of this see Sami Zubaida, 'Human rights and culture difference: Middle Eastern perspectives', Reza Afshari 'An essay on Islamic cultural relativism in the discourse of human rights', and Bassam Tibi, 'Islamic law/*Shari'a*, human rights, universal morality and international relations' both of the latter in *Human Rights Quarterly*, 16 (May 1994). For a comparable argument on the *cultural* obstacles to individualism, rationality and modernity within Islam see Darius Shayegan, *Cultural Schizophrenia* (London, Saqi, 1992). Tibi's own argument is developed further in his *The Crisis of Modern Islam* (Salt Lake City, University of Utah Press, 1988). A broader onslaught on the religious and anti-modernist political culture of the Middle East,

those within and without the Muslim world for such a liberal reading are, in some cases, realistic and have already shown their theoretical and practical potential: but they can, at times ignore (illiberal) context in favour of (somewhat flexible) text.

This issue of culture relates directly to the third constituent of incompatibility, namely instrumentality, or, more bluntly, the relation of state to society. In sum, states in the contemporary Islamic world, like their predecessors, have denied autonomy to society and to the legal and other constituents of a human rights practice: as has been well shown by Simon Bromley, this dictatorial practice, often ascribed to 'Islam' has other, secular, and changing, roots, the modern state having as much to do with oil, repressive technology and inter-state war as with any cultural continuity.[30] But the fact is that in a context where states deny an autonomous civil society, and where, among other forms of demagogy, they seek to promote their own spurious human rights rhetoric, the development of respect for human rights has little hope: the objective, historical and political, preconditions for it are not there and it is illusory to pretend they are.

The final suggested component of collision is that of secularism itself, i.e. the insistence on the exclusion of religion from public, including legal and constitutional, life. Although Islamists are keen to focus on this issue, and to denounce the influence of secularism in Western and Islamic societies,[31] writers on Islamic attitudes to human rights seek to fight shy of this question, preferring to hope for the triumph of 'liberal' interpretations of human rights but within an Islamic vocabulary and framework. The most notable exception to this reluctance has been that of the secularist tradition in Turkey, formulated by Ziya Gokalp and implemented by Kemal Ataturk. Discussion of secularism is all the more difficult because, as with issues mentioned above, the Western definition and policy on it are open to criticism and less solid than might at first appear. Islamist thinkers often go further and argue that, in another case of misleading Western propaganda, the continuing hold of religion on Europe and the USA is not recognized.[32]

Despite all these difficulties, however, the issue of secularism lies at the heart of the whole story, and justification, of human rights and democracy and of the difficulties that Islamic societies have in formulating, and implementing, policies in this regard. Secularism is part of, but conceptually distinct from, the issues of political culture and state-society relation mentioned above: it involves not only limiting the claims of religion in the public sphere, but a climate of tolerance of debate, and the application of reason to social and legal life. Without it, not only can recourse be made to particular authoritarian texts, but, more importantly, there is available an authority and atmosphere that denies the scope either for individual challenges to the state or for reasoned, free, discussion of the rights issue. A liberal interpretation of Islam is certainly

from a radical Palestinian nationalist standpoint is Hisham Shirabi, *Neo-Patriarchy* (Oxford, Oxford University Press, 1988). All of these (Middle Eastern) writers will no doubt be dismissed as 'ethnocentric, 'orientalist', 'essentialist', 'reductionist' etc. by those who disagree with them.

[30] Simon Bromley, *Rethinking Middle East Politics* (Oxford, Polity, 1994).

[31] E.g. M. al-Ahnaf and others, *L'Algerie par ses islamistes* (Paris, Karthala, 1991) pp. 100–17.

[32] E.g. that the Queen of England is the head of the Anglican church, no Jew has ever been president of the USA, Muslim schools and holidays are not on an equal footing with Christian etc. But these criticisms themselves presuppose a universal principle.

preferable to an illiberal one: but the long-term issue is not that of finding some more liberal, or compatible, interpretation of Islamic thinking, so much as that of removing the discussion of rights, as of other issues, from the claims of religion itself. As long as this fails to be the case, the multiple levels of limitation identified here – text, culture, instrumentality and religious hegemony – will prevail. It is this question above all which those committed to a liberal interpretation of Islam seek to avoid – albeit, for very good practical, as well as philosophical, reasons.

Conclusion

The above argument may lead to some uncomfortable, but arguably unavoidable, conclusions about the contemporary debate on human rights. If it suggests that discussion on an 'Islamic' approach to human rights has often been confused, when not straightforwardly manipulative, it also suggests that there is no easy resolution of this question, given the forms of ideological domination prevailing in the Islamic states of the Middle East, and the absence of the preconditions for an effective discussion, or policy, on rights. What this suggests is a long-term, possibly dispiriting, defence of human rights and a simultaneous encouragement of those broader processes of social and political change that make rights a practical possibility. Insofar as there are those within the Muslim world, liberal Muslims or secularizers, who do accept the implications of international conventions and practice on human rights there should be no obstacle to collaboration with them. The hope for the improvement of respect for human rights in these states may, for the foreseeable future, rest as much with the elaboration of a liberal Islamic understanding of the issue as it does with the strengthening of secularism.[33]

The case of the Islamic countries should also encourage us to question the prevailing trend towards relativism, which is evident in much human rights discussion as in many areas of the social sciences and of moral philosophy.[34] One can recognize at least three distinct sources of this relativism – anti-imperialist concern about the 'ethnocentric' nature of universal values, postmodernist rejection of any claim to rationality and universality, and philosophic doubts about the possibility of asserting universal entitlements. The first is prey to the fallacy of origin: the fact that a set of ideas were produced in one particular context says little about their subsequent validity.[35] The second is a debilitating intellectual fashion indulged in by people who give the impression of having never been near a human rights violation.[36] The third is, for all the solemnity of its utterance and the genuine philosophic concern it

---

[33] Secularism has, as much as anything, meant tolerance or legal neutrality *as between* different religions; but what is being required here is as much tolerance – of free speech, diversity, even renunciation – *within* religions. I am especially grateful to Kevin Boyle for this point.

[34] Alasdair Macintyre, *Beyond Virtue* (London, Duckworth, 1984); Stuart Hampshire, *Innocence and Experience* (London, Penguin, 1992).

[35] I have gone into this in greater detail in my ' "Orientalism" and its critics', *British Journal of Middle Eastern Studies*, 20.1 (1993).

[36] It may, however, be worth noting the life-long practical commitment of Michel Foucault to human rights causes [David Macey, *The Lives of Michel Foucault* (London, Vintage, 1994)] especially ch. 8, 'South', which recounts Foucault's courageous, and, for him, dangerous support for human rights in Tunisia: no trace of relativism, or anti-imperialist non-intervention, in this instance.

reflects, a political and legal abnegation that corresponds rather weakly to the requirements of much of humanity.

There are many aspects of these relativisms which cannot be dealt with here: however, insofar as the case of the Islamic countries is often invoked to justify such relativism, in one or all of its above variations, or to legitimate or illustrate arguments that rely upon a concept of 'tradition' or historically produced 'community', it is to be hoped that the above discussion will, at the least, indicate that 'Islam' provides no such succour. Whatever else they may be, or interpreted to be, the Islamic discourses and practices of the countries of the Middle East are not examples of relativism, or mutually tolerant communitarianism, as those who are subjugated to their various contemporary political and social manifestations are all too cruelly aware.

Human Rights in the Processes of Transition and Consolidation of Democracy in Latin America

Francisco Panizza

Much has changed in Latin America since the first countries of the region returned to civilian rule in the late 1970s and so has the situation of human rights in the continent. The pace and the direction of change have not been uniform though. While some countries – like Bolivia – have gone through four democratic elections since shaking off their military rulers, others – Mexico, Guatemala, El Salvador – are still in transition to democracy or on the verge or in the aftermath of peace processes. Venezuela, formerly a model of democratic stability in the region, was badly shaken by two military uprisings in 1992 and early in 1994 was placed under a state of emergency, under the shadow of financial collapse and social unrest. Perú returned to democracy in 1980 only to suffer a *civico-military coup* in 1992 and is now heading towards new presidential and parliamentary elections in 1995. After a short democratic interlude Haiti went back in 1991 to a regime of military terror and although president Aristide was restored to office by a US-sponsored military operation in 1994, the future of democracy is still uncertain in the country.[1]

Drawbacks and exceptions notwithstanding, the direction of change is, however, clearly set. It would be naive to rule out new breakdowns of the constitutional order in the region. The quality and limits to democratic rule can and should be put into question. Armed conflicts and social unrest still affect a number of countries. But liberal democracy is now established in the region more broadly than at any time in the past and it is within its framework that the human rights issues should be considered.[2] But it is not just changes in the political system that affect the situation of human rights. Significant cultural, economic and social changes as well as changes in the international environment have affected the conditions under which most people live, including their chances of effectively enjoying basic human rights. In this paper I will argue that while democratic governments have adopted the discourse of human rights, still a considerable gap remains between the rulers' pledge to protect human rights and their full respect in the region.

---

[1] Some countries have not changed or at least are not changing in a democratic way. However, by refusing to move gradually towards a more open political system, Cuba is likely to experience the most traumatic change in the region.

[2] In this paper I limit myself to the discussion of civil and political rights, particularly those associated with the right to life, without considering broader social and economic rights.

Human Rights in the Struggle against Dictatorship

It was during the military dictatorships of the 1970s and 1980s that human rights first became a political issue in Latin America.[3] This is not to ignore the fact that before the era of military rule human rights were part of the region's juridical order. Nor, of course, were the 1970s and 1980s military rulers the first governments guilty of serious human rights crimes in the history of the region. It was rather the massive and unprecedented nature of human rights abuses committed by the military governments that made human rights a crucial component of public debate in the region. However, it was not just the gravity of the crimes committed by the military that explains the new centrality of the discourse of rights in the 1970s and 1980s. Under conditions that made open political opposition almost impossible, the discourse of human rights was the only oppositional political language that proved difficult to suppress or neutralize.

During the years of military rule the struggle for human rights became a unifying element in the struggle for democracy. Demands for human rights constituted a focal point for both traditional and new political actors of different ideological complexion. Among the latter, for the first time in modern Latin American history, women, most notedly but by no means only the Mothers of Plaza de Mayo, were at the forefront of the struggle for human rights. Their action effectively put into question the dividing line between the personal and the political: their grief as mothers became the first intensely private issue to reconstitute a public space hitherto closed by the government. But women's groups were not the only new social actors that gained prominence in the struggle for human rights. Many other non-governmental organizations (NGOs) were constituted under the umbrella of the defence of human rights. The Catholic Church played a prominent role in countries like Chile, denouncing human rights violations and defending their victims. Among the traditional political actors, mainstream politicians used the question of human rights to vindicate a past political order in which human rights were formally guaranteed in the constitution. The left, which previously had regarded human rights as an issue of bourgeois ideology and suffered the blunt of repression under the military, found in the defence of human rights a vital lifeline for political survival as well as for the physical survival of its militants.

It was not only internally that human rights became a crucial element in challenging the power of the military. Independent international organizations like Amnesty International, set up in 1961, played an increasingly prominent role in raising public awareness about human rights violations in Latin America. The massive influx of political refugees into Europe, the US, Canada and other countries brought with them testimonies of their terrible human suffering. Latin American solidarity groups in the developed countries found in the denunciation of human rights violations the possibility of appealing to a much broader public opinion than those specifically interested in Latin American politics.

The articulation of new and old political elements that characterized the struggle for human rights during the years of military rule anticipated further changes in the political landscape in the transition to democracy. During

---

[3] I. Cheresky, ' La emergencia de los derechos humanos y el, retroceso de lo político', *Punto de Vista*, (August 1992), 42–8.

transition, the revalorization of constitutional liberalism and human rights, came together with the emergence of new social actors less dependent on the state than in the past and, above all, of a new political culture more receptive to human rights. The return of thousands of political exiles whose survival had been in many cases greatly assisted by human rights organizations in their countries of exile, increased domestic awareness of the international dimension of human rights. And the fact that denunciations of human rights violations contributed to the de-legitimation and ultimately to the downfall of right-wing political regimes gave an ideological twist to what had before been conceived mainly as an instrument of cold war politics.

Human Rights in the Transition to Democracy

During the transition to democracy the human rights debate was almost entirely centred around how to deal with the human rights crimes committed under military rule. As Manuel Antonio Garretón put it, the concern was not so much with the present and future conditions that would assure the achievement of human rights, which in some way were considered to have been secured with the disappearance of the military regime and the installation of a democratic one, as it was with the imperative to deal with an unresolved issue: 'Nunca Más was less a programme for the future than a denunciation of the past, since the future seemed guaranteed by the very condition of all democracies'.[4] Time would show that this was a simplistic assumption.

The issue that first made apparent the tensions between democracy and human rights was the demand for the punishment of military officers accused of gross human rights crimes. This issue generated a debate that exposed the ambiguous relationship between morality, justice and politics. While few outside the military and their closest allies defended the morality of the actions of the 'dirty wars' and there was little doubt that serious crimes were committed, it was naive to ignore the fact that the punishment of the perpetrators of serious human rights violations was, above all, a political matter and that politics would ultimately determine the limits of justice. And as with any other political issue matters of interest, power and hegemony ultimately determined its outcome.

Politically the debate about past human rights abuses was related to another issue, namely how can emergent democracies establish the rule of law and build up human rights guarantees into a new system that prevents the recurrence of abuses? For some, particularly human rights activists, the punishment of perpetrators of past human rights crimes was not just a moral obligation and a matter of justice but also an essential act of deterrence against the repetition of such crimes: if a transition to democracy occurs without ensuring justice for past violations of human rights, what would this imply for the respect of human rights in the future? It was stressed that the military needed to be aware that if they attempted again to have recourse to violence they would be called to account. Furthermore, it was argued that under the rule of law there was a need to individualize responsibility. Otherwise a whole institution – the armed forces – would remain tainted with the crimes of a number of individuals.

---

[4] M. A. Garretón, 'Human rights in processes of democratization', *Journal of Latin American Studies*, 26 (1994), 221–34.

Finally, it was argued that punishment according to the law was necessary to demonstrate the change in the type of political system.

On the other hand, those advocating leniency argued that after a period of upheaval there was a need for a fresh start. The return to constitutional order called for national reconciliation, no balance sheets. They claimed that people preferred clean breaks rather than trials that would drag on for years bringing with them uncertainty and polarization. It was further argued that trials would make martyrs out of villains. Besides, trials could never be fair as it would be impossible to bring all perpetrators to court. It was also claimed that ultimately everybody was guilty, if not of human rights crimes as such, at least of the political mistakes that led to violence and authoritarianism. As for the future, the military and the police needed education rather than punishment.[5] Ultimately, the main argument against bringing the perpetrators of human rights crimes to justice was that, rather than by bringing to justice military and police officers, the consolidation of a democratic regime was the only guarantee of avoiding new human rights violations in the future. Hence, *politically*, the human rights issue needed to be subordinated to the democratic issue, because a successful transition from authoritarianism to democracy was paramount.[6]

Leaving aside, if that is possible, considerations of morality and justice the decision to prosecute or to pardon was less straightforward than campaigners for human rights would like to believe. As David Pion-Berlin has pointed out, because the policies under authoritarian rule had so polarized these societies, finding a win-win strategy was virtually impossible and midpoints between the two options were not necessarily the most desirable.[7] Virtually nobody believed that the trial of every military and police officer involved in human rights crimes was feasible. However, human rights lawyers argued that, as a minimum, prosecutions should not be symbolic but include every rank and position. At the end, not even this minimum standard was achieved in any country.

Within certain clear limits there were, however, significant differences in the way each country dealt with past human rights crimes. They ranked from the trial and condemnation of some high ranking military officers in Argentina, to the setting up of 'truth commissions' with different briefs in Chile and El Salvador, to the sanctioning of an amnesty, ratified by a plebiscite, for those responsible for human rights violations in Uruguay. Two questions arise from this variety of strategies: (a) how to explain these differences in the handling of the problem? and (b) what were the consequences of the differential treatment of those responsible for past human rights crimes for the observance of human rights in the future?

To answer the first question it is important to consider the different ways transitions to democracy took place in the region. In a typology that has become classical in the comparative literature on the subject, Guillermo O'Donnell distinguishes between transitions that occur by collapse and

---

[5] These arguments were outlined by Francoise Hampson in her presentation to the Workshop on 'Impunity and Governability in Latin America', that took place in the Institute of Latin American Studies, London, April (1994).

[6] Garretón, 'Human rights in processes of democratization' p. 224.

[7] D. Pion–Berlin, 'To prosecute or to pardon? Human rights decisions in the Latin American southern cone', *Human Rights Quarterly*, 16 (1994), 105–30.

transitions that occur through transaction.[8] In the former case, a series of crises and failures of the authoritarian regime lead to an accumulation of pressure, until the rather sudden emergence of massive and active opposition or defeat in an external war forces the armed forces to a hasty retreat to the barracks. Transitions by collapse – O'Donnell points out – are short. The authoritarian incumbents have comparatively little control over who will become the main actors in this process and are unable to extract guarantees from the opposition that their crimes will not be investigated.

In turn, transitions by transaction occur when the incumbents of the authoritarian regime decide to open up the situation gradually. A process of negotiations with opposition forces follows, in which the armed forces retain a variable degree of control over the situation and are able to impose certain conditions for surrendering power. Often, a crucial guarantee is that the democratic government will not investigate the authoritarian past. O'Donnell concludes that while democratic governments resulting from a transition by collapse have fewer policy constraints than those that result from a transacted transition, the other side of the coin is that transitions by collapse tend to be more seriously threatened in their survival by powerful, disaffected actors who, in contrast with the transacted cases, have not had their crucial interests adequately accommodated in the new situation.[9]

O'Donnell's typology appears to provide an explanation for the new democratic governments' different attitudes towards past human rights violations. As a result of its military defeat in the Malvinas/Falkland wars Argentina was the only case of 'transition by collapse' in the region. Accordingly, it was possible for the newly elected Argentinian government to bring a number of military officers to court, a decision that was beyond the powers of other governments under higher constraints. Moreover, the military uprisings that the Argentinian government had to face and that led to a number of statutes of limitation of responsibility and eventually to the pardon of those condemned for human rights crimes, give further support to O'Donnell's claim.

Different types of transition, however, certainly influenced but did not fully determine the new democratic governments' attitude towards past human rights violations. The Argentinian government may have had more freedom than other newly democratic regimes to impose its will on the military, but it was by no means bound to bring the suspects of human rights atrocities to justice. During the first electoral campaign the Peronists, widely tipped to win the election, were accused by their political rivals of having clinched a deal with the armed forces that guaranteed the military that there would be no prosecution for past crimes. The denunciation of the Peronista-military pact became the main theme of the Radical party candidate Raúl Alfonsín's electoral campaign. Alfonsín – a human rights lawyer – discursively divided the political arena between those favouring the 'new democratic Argentina', committed to justice and human rights, which he claimed to represent, and the 'old' corporatist and authoritarian Argentina embodied in the alleged Peronist-military pact. This strategy put the Peronists totally on the defensive and led to

---

[8] G. O'Donnell, 'Transitions to democracy: some navigation instruments' in R. A. Pastor (ed.), *Democracy in the Americas. Stopping the Pendulum* (New York and London, Holmes and Meier, 1989), pp. 62–75.

[9] O'Donnell, 'Transitions to democracy', pp. 63–4.

their defeat. In keeping with his electoral promises, once elected, Alfonsín brought the members of the military juntas and a number of other high ranking military officers to trial. It is very doubtful that the Peronist candidate, Italo Luder, would have followed the same path.[10]

The importance of political agents' perceptions and decisions regarding past human rights violations is stressed by David Pion-Berlin in his comparative study of the Southern Cone governments' policies towards human rights crimes.[11] Pion-Berlin argues that variations in the gravity of the crimes committed by the military and the civil-military balances of power alone or combined cannot sufficiently explain the divergence in human rights policies. He introduces as further variables élite preferences, organized interest group pressures and strategic calculation. Within the boundaries set up by the legacies of authoritarianism and the resultant balance of power between soldiers and civilians, Pion-Berlin concludes that it was the commitments, perceptions and calculations of the political leaders that led to different policies.[12]

The Right to Truth

If the right to justice was blocked by the not so residual powers of the military and by governments unwilling or unable to risk challenging them, the military were less successful in concealing their crimes. The so-called 'truth commissions' became the main instruments in the inquiry into the fate of the thousands of 'disappeared', extrajudicially executed and tortured in the years of the dictatorships. The first official report on past human rights crimes was that of the Argentinian National Commission on the Disappeared Persons, *Comisión Nacional Sobre la Desaparición De Personas*, CONADEP, which in 1984 published its report 'Never Again, '*Nunca Más*'. CONADEP's report catalogued 8961 cases of unresolved 'disappearances' and warned that the true figure might be even higher. CONADEP drew up files comprising the complaints of relatives of 'disappeared' prisoners, testimonies of people released from secret detention centres and statements from members of the security forces who participated in the repressive activities it described. In Brazil an unofficial report was issued in 1985 by the archdioceses of Sao Paulo.[13] In Chile, an officially appointed Commission for Truth and Reconciliation had as its brief investigating human rights violations that resulted in deaths or disappearances. Its findings, the so-called 'Rettig Report' – after the Commission's president – was published in 1991.[14] The report went beyond the

---

[10] Conversely, the unsuccessful military uprisings did not make the president Carlos Menem's pardon of those condemned inevitable.

[11] In Argentina, President Raúl Alfonsín (1983–9) authorized an official investigation into the plight of the disappeared, '*los desaparecidos*', followed by judicial proceedings against a limited number of alleged perpetrators; in turn Chilean President Patricio Alwin (1990–4) called for an inquest but not trials; finally, Uruguayan President Julio María Sanguinetti (1985–90) called for no investigation and no trials.

[12] Pion–Berlin, 'To prosecute or to pardon?', pp. 107 and 129–30. However, the fact that in the Southern Cone, outside Argentina, no military officer has been brought to justice and that even in Argentina none of the officers condemned served his full sentence, highlights the relatively narrow limits of variation of governments' approaches to past human rights crimes.

[13] Arquidiosece de Sao Paulo, *Brasil Nunca Mais* (Petrópolis, Vozes, 1985).

[14] Secretaría General de Cultura, Secretaría General de Gobierno, '*Informe de la Comisión Nacional de Verdad y Reconciliación*' (Santiago de Chile, 1991).

investigation of past crimes to analyse the causes of human rights violations, analyse the behaviour of the security services, the armed forces and the judiciary, and propose a series of measures to ensure that there would be no repeat of the massive human rights violations.[15]

Through the pioneer work of bodies like the CONADEP and the Chilean Commission for Truth and Reconciliation, the 'right to truth', a right as such not codified in the main international human rights treaties, was established. This right became a major element in future peace processes and processes of transition to democracy elsewhere in Latin America. Accordingly, it was in the Salvadorian peace process that the importance of the 'right to truth' became more apparent through the work of the UN-appointed Truth Commission. The setting up of a Truth Commission as a result of the peace accords was in itself an unprecedented initiative, the first time that a national government and opposition group mandated a body made up of international personnel to carry out investigations into past human rights abuses. The Commission's mandate was to clarify the most serious human rights abuses committed by both sides in the context of the civil war. Its brief also included examining the pattern of impunity within which abuses by government forces were committed and to make legal, political or administrative recommendations to prevent a repetition of past abuses and to stimulate reconciliation. Both the government and the opposition Farabundo Martí Liberation Front (FMLN), *Frente Farabundo Martí para la Liberación Nacional*, formally agreed to abide by the Commission's recommendations.[16]

The Commission collected information about over 20,000 victims of human rights abuses of which 30 were selected for in-depth investigations. Its report, published in March 1993, established that the Salvadorian armed and security forces and paramilitary groups were responsible for human rights crimes on a large scale, including massacres, torture and 'disappearances'. It concluded that 'death squads' linked to state structures became an instrument of terror responsible for the systematic physical elimination of political opponents. The FMLN was also held responsible for a number of human rights crimes although on a much lesser scale. Where appropriate those responsible for the crimes were named.[17]

The Commission did not limit itself to investigating the past but made a number of recommendations aiming at the protection of human rights in the future. Among the recommendations were the removal from office of all military and judicial officials named in the report; the banning from public office for ten years of the above and also of FMLN members held responsible for abuses, and an urgent investigation into 'death squads', as it perceived these groups as still posing a threat to society. Significantly, the report cited the judiciary as bearing a great responsibility for the impunity with which the abuses had been committed and the extensive reform of the judiciary was prominent among its recommendations. The serious deficiencies of the Salvadorian judiciary, however, prevented the Commission from recommending

[15] Garretón, 'Human rights in processes of democratization' p. 227.

[16] Amnesty International, *El Salvador. Peace without Justice* (London, 1993, AMR 29/12/93), pp. 1–2.

[17] See S/25812/Ad.3, *Report of The Secretary General on the United Nations Observer Mission in El Salvador*, 25 May (1993). The decision to name those responsible in the report was met with considerable opposition by the government and the armed forces.

prosecutions of those responsible for human rights abuses. The Government's immediate response to the report was the promulgation of a sweeping amnesty law in favour of the perpetrators of human rights crimes.

The Legacy of Transition

It would be tempting to sum up the legacy for human rights of the processes of transition to democracy in Latin America in a single word: *impunity*. Laws of political amnesty or to the same effect were passed in Brazil, Chile, Argentina, Uruguay, El Salvador and Honduras. These laws effectively exempted members of the military and in some cases also members of armed opposition groups, from prosecution for past abuses. The lack of effective legal punishment for those responsible for serious human rights crimes sanctioned by the amnesty laws has been regarded as a failure for the human rights movement and as a dangerous legacy for the new democratic governments.

Impunity however is a concept both too broad and too narrow to give an adequate picture of what were highly complex and changing situations. *To a certain extent* the failure to bring the military and their allies to justice was perhaps to be expected, if not justified. At the best of times it is difficult to translate moral imperatives into political realities. And while the justice of the demands for the punishment of human rights crimes can hardly be disputed, those demanding justice never seemed to have a coherent political strategy to achieve their aims. In some cases, in their radical rejection of any kind of compromise, human rights' groups showed a contempt for politics which was not radically different from that of the former military rulers and became equally isolated from society, as the current plight of the Mothers of Plaza de Mayo illustrates.[18] As David Pion-Berlin points out,

> In the abstract, seeking justice for the victims of state terror may seem imperative, the right thing, perhaps the only thing to do. But moral 'dos and don'ts' should not be lifted and then divorced from the political context. As worthy as the human rights cause may be, it must still be placed against a backdrop of specific, political realities that often preclude optimal solutions.[19]

Politically, impunity eroded the legitimacy of the new governments by blatantly violating the principle of equality before the law which every democratic government is bound to uphold. However, as shown by the outcome of the Uruguayan referendum, many people clearly feared that the prosecution of military personnel responsible for past human rights crimes would represent a greater danger for democratic stability than impunity. Moreover, concerns for impunity were not adequately channelled into broader demands for institutional reform of the security forces and, above all, of the judiciary, that are crucial for the enjoyment of human rights under the new democratic governments.

Moreover, impunity did not mean that everything was lost for human rights during the transition to democracy. Amnesties, even under the shadow of the

---

[18] F. Panizza, 'Human rights: global culture and social fragmentation', *Bulletin of Latin American Research*, 12 (1993), 205–6.

[19] Pion-Berlin, 'To prosecute or to pardon?' p. 130.

military, should not be confused with amnesia. Through the findings of the 'truth commissions', the right to truth, *el derecho a la verdad*, became a significant achievement in the struggle for human rights. Advocates of the 'right to truth' ground it in the 'right to identity', arguing that while death is the end of human life, it is not the end of the person's right to identity. This right includes the right to know how a person's life came to an end. Furthermore, the public disclosure of information about the fate of the victims of human rights crimes was an important element of the emotional healing necessary to 'turn the page without closing the book'.

The other area in the field of human rights in which important progress was made over this period was that of the role of international organizations and international law. Already during the years of military rule, the fact-finding mission of the Inter American Commission of Human Rights' (IACHR), *Comisión Interamericana de Derechos Humanos*, to Argentina in September 1979 was a turning point in breaking the officially imposed conspiracy of silence about the fate of the 'disappeared'.[20] After the return to democracy, a landmark report by the IACHR concluded that the Argentinian laws No 23.492 and 23.521 and Decree No 1002/89 that put to an end criminal investigations for past human rights violations were in violation of the American Convention on Human Rights. But perhaps the most important contribution of the international community to the observance of human rights in the region has been the role of the United Nations in the peace processes of El Salvador and Guatemala.[21] The report of the Truth Commission in El Salvador and the setting up of a corps of human rights observers to monitor compliance with the peace agreements have added an international dimension to these processes, which counterbalances the still very considerable powers of the armed forces and their allies.

Human Rights and the Consolidation of Democracy

The central dilemma during processes of transition to democracy was how to balance demands for justice and retribution with the need to safeguard the democratic transition itself. Later, as most countries of the region move away from transition towards 'actually existing democracy', new human rights concerns have emerged. It is to these concerns that I turn next.

Crimes on a massive scale like the over nine thousand 'disappeared' in Argentina, the thousands of political prisoners in Uruguay, the torture of political prisoners in Brazil and the thousands of political killings in Chile are thankfully over. Freedom of expression and of political association, almost

[20] I. Cheresky, 'Derechos humanos y régimen político. Una genealogía de la idea democrática moderna', *Sociedad*, 2 (May 1993), 115–25.

[21] The UN Observer Mission in El Salvador (ONUSAL), began its operations in El Salvador in July 1991 and was set up to monitor the observance of the peace accords. Its Human Rights Division was specifically mandated to verify implementation by both sides of the 1990 San José Agreement, which committed the two parties to eradicating human rights violations and other abuses. Since it began its work, the Human Rights Division has issued six reports documenting patterns and cases of human rights violations and the implementation of other agreements directly related to the protection of human rights in El Salvador. ONUSAL has made numerous recommendations to the government on individual cases it has investigated, on patterns of abuses and on institutional reforms, many of which have not so far been implemented. Amnesty International, *El Salvador. Peace without Justice*, p. 4.

non-existent before, are widely enjoyed in most countries. Within this new climate of freedom, denunciations of human rights abuses are often vigorously followed by independently-minded journalists and taken up by human rights organizations. However, welcome as they should be, these improvements have not put an end to serious human rights violations in the region.

Some of the most serious contemporary human rights abuses are reported in countries that were until very recently under military rule or have not yet fully completed their transition to democracy. In 1993 and the first half of 1994 hundreds of people in Haiti 'disappeared' or were extrajudicially executed by the army or their armed civilian auxiliaries, especially during crackdown on suspected supporters of exiled President Jean-Bertrand Aristide.[22] During the same period, in Cuba, at least 500 prisoners of conscience were believed to be held, some serving sentences as long as 13 to 15 years' imprisonment. Scores of non-violent government opponents such as members of unofficial political parties, trade unions or human rights groups were routinely arrested for short periods of time. Detention and trial procedures in all political cases fall far short of international standards.[23] In Guatemala, nearly 150 extrajudicial executions and several 'disappearances' were carried out by the security forces and their civilian agents in 1993.[24] After the 1992 peace accord in El Salvador there has been a series of killings of members of the former armed opposition and dozens of other killings which appear to have been carried out by 'death squads' linked to the armed forces.[25]

In other countries, human rights abuses have been reported in the context of counter-insurgency operations. In Colombia, over 120 people 'disappeared' in 1993 after being seized by the security forces or paramilitary groups and many hundreds were the victims of extrajudicial executions by the armed forces.[26] In Peru, during the 13 months from April 1992 through to April 1993 Amnesty International documented the cases of 209 people who 'disappeared' following detention by the security forces. The fate of 139 of these people remain unknown and 28 were subsequently found dead. During the same period Amnesty International documented 57 extrajudicial executions and at least 40 cases of torture. Furthermore, at least 4000 political prisoners were awaiting trial or were tried under judicial procedures which fell short of international standards.[27] In Mexico human rights abuses by the army, including extra-judicial executions and torture, were reported during the short armed confrontation between the armed forces and the Zapatista insurgents in January 1994.

Human rights violations are not limited, however, to situations of armed conflict or unfinished transition to democracy. Torture and ill-treatment of common prisoners has been widely reported in many countries of the region, including Mexico, Argentina, Venezuela, Chile, Perú and Colombia. Prison

[22] See Amnesty International, *Haiti. On the Horns of a Dilemma: Military Repression or Foreign Invasion?* (AI Index: AMR 36/33/94, August 1994).

[23] Amnesty International, *Amnesty International Report 1994* (London, Amnesty International, 1994), pp. 111–4.

[24] Amnesty International, *Report 1994*, pp. 142–5.

[25] Amnesty International, *Report 1994*, pp. 123–6.

[26] Amnesty International, *Political Violence in Colombia: Myth and Reality* (London, Amnesty International, 1994).

[27] Amnesty International, *Perú: Human Rights since the Suspension of Constitutional Government* (London, Amnesty International, 1993) and Amnesty International, *Report 1994*, pp. 238–41.

conditions amounting to cruel, inhuman and degrading treatment are common throughout the region. Scores of prisoners were killed in Venezuela and Brazil in violent incidents, including protests against prison conditions. Social struggles, particularly the struggle for land, have resulted in serious human rights abuses. Peasants and rural union leaders have been the victims of the violence of the state or of landowners in several countries, including Brazil, Mexico and Guatemala.

It would be misleading but not untrue to claim that the transition from military to civilian governments in the region has only put a stop to the killing of the sons and daughters of the, mostly middle class, opponents of the military juntas in Argentina and Chile but has not prevented the killing of thousands of poor children and adolescents by death squads in urban Brazil and Colombia. 'Social cleansing' is a feature of life in the sprawling shanty towns of some of the region's largest cities. In the major cities of Brazil, hundreds of adolescents, street children and adults are killed or 'disappeared' every year by the police and death squads, which often include off-duty police officers.[28] In Colombia 'death squad' style killings of people regarded as 'disposable' is common in urban areas.[29] Children and adolescents in the care of the state are abused and subjected to inhuman and degrading treatment in state institutions throughout the region.

Why, after more than a decade of democracy, is there still this high level of human rights abuse in the region? As it has been suggested above, some of the human rights problems are the legacy of the years of military rule or ongoing civil conflicts. Others derive from the weakness of existing democratic institutions. Still others are rooted in deeper social changes that affect people's relations with state institutions. It is on these changes and their significance for human rights that I will concentrate below.

Changes in the region have not been limited to the election of governments through regular, open, elections. In most countries, the return to democracy has coincided with the abandonment of the state-centred matrix of economic development and the corporatist structures of state control that were constitutive of Latin American societies for over 30 years, between the 1940s and the 1970s. This dirigiste model of economic development has given way to market oriented economic policies with the corresponding changes in the public-private divide, often accompanied by a drastic reduction in the public sector, the privatization of services and the opening up of the economies of the region to external markets. So far, the results of these changes have been economically mixed and politically ambiguous.

Economic Reforms, Human Rights and Inequality

Market-oriented reforms have been demonized by their critics as an unqualified evil. 'Neoliberalism' has substituted for 'imperialism' and 'the oligarchy' in the discourse of some sectors of the left as a term signifying the oppression of the people. It would, however, be economic reductionism of the worst kind to claim a direct, causal, relationship between neoliberal economic policies and contemporary human rights violations in the region. For once,

---

[28] See US State Department's Human Rights Report for 1993.
[29] Amnesty International, *Political Violence in Colombia: Myth and Reality*, pp. 16–24.

business, particularly international investors whom every government in the region seeks to attract, do not favour authoritarianism any more. On the contrary, advocates of neoliberal reforms present free markets as the only economic system compatible with liberal democracy. The potential implications of economic liberal discourse for human rights is sometimes not taken up by its critics. Whatever the differences between the legislation that business would sponsor and the laws that the defenders of human rights would like to be passed, the fact remains that the rule of law enforced by an independent judiciary is a condition for modern market economic relations and the protection of human rights alike. 'Markets need laws' claimed a businessman in a recently Confederation of British Industry, CBI-sponsored, seminar on investment opportunities in Latin America, criticizing the pervasive inefficiency and corruption of the judiciary in the region. 'Human rights need laws as well, although of a different kind' it could have been added.

Market economics, however, do not just favour the rule of law but also bring about the exclusion and marginalization of all those who do not have the necessary skills to adapt themselves to the market economy. Economic reform has been centred around the International Monetary Fund (IMF) sponsored policies of 'structural adjustment'.[30] The results of these policies have varied considerably from country to country.[31] However, even the most optimistic growth projections would be barely enough to absorb the growth in the economically active population, still less to tackle the backlog of social deficiencies that has accumulated over the years. Furthermore there is ample evidence that social inequity is one of the main unsolved problems of the region. Even in those countries like Chile, Mexico and Argentina that have experienced among the highest rates of economic growth over the past four years, the level of poverty is higher now than it was in the 1980s.[32] In many countries, state provisions in areas like health, education and social security have deteriorated, affecting the traditional poor but also a new and growing class of urban poor as well as large sectors of the lower middle class. A new informal sector of unemployed, semi-employed and self-employed has swelled the decaying inner cities and urban slums alike.

The fall in unemployment produced by the economic growth of the last three years has not been enough to improve the standard of living of the majority of the population. There is now a higher percentage of young people who neither work nor study than at the beginning of the 1980s. For example, in Caracas the number of young people who neither work nor study has risen from 15 to 21% in the past five years. According to PREALC, by the end of the century there will be an estimated 82 million more people in the region. By that time 80% of

---

[30] Although with considerable variations in depth and pace from country to country, structural adjustment programmes have in general involved the following aspects: macroeconomic stability, deregulation, privatization, openness to trade and financial efficiency. See D. E Hojman, 'The political economy of recent conversions to market economics in Latin America', *Journal of Latin American Studies*, 26 (1994), p. 194.

[31] After the so-called 'lost decade' of the 1980s in which, for the first time in the post-war years, the region's gross domestic product grew less than its population, the Latin American economies are experiencing an upturn in the 1990s. For three consecutive years, between 1991 and 1993, the region has been growing by more than 3 per cent a year. Growth projections for the rest of the decade are of continuous moderate GDP per capita growth of about 2 per cent per year. Source: World Bank, *Global Economic Prospects and the Developing Countries* (1993).

[32] *Latin American Weekly Report*, (LAWR) WR–94–17, 12 May (1994), p. 200.

the population will be aged between 15 and 64, which implies a massive incorporation into the labour market.[33] I will come back to the relations between economic exclusion and human rights violations below.

Democratic Disenchantment

Out of the struggle against the dictatorship and of the wide ranging social changes of the last decade has emerged a more autonomous civil society. Non-governmental organizations (NGOs), often with close links with international civil society[34] interact with the state on very different terms than the old state-controlled popular organizations. Rather than the exchange of state economic and political handouts for the political allegiance of its members, many modern NGOs seek to influence policy formation. Human rights organizations are part of this new civil society. Although the human rights movement has lost much of the centrality it had during the years of authoritarianism and in the process of transition to democracy, human rights organizations are established in most countries of the region. Citizens' participation in this more autonomous civil society is, however, limited and democracy in the region is far from being a participatory democracy. It is perhaps not surprising that after the initial euphoria of the return to democracy, a mood of 'democratic disenchantment' is detectable throughout the region.[35] This is not a yearn for authoritarianism, but a result of the loss of confidence by the citizens in their rulers and political institutions.

Disenchantment is partly a natural result of the frustration of popular expectations about a rapid improvement of living standards after the return to democracy. Political corruption has contributed to the mood, eroding public confidence in the new democratically elected governments. 'Disenchantment', however, has deeper roots. To a considerable extent it is the product of the 'power deflation' experienced by the states of the region vis-a-vis the market and international economic agents. Increasingly, decisions affecting the well-being of the population are being taken or are perceived to be taken outside the democratically elected government by powerful private agents. As José Nun put it, for many citizens, 'democratic disenchantment' has translated into 'a defensive withdrawal into the private sphere, public apathy, and a rapid widening of the gap between legality and legitimacy'.[36] However, rather than leading to calls for a return to authoritarianism, the loss of public confidence in

---

[33] PREALC, *Programa de Empleo para América Latina*, is the Latin American arm of the ILO's World Employment Programme. A few social and economic indicators will help to visualize the social problems of Latin America. The Economic Commission for Latin America (ECLAC) calculates the current number of people under the poverty line in Latin America at 196 million, or 46 per cent of the population. Moreover, the numbers of the poor are growing at an annual rate of 3.6 per cent. Income distribution has also worsened. In the majority of the countries in the region the top 5 per cent have seen their income grow or at least mantained, whilst the lower 75 per cent have seen their income reduced, thus widening the chasm between poverty and well being. The percentage of people classed as extremely poor grew. Figures quoted in *LAWR*, WR-93-42, pp. 498–9.

[34] See D. Lehman, *Democracy and Development in Latin America* (Cambridge, Polity, 1990), pp. 148–89.

[35] See R. Munck, 'After the transition: democratic disenchantment in Latin America', *European Review of Latin America and the Caribbean*, 55 (December 1993), 7–19.

[36] José Nun, 'Democracy and modernization, thirty years later', *Latin American Perspectives*, 20 (1993), 7–27, p. 17.

traditional political parties and leaders has led in some countries (and may be even more the pattern in the future) to the emergence of neopopulist political leaders whom, while democratically elected, govern in a highly personalistic way with little regard to party structures, parliamentary processes or legal procedures and with very limited effective account-ability.[37]

Changes in Political Culture

While social and political changes have, as will be made more clear below, a significant bearing on the condition of human rights, changes in political culture are perhaps the ones that may more directly affect the prospects for human rights in the region. In this sense, it can be argued that the return to democracy brought about a radical shift in the region's political culture. This change has little to do with the restoration of constitutional provisions for the protection of rights. Civil and political rights have been contemplated in the region in law, although hardly in practice, since independence.[38] Rather, changes in political culture refer to the demise of collectivist and authoritarian notions of 'the rule of the people' and of 'people's democracy' characteristic of the populist and corporatist forces that dominated politics in the region since the 1930s. Against the primacy awarded by populist and corporatist ideologies to the 'right of the people' and to social and economic rights over citizens' rights, it is argued that the new democratic culture privileges individual rights, the primacy of individual freedom and the rule of law over the will of the leader.[39]

Perhaps a symptom of this cultural change is that in the 1990s, for the first time in history, most governments of the region speak the language of rights. While in almost no case had perpetrators of past human rights abuses been brought to justice, nonetheless the new civilian authorities declare their commitment to human rights. As a signal of their democratic credentials the new governments often hurry to accede to regional and international human rights covenants. New government agencies ('Procuradurías', 'Comisiones', 'Secretarias') are set to monitor and uphold human rights. Human rights violations are often openly acknowledged, although always attributed to forces or events beyond the government's control. International human rights organizations have regular access to high ranking government officers.

Political Strategies and the Future of Human Rights

What do the economic, political and cultural changes outlined above mean for the future of human rights in the region?

[37] Examples of 'neopopulist' leaders are presidents Alberto Fujimori of Perú and Carlos Menem of Argentina and former president Collor de Mello of Brazil. For a view on this issue see L. Whitehead, 'Alternatives to liberal democracy: a Latin American perspective', *Political Studies*, XL, Special Issue (1992), 146–59. Also Nun, 'Democracy and modernization' pp. 17–8.

[38] See F. Xavier-Guerra, 'The Spanish-American tradition of representation and its European roots' *Journal of Latin American Studies*, 26, (February 1994), 1–35.

[39] I. Cheresky, 'La emergencia de los derechos humanos y el retroceso de lo político', *Punto de Vista*, (August 1992), 42–8.

There are good reasons to believe that there will be no generalized return to a new wave of authoritarianism.[40] It is also unlikely that political movements or counter-ideologies would emerge that will radically challenge the current hegemony of liberal-democratic political principles. No Asian-style 'anti-human rights alternative' to the discourse of rights is likely to be adopted by countries which are historically children of the French and American revolutions.

However, in most countries of the region democracy will remain unstable and subject to periodical crises and explosions of social protest. While less pervasive than before, political violence is still part of the region's political landscape. In Perú and Colombia armed opposition groups are still active, with unclear prospects for peace in the immediate future. In Guatemala and Nicaragua old conflicts still flare up in sporadic armed clashes between the government and armed opposition groups. The Zapatista uprising of January 1994 in Mexico shows that armed opposition groups of a new type can emerge as successors of traditional guerrilla movements.

Protest will not be expressed in the same way in every country and will not necessarily involve traditional social forces like the trade unions. It will rather involve those excluded from the market-oriented modernization: the young, the unemployed, unskilled and deskilled workers, displaced peasants, indigenous people and even disaffected sectors within the military.[41] The urban riots that shook the Venezuelan government in 1989, the riots in Argentinian Northern provinces in 1993, land conflicts in Brazil and widespread trade union and peasant protests in Paraguay and Bolivia are only the most visible manifestations of social tensions which, in more or less acute forms, affect most countries of the region. Meanwhile in urban areas there is widespread public anxiety about crime, partly as a result of deteriorating social conditions but also of other factors, like the rise in organized crime and the deterioration of the bonds that keep families and communities together. Together with its more political manifestations the unravelling of social order may lead to a considerable breakdown of the social fabric, particularly in the big cities but also in some rural areas or backward regions.

Faced with these conditions, the Latin American governments are likely to have recourse to a variety of strategies which will directly affect the human rights of their people. These strategies can be labelled as 'instrumental authoritarianism', 'legal fetishism' and 'paralegality'.

'Instrumental authoritarianism' refers to the fact that, while as expressed above, it is unlikely that governments will challenge the discourse of rights on ideological or philosophical grounds, authoritarianism in Latin America has always been more grounded in political practices than on philosophical foundations. In other words, rather than as an alternative set of political principles and institutional arrangements to those of liberal constitutionalism,

---

[40] There are many reasons for believing that the current wave of democratization in Latin America will be more long-lasting than previous similar ones (1944–8, 1955–62). Among others, the end of the Cold War, the loss of appeal of the Cuban revolution, the failure of past authoritarian projects, the 'deradicalization' of the left, the lack of support for military intervention among the economic élites, the 'contagion effect' of successive transitions to democracy etc.

[41] Or military rebels turned into politicians like Cnel Aldo Rico and his 'carapintadas' in Argentina.

authoritarianism has historically been presented as a provisional device to overcome alleged obstacles towards a fully democratic society: as an 'unwanted but unavoidable situation', as an interim arrangement, 'forced by circumstances' (the rise in crime, political corruption, heightened social divisions etc.).

In other words, 'instrumental authoritarianism' is not the negation of democracy and rights in the name of an alternative ideology but its partial, *de facto*, abrogation or temporary deferment. If past history is a guide, in conditions of social polarization and political turmoil, democratically elected governments would not hesitate to have recourse to arbitrary and authoritarian means to impose social order. Instrumental authoritarianism can also be a feature of societies that, while not facing political violence, are facing social disintegration and high levels of criminality. In those cases, extrajudicial executions, 'disappearances' and torture could be regarded as a regrettable but unavoidable consequence of the growing threat to public order. According to each country's conditions, instrumental authoritarianism could vary from systematic excessive use of force by the police, suspension of constitutional guarantees, deployment of the armed forces in certain regions of the country or quarters of a city etc.

'Legal fetishism' has also been a historical feature of Latin American political systems and is likely to continue to be so in the future. It refers not only to the excessive legalism in which public debate is conducted in most countries of the region, but to the combination of legal provisions that regulate every aspect of social life, including constitutional and legal provisions for the protection of human rights, with the practical disregard for the rule of law. The politicization of the judiciary, its lack of real independence and the frequent violation of the principle of equality before the law are some of the means by which the law is used as an instrument of domination rather than as a guarantee of justice.[42]

Legal fetishism is thus the opposite of a good legal order. It often operates under the pretension that passing a legal norm amounts to upholding the rule of law. It is significant that, as a rule, the return to democracy in most Latin American countries has not brought about judicial reform or resulted in a more assertive and independent judiciary. In addition to these historical aspects, 'legal fetishism' has a number of features that are likely to continue in the future. Among these are the following:

(a) The 're-legalization' of political repression. This feature is already apparent in countries like Peru and Colombia, where special courts and draconian anti-terrorist legislation has led to the expedient trial of thousands of alleged 'subversives', many of whom are not members of armed opposition groups. This has led to a new twist in those countries' pattern of human rights violations. While in the 1980s 'disappearances' and 'extra-judicial executions' were the most usual means of getting rid of alleged subversives, the 1990s witnessed an increase in the number of prisoners of conscience,[43] condemned

---

[42] For a history of the use of the rule of law to perpetuate an exclusionary society in Latin America see C. Anglade, *Sources of Legitimacy in Latin America. The Mechanisms of Consensus in Exclusionary Societies* (Paper presented at the XI World Conference of Sociology, New Delhi, 1986).

[43] I.e. people imprisoned for their political beliefs who have not resorted to violence or advocated the use of violence.

by special courts and anti-terrorist legislation which fell well short of international standards for fair trial.

(b) The setting up of human rights bureaucracies. After returning to democracy many Latin American governments set up a number of agencies or watch dogs to protect human rights. So, Argentina has now an Under Secretary of State for Human Rights. In El Salvador a National Council for the Defence of Human Rights was established in 1992. In Perú there is a Special Attorney for the Defence of the People and Human Rights in the office of the Public Ministry. Similar bodies have been established by the new Colombian Constitution and in Mexico a high profile, well endowed, National Commission of Human Rights was created in 1990.

The establishment of human rights agencies should be broadly welcomed. Although the attributions, power, resources and effectivity of these agencies vary from country to country, in many cases their office holders are seriously committed to the protection of human rights. However, these agencies may also perform a more ambiguous role. At best they are no substitute for the governments' lack of political will to uphold human rights under the rule of law enforced by an independent judiciary. At worst these agencies may become little more than lightning conductors to shield governments from taking direct responsibility for human rights violations.

But it is the rise in 'paralegal' forms of social control that is behind some of the most serious human rights violations in contemporary Latin America. The term 'paralegality' was originally used to describe the clandestine operation of the Argentine military during the 'dirty war'.[44] It signified a permissible illegality, because, while still illegal, it remained unpunished and was both denied and admitted. In post-dictatorial Latin America, 'paralegality' refers not so much to the military regimes' anti-subversive strategy but to the fragmentation and loss of state authority and to the erosion of the dividing lines between legality and illegality. The rise in 'paralegality' characterizes countries like Brazil, Colombia, Venezuela as well as a number of Central American countries. It is not so much, as in the past, the threat of new forms of totalitarianism but the emergence of parallel powers in a context of social disintegration that imposes its own forms of social regulation. In contemporary Latin America, 'paralegality' normally takes the form of an alliance between the forces of the state and those of private individuals and organized crime, often in collusion with local traders and politicians.[45]

'Paralegality' takes different forms in different countries of the region. The case of Colombia is perhaps the most paradigmatic, as it entails the articulation of traditional forms of 'paralegality', associated with the anti-subversive strategy of the military, combined with 'new forms' related to the activities of organized crime and death squads which in the country is labelled as 'social cleansing'. As a recently published Amnesty International report states:

> The military's management of repression, so that plainclothes agents of the state are virtually indistinguishable from common criminals (and may indeed be both), provides the government with a second line of defence

---

[44] L. Zac, *The Politics of Silence: Logical Resources and the Argentinian Military Discourse (1976–1980)* (University of Essex, 1989, unpublished).

[45] Panizza, *Human Rights: Global Culture and Social Fragmentation*, p. 211.

against accusations of human rights violations. Successive governments have claimed that the paramilitary groups are independent organizations over which they have no control and thereby abrogated responsibility for thousands of political killings and 'disappearances'.

(...)

This terrifying alliance between the forces of the state, and those of private individuals and organized crime is one of the key factors underpinning the cycle of violence in Colombia.[46]

In El Salvador, the activities of paralegal organizations are not any more related to the country's armed conflict – as is still the case in Colombia – but to its aftermath. Dozens of unclarified killings, some of them with clear political overtones, have followed the 1992 peace accords, which ended 12 years of armed conflict between the government and the *Frente Farabundo Martí Para la Liberación Nacional* (FMLN), Farabundo Martí National Liberation Front. In December 1993, following growing concerns for these killings, the newly elected government announced the creation of a commission to investigate the existence of illegal armed groups.[47]

In July 1994 the group, known as *Grupo Conjunto*, Joint Group, released its report. Among the conclusions from the investigations is that in the country there are currently groups and individuals who continue to have recourse to violence in order to obtain political results. The report concludes that 'the broad network of organized crime which is plaguing the country cannot be separated from many of the violent actions with political goals'. It further establishes that the so-called 'death squads' have been transformed into highly organized groups which are dedicated to 'other types of crimes', but which maintain their structures intact, as well as their abilities to take on – when the circumstances so require – the role of executors of politically motivated criminal actions. The report concludes that criminal structures, such as those which are currently prevalent in the country, cannot exist without support from some active members of the State security forces.

In Brazil, where there are no armed opposition groups, the activity of paralegal organizations is more clearly linked to the country's entrenched social problems. In urban areas, police and vigilante groups, often composed of members of the police force, are responsible every year for hundreds of killings of criminal suspects, street children and slum dwellers.[48] Death squads vary considerably in their size, composition and methods. Some are criminal gangs engaged in drug-trafficking and other criminal activities. Others operate as part of large criminal networks with sophisticated organizations. Others, in turn, are local vigilante groups which have little to do with organized crime, but impose their own social and political control over their own neighbourhood. Their relation with the poorest sectors of the population is highly ambiguous as they appear at the same time as a threat and as protectors.

[46] Amnesty International, *Political Violence in Colombia*, pp. 5–6.

[47] Amnesty International, *Report 1994*, pp. 123–6.

[48] See the chapter on Brazil of the US State Department's Human Report for 1993. In Rio de Janeiro alone, where the death squads are more active, 1200 people were reported to have been killed by these organizations between September 1993 and June 1994. Killings of criminal suspects and minors by vigilante groups, usually go unpunished. Nine out ten of these cases remain unresolved. See also: Amnesty International, *Beyond Despair: an Agenda for Human Rights in Brazil* (London, Amnesty International, September 1994, AI Index AMR 19/15/94) p. 3.

The paralegal justice of the death squads has its roots in the country's history of authoritarianism and in the failure of a cumbersome and ineffective administration of justice.[49] However, contemporary social developments, like the rise in unemployment and the emergence of well organized drug gangs, have contributed to the spread of death squads' activities.[50] In common with the paralegal organizations of Colombia and El Salvador, death squads in Brazil are not engaged in purely private criminal violence. Not only is the police heavily involved in their activities, but local politicians often protect and support the death squads. In the poor quarters of some of Brazil's main cities, like in the Baixada Fluminense region of Rio de Janeiro, local mayors, municipal councillors and state and federal deputies have all been linked with death-squads violence. Some people under prosecution for death squad-style crimes work openly for local politicians. In turn, local politicians use the control exercised by *justiceiros*, as death squad members are known, over the local population to canvass for votes and to intimidate political opponents.[51]

Conclusion: Modernity, Post Modernity and Human Rights in Latin America

The question of human rights is at the heart of the processes of transition and consolidation of democracy in Latin America. Its status raises significant theoretical and practical questions about the nature of these processes, which I would like to address by way of conclusion.

The return to democracy in Latin America is closely linked to notions of modernity and modernization. To a significant extent the appeal of the current wave of democratization in Latin America is that 'being a democratic society' is perceived as belonging to the commonwealth of modern nations and so is promoting market-oriented reforms. For governments 'to speak the language of rights' is part of this appeal, addressed both to domestic and international public opinion. However, while there have been significant advances in the struggle for human rights, there is still a considerable gap between governments' promises and reality.

If human rights are today regarded as part of a process of modernization in the region, this has not always been the case, nor are modernization projects always conceived as compatible with the respect for human rights. The military regimes of the 1970s were modernizing regimes that explicitly maintained that democracy and human rights were incompatible with socio-economic development.[52] Today, highly successful modernizing regimes in Asia dispute the notion of the universality of human rights.

The project of modernity to which the notion of human rights is associated is one among many through history. Through the influence of the American and French revolutions, this project inspired the onset of independence in Latin America. Civil and political rights were incorporated into the region's

---

[49] P. Flynn, 'Brazil: conflict or conciliation' *Conflict Studies*, 265 (October 1993), 1–33.

[50] There is evidence that a significant proportion of the murders of adolescents is related to the drug trade. See C. Milito, H. Raimundo Santos Silva and L. E. Soares, 'Murders of minors in Rio de Janeiro State (from 1991 through July 1993)'. Report conducted as part of project *If This Street Was Mine* (Rio de Janeiro, FASE, IBASE, IDAC, ISER, 1993).

[51] Amnesty International, *Beyond Despair*, p. 6.

[52] And so did some US academics in the 1960s and 1970s. See S. P. Huntington, *Political Order in Changing Societies* (New Haven, Yale University Press, 1968).

nineteenth century post-independence constitutions which set up the juridical framework of the emerging nation-states. However in a narrow interpretation of what a holder of rights was supposed to be, the liberal élites who ruled in nineteenth century Latin American associated cultural diversity with barbarism and denied those who did not conform to a certain cultural tradition the condition of holders of certain rights, including the rights to their own identity. Hence, the great nineteenth century, liberal-inspired dividing line between civilization and barbarism that traversed Latin American societies.

In nineteenth century Latin America, modernity was connotatively associated with European culture, regarded as the universal form of civilization. Today it is linked to the homogenizing influences of international forms of material and symbolic consumption, brought about by the transnationalization of capital and the globalization of communications. Increasing travel and communication facilities have brought nearer to reality the notion of a 'global citizenship' of which the respect for human rights and the environment are paramount concerns.[53] But not all the people in Latin America have access to this 'universal community of humankind'. Integrated into international economic and cultural processes, contemporary Latin American societies are simultaneously more homogeneous and more fragmented than in the past. In the nineteenth century the liberal political order excluded the culturally, ethnically and socially different, mainly the peasants and the indigenous population. Today, the market-led project of economic modernization excludes those who lack the necessary skills demanded by the market. These include not only the traditional rural poor but also important sectors of the urban middle classes and a growing number of unemployed and mostly unemployable youths. Many of those excluded from formal labour markets have no option but to become part of the so-called informal sector, which, by its very existence, blurs the dividing line between legality and illegality. The rule of law, restored by democracy, is undermined by the spread of unregulated social spaces and the emergence of paralegal forms of social control. Chaos and unpredictability rather than revolution are likely to be the main threats to social order in the future.

Presiding over societies that are more unequal and complex than before, the Latin American states have lost their nineteenth century civilizing optimism and their mid-twentieth century development and welfare sense of mission. These have been replaced by a reassertion of constitutional liberalism in which the state is supposed to set up the framework for the development of market forces and a self-regulated civil society. In many countries, since their return to civilian rule, there is indeed an increasing space for the operation of non-governmental organizations. In turn, stronger civil societies mean that human rights victims are not at the mercy of the state as easily as in the past. Furthermore, the state is not any more the monolith entity it was during the years of dictatorship. Openings have been created for a dialogue between the human rights movement and government institutions.

To be effective, however, the human rights movement should reach beyond established state institutions. Internally fragmented and subjected to external and internal forces beyond its control, the state has lost much of its ability to

---

[53] S. Serra, *'Multinationals of Solidarity' International Civil Society and the Issue of the Killing of Street-Children*, paper submitted to the IAMCR Conference, Dublin, June (1993).

act as regulator of a well ordered society. This failure of the state brings about social unease and political disenchantment and may ultimately weaken governments' legitimacy. In this context, human rights in Latin America are at a crossroad: they are part of a project of modernity that has to face up to the problems of post modernity.

Human Rights and Democratization in Africa

SIDGI KABALLO

Towards a Theoretical Formulation

Democracy in modern societies, unlike in the ancient Greek or Roman societies, is, by definition, organically linked to the civil and political human rights of all people. This is mainly because modern societies are based on the freedom of the individual and the equality of citizens before the law. The dismantling of the apartheid regime in South Africa has concluded a complete historical era and has, at last, accomplished the universality of the aims that were first put forward by the French Revolution two centuries ago.

Democracy in this paper is used to mean the people's participation in decision making through the choice, accountability and change of their representatives and governments. Choice presupposes the presence of alternatives to choose from, and the right to information about these alternatives (whether they are political parties, individuals or political programmes) and at the same time suggests the right of the alternatives to expose and introduce themselves, not only by making known their own policies and programmes but also by explaining how these differ from each other. Accountability also presupposes the right to information and to freedom of thought and expression. Choice, accountability and change could only be practised through free periodic elections. Within this understanding of democracy, there is nothing like 'democracy without human rights'[1] or 'democracy for the people and a dictatorship against the enemies of the people'.[2] Whether under the cover of artificial multi-party democracy or the argument of the relativity of human rights, democracy without universal human rights is a contradiction in terms. One cannot imagine how a multi-party democracy could be established without the respect of basic human rights. These include the right to free association (including all civil society free associations such as political parties, trade unions, cultural and intellectual societies, students' organizations, co-operatives, etc.). They include the right to free expression and to free access to and free flow of information, etc. David Beetham has rightly noticed that securing these rights in accordance with special legal or constitutional protection is one of the necessary components of

---

[1] A. Aidoo, 'Africa: democracy without human rights?' *Human Rights Quarterly*, 15 (1993) 703–15.

[2] This was one of the slogans of the Chinese Revolution which was presented by Mao as the people's democratic dictatorship.

democracy.[3] Beetham, being aware of the fact that 'not all individual rights are democratic rights', argues:

> ... without the guaranteed right of all citizens to meet collectively, to have access to information, to seek to persuade others, as well as to vote, democracy is meaningless. *Democratic rights, in other words, are those individual rights which are necessary to secure popular control over the process of collective decision-making on an ongoing basis, and which need protection even when (or especially when) their exercise involves opinions or actions that are unpopular, whether with government or society at large.*[4]
> (Italics added.)

Those who argue for the relativity of human rights on the grounds of their individualistic origin overlook the necessity of individual rights for establishing and sustaining an effective democracy. They are also typically vague about which rights can be dispensed with, as is clear when the discussion shifts from an abstract level to consideration of a definite bill of rights. For example, what is relative about the right to life? Should people be arbitrarily detained and remain indefinitely in custody without trial? Should people have the right to speak their mind, elect and change their government, etc.?[5]

In Africa the relativist approach, as Rhoda Howard[6] rightly argues, alleges three value differences between African and Western societies. African societies are said to be communal in their orientation, consensual in their process of decision making and distributive of the surpluses they generate. These values are held to be contradictory to Western societies, which are described as individualistic in orientation, competitive in decision making and profit maximizing and accumulative of surplus generated. Such an approach to culture suffers from many shortcomings. First it assumes that culture is a static unitary whole unaffected by changes in economic and social structures. In reality cultures change due to changes in economic and social structures, to education and to interrelation with other cultures. Cultures are not closed systems, though they differ in their degree of openness and the speed and extent to which they respond to changes. Among the economic and social changes that could not be disputed as taking place in Africa are the changes in the relative size of commodity production, capital accumulation, income distribution and the class structure. African societies are not any more communal, consensual or egalitarian. The second shortcoming of the relativist approach is that it is inconsistent in dealing with other cultures, especially Western culture. The authoritarian élites select what they adopt and what they reject of 'Western culture'. For example, their lists of favourable items include some items of the culture of repression created and practised by colonial and fascist states as well as items of luxurious life and conspicuous consumption. While driving a Mercedes Benz and using tear-gas are not considered strange

---

[3] D. Beetham, 'Liberal democracy and the limits of democratization', *Political Studies*, XL (1992), p. 41.

[4] Beetham, 'Liberal democracy and the limits of democratization', p. 41.

[5] For a more illustrated discussion, see Fred Halliday in this volume.

[6] R. Howard, 'Is there an African concept of human rights?' in R. J. Vincent (ed.), *Foreign Policy and Human Rights* (Cambridge, Cambridge University Press, 1986), pp. 11–32.

to African culture, civil rights are. Herman Cohen, the ex-Assistant Secretary of State got it right when he argued:

> We ... realize that each nation in Africa has its own conditions, its own needs, and its own range of viable political options. We will try not to indulge in cultural arrogance by claiming that only the American system is appropriate for Africa. But the right to participate, the right to speak out and the right to associate are essential elements in any democratic system, regardless of culture.[7]

Even when universal human rights are acknowledged, some countries continue to argue for what is, in reality, a relativist argument regarding implementation and international monitoring of human rights in these countries. For example, the Asian-African Legal Consultative Committee[8] in its Kampala Declaration on Human Rights prepared for the Vienna World Conference on Human Rights argued:

> The primary responsibility for implementing and giving effect to human rights is at the national level. Consequently, the most effective system or method of promoting and protecting these rights has to take into account the nation's history, culture, traditions, norms and values. There is no *single universally valid prescription model or system*. Whilst the international community should be concerned about the observance of these rights, *it should not seek to impose or influence the adoption of their criteria and systems on developing countries*. It should be sensitive to the unique aspects of each situation and establish impartiality and genuine concern on human rights problems by objective and acceptable factual analysis of events and situations.[9]

Accepting the distinctiveness of local traditions and values is fine where these are not incompatible with basic human rights standards. But the argument for local distinctiveness can all too easily become a justification for 'the repression and elimination of political opposition and dissent, the desecration of the rules of democratic competition and the consequent exhaustion of political legitimacy'.[10] These are characteristic symptoms of authoritarian tendencies. That is why it is necessary for democrats, in their fight against such tendencies before they are consolidated, to win the ideological and cultural battle against any justification of violation or confiscation of human rights. Democratic culture is not just inherited or rises automatically with changes in economic and class structures: it has to be created, spread and, even, fought for on all levels of civil society's institutions.

Ethnicity and Democracy

It is particularly important to insist on the link between democracy and human rights in the context of claims that multi-party democracy will endanger

---

[7] Quoted African Association of Political Science, *Newsletter*, 4 (September 1991), p. 1.

[8] It is an intergovernmental organization comprised of 43 Asian and African countries established as a result of the Bandung Conference in 1955 and based in New Delhi, India.

[9] United Nations, General Assembly, A/conf.157/pc/62/add.9, 20 April 1993, p. 5.

[10] L. Diamond, 'Introduction: roots of failure, seeds of hope' in L. Diamond, J. Linz and S. M. Lipset (eds), *Democracy in Developing Countries, Volume Two: Africa* (Boulder CO, Lynne Riener and Adamantine, 1988), p. 5.

national unity and rehabilitate ethnic conflicts. According to this argument, which is a favourite argument of President Moi of Kenya, electoral competition is too divisive for African societies, since political parties tend to be formed on an ethnic or tribal basis, and democracy therefore intensifies these divisions. However, the evidence that ethnic rivalries can be stimulated as a conscious instrument of policy by political leaders, and even to discredit multi-party competition itself, as in Kenya, should make us suspicious of the use of ethnicity as a means of 'denying demands for social justice and democracy or asserting group interests at the expense of individual citizenship'.[11]

Following Maré we define an ethnic group as a group of people who share a belief of a common origin, a specific cultural practice, a unique set of symbols and beliefs and a sense of belonging to each other as a group distinct from other groups. According to this definition, ethnic groups are not political entities, but they can be politicized for different reasons to serve different interests, including and excluding the interests of the ethnic group itself. While conflict between ethnic groups is not inevitable, given that different ethnic groups can live together in peace and share common interests, ethnic conflicts may arise out of uneven distribution of wealth and resources and unequal sharing of power, regardless of the kind of political system.

However, only a democratic order which takes human rights seriously will be capable of avoiding or resolving ethnic conflict. These rights include the rights of ethnic groups, both as groups and as individual citizens. Such rights have recently gained international recognition and support in the UN Declaration on the Rights of Persons belonging to National or Ethnic, Religious and Linguistic Minorities adopted by the General Assembly in 1992. The respect of universal human rights is one of the first measures to combat ethnic conflicts because individuals from different ethnic origins will be treated as equal citizens who have equal rights before the law. However, this is not enough on its own to combat problems of power and the sharing of development benefits, especially where there is a dominant ethnic group or an inherited uneven regional economic development or uneven distribution and allocation of resources and services. These need to be resolved by constitutional and institutional arrangements, regional development programmes and equitable allocation of resources and distribution of benefits. Larry Diamond concludes from studying the experience of Nigeria that 'a structure that ensures some degree of group autonomy and security while crosscutting major ethnic solidarities can do much to prevent the polarization of politics and ethnicity'.[12]

Authoritarianism and the Right to Development

The history of most African countries since independence has been one of collapse into authoritarian rule. In Algeria and the ex-Portuguese colonies (Angola, Mozambique, Guinea Bisseau and Cape De Verde), a single party took power after the success of the national liberation war. Almost all the other

[11] M. Szeftel, 'Ethnicity and democratization in South Africa', *Review of African Political Economy*, 59–61 (1994), 185–89, p. 188.

[12] L. Diamond, 'Nigeria: pluralism, statism, and the struggle for democracy', in Diamond, Linz and Lipset, *Democracy in Developing Countries, Volume Two: Africa*, pp. 33–91, p. 69.

African countries had at the beginning of their independence multi-party democracies based on constitutions that contained bills of rights and independent judiciary systems to safeguard those rights. The dismantling of these multi-party democratic systems was carried through in one of two ways: either a military coup d'état or a civilian coup in which the ruling party became the only party in the country. Some of the military governments formed their own parties and established single party systems. Both experiences were linked with the confiscation of basic civil and political rights. The confiscation of at least one of these rights was common among all: the right to free association.[13] It was not the right to form political parties and organizations that was the only one to be confiscated, but the right to form other civil associations and organizations was seriously violated. The intervention in the trade union and students' movements by the governments or the ruling party was a common practice in all single-party regimes.[14] The freedom of expression and especially the freedom of the press came under intensive and extensive security control. 'National' or 'state' security acts were promulgated in most of the African countries to outlaw any kind of opposition and to establish special courts (state security courts) to deal with 'crimes' alleged to have been committed under such acts.[15]

Such denials of civil and political rights have been justified on the grounds of the 'right to development' or the demand for 'a new international order'. Yet the lessons of the last three decades in Africa have shown that development without the participation of the people has been an illusion. In the Horn of Africa, Sudan, Rwanda, Liberia, Chad, Angola and Mozambique, the result of the absence of civil and political rights was civil wars, famines and genocide. Without parliamentary sovereignty (and eventually accountability), and the right to information and the right to expression (especially the free press), not only were resources misused and corrupt practices became dominant, but the flight of national capital from Africa became a permanent feature. Where the human being was not taken as the subject and object of development, development ended in white-elephant projects and luxurious lifestyles for the élites and dominating class. The UN Declaration on the Right to Development defines development as, 'a comprehensive economic, social, cultural and political process, which aims at the constant improvement of the well-being of the entire population and all individuals on the basis of their *active, free and*

---

[13] Except for Kenya where KANU became a *de facto* single party in 1969 when the government banned KPU (the Kenyan Peoples Union), almost all other countries with one party systems had legislation which outlawed the formation of other political parties and which explicitly mentioned the single party as the only political party (e.g. The Permanent Constitution of the Democratic Republic of the Sudan of 1973).

[14] All the single-party regimes were authoritarian and were not keen on developing any independent mass movement. For example, Nasser succeeded in destroying any significant independent political or trade union movement as early as 1953 when parties were dissolved in Egypt.

[15] See, for example, the following reports by Africa Watch: Kenya: *Taking Liberties*, 1991; *Where Silence Rules: the Suppression of Dissent in Malawi*, 1991. In the latter country, the 1965 Public Security Regulations empowered the President to detain any one without charge. Similar regulations and acts were found in almost all African countries: e.g. Zanzibar Preventive Detention Act of 1964, Tanzania Preventive Detention Act of 1975, in Sudan the 1973 State Security Act until 1985 and the State of Emergency from 1989.

meaningful participation in development and in the fair distribution of benefits resulting therefrom' (italics added).[16]

The African Charter of Human and Peoples Rights clearly states that all people 'shall freely determine their political status and shall pursue their economic and social development according to the policy they have freely chosen'.[17] Both statements underline the integral connection between the goal of socio-economic development for all, and participation and political freedom. The main argument used to justify the undemocratic regimes in Africa was that African countries needed fast development and 'liberal' democracies would not allow that. Instead an Eastern European model of a single-party system was established by radical as well as conservative regimes. A Chinese rhetoric of 'democracy for the people and dictatorship against the people' was used by single parties both on the right and on the left. By the end of the seventies it was clear that no development was achieved and 'democracy for the people' turned out to be aggressive dictatorships against the people. One has only to look into Amnesty International and Africa Watch reports and the minutes of the United Nations Human Rights Commission to recognize the extent of the violation of human rights in Africa. On the other hand, a look at the UN specialized organizations (FAO, WHO, UNESCO etc.), World Bank and the IMF reports and statistics will show how poor, if any, was the outcome of the development effort in these countries. Economic crisis, debt crisis and famine were the result. Ten years ago the World Bank's president wrote that 'Sub-Saharan Africa today faces acute difficulties',[18] and a prominent African political economist wrote at the beginning of this decade:

> If the 1960s were characterized by the great hope of seeing an irreversible process of development launched throughout what came to be called the Third World, and in Africa particularly, the present age is one of disillusionment. Development has broken down, its theory is in crisis, its ideology the subject of doubt.[19]

Forgoing democracy to achieve development did not work in Africa.[20] On the other hand, establishing democracy will not lead automatically to economic development. Both need real effort to sustain. At the same time the struggles on the part of subordinate groups for economic improvement and for democratic rights go hand in hand. The struggle for better salaries, wages and working conditions has to pass through a struggle for independent trade unions and mass organizations, and the struggle for the right to assemble, to demonstrate and to strike. This struggle has given the democratization process two important features. The first is that it is mainly a mass movement of the dominated classes, and the second is that it is a human rights movement for civil liberties. The harsh response of the authoritarian state to such movements

[16] Declaration on the Right to Development, G.A. Re. 41/128 of 4 December 1986, 41 U.N. Supp. (No. 53) at 186, Un Doc. A/41/53 (1986).
[17] African Charter on Human and Peoples Rights, Article 20 (1).
[18] The World Bank, *Towards Substantial Development in Sub-Saharan Africa, A Joint Program of Action* (Washington DC, World Bank, 1984), p.v.
[19] S. Amin, *Maldevelopment: Anatomy of Global Failure* (Tokyo, United Nations University Press and London and New York, Zed, 1990), p. 1.
[20] Whether it has worked in other countries is a matter which has given rise to a lot of discussion in development literature especially about the experiences of South Korea and Chile.

(arbitrary detention, martial and special courts, emergency regulations and state security acts, news blackout and censorship on the news of strikes and demonstrations) has only served to widen the struggle by enlisting new forces (especially lawyers, students and intellectuals) and has deepened its human rights character to involve demands like abolition of arbitrary detention, the independence of the judiciary, the rule of law and the freedom of the press.

The Current Democratization Process

When the Sudanese people began their uprising in March 1985 that led to a bloodless coup in April and the restoration of democracy, no one thought that was the beginning of a new era in Africa. It is true that the March–April uprising in the Sudan was mainly an internal event that had no link to the international changes towards democracy that followed. Yet it was clear evidence that the struggle for democracy in Africa did not start as a response to the changes in Eastern Europe. Hence one can argue that the current democratization process is not just a response to changes in Eastern Europe or one that is imposed by donors or international pressure. In almost all the countries that have witnessed a sort of democratic change there were internal forces that were struggling for democracy and human rights.[21] The new international situation that has resulted from the changes in Eastern Europe has given a new momentum for democratization and has assisted the forces already struggling for democratic change. In some countries, like Malawi, the democratization process would not have begun at the specific time (1992) and would not have taken the same speed if the donors had not put their pressure on Banda's regime. Yet it is not correct to see the democratization process in Africa as imposed by foreign powers. In Kenya for example the struggle for democracy was a long and hard one. The 1990 events were only the climax of that struggle. Africa Watch reported:

> In Kenya, the calls for greater democracy and a multi-party system that followed were not inspired by Eastern Europe, as it has so frequently been claimed, but emboldened. There have been calls for political pluralism during both President Kenyatta's and President Moi's rules, but they have gone unheeded and unpublicized. The difference of the 1990's was that intellectuals, the church, the lawyers and activists were uniquely tuned to the collapse of one-party states. Critics could challenge the West on its continuous support of the single-party state in Kenya.[22]

Yet in Kenya, the role of donors 'was crucial in President Moi's decision to repeal the article in the constitution making Kenya a one party state and to call for elections'.[23] The situation in other African countries was not different. The local movement for democracy seized the opportunity provided by the new international changes towards democratization.

---

[21] For a discussion of the African struggle for democracy, see P. Anyang Nyongo (ed.), *Popular Struggles for Democracy in Africa* (London and New Jersey, Zed, 1987).

[22] Africa Watch, *Kenya Taking Liberties* (New York, Washington and London, Africa Watch, 1991), p. 37.

[23] Human Rights Watch, Africa: *Kenya: Multipartyism Betrayed in Kenya* (Washington and London, Human Rights Watch, 1994), p. 2. The most important pressure was the suspension of bilateral aid to Kenya by its 'consultative group' in November 1993.

Transition to Democracy: Genuine Reforms

Some of the countries did not bother to carry meaningful reforms in their constitutions and legal systems and institutions to adapt to the requirements of multi-party democracy and free and fair elections. Such requirements are defined by the UN Centre for Human Rights as prerequisite rights. The Centre singled some rights enunciated in the international human rights instruments as taking 'additional importance for election purposes'. According to a handbook produced by the Centre these are 'the rights to free opinion, free expression, information, assembly and association, independent judicial procedures and protection from discrimination'.[24]

Malawi and Benin sought the technical assistance of the UN Centre for Human Rights to prepare for the transition from single-party rule to multi-party democracy. The technical assistance was required to amend legislation including the constitution, to suggest reform in institutions and provide training and education in aspects of human rights and elections for official personnel, politicians and ordinary citizens. Both countries reached agreements to implement technical assistance programmes after the elections.

From a human rights perspective genuine institutional, legal and policy reforms are needed to enable African countries to meet their human rights' obligations. These obligations are of three kinds.[25] The first is the obligation to respect, which requires the government of the country to abstain from doing anything that violates human rights. This requires that the government abides by the universal human rights standards set in international institutions. The second obligation is to protect, which requires taking all the measures to prevent other individuals or groups from violating the standard human rights. This requires that these rights become part of the basic organic law of the country (a bill of rights in the constitution). It also requires the formation of an independent judiciary which is empowered by the constitution to protect these rights, including the protection from being violated by the government and other state organs. The case in some African countries shows that courts' decisions in this aspect are not respected by governments. The third obligation is to fulfil and promote the enjoyment of these rights by taking necessary measures that enable any person within the jurisdiction of the state to obtain the maximum possible satisfaction of these rights. This last measure is particularly important when it comes to the enjoyment of economic and social rights, some of which could not be secured by personal efforts.

What pressures are there on governments to maintain human rights standards? These come from three different sources. First is the African Charter on Human and Peoples Rights that entered into force on 21 October 1986. Under the Charter an African Commission on Human and Peoples Rights was established in 1987. Though the Commission is assigned the task of promotion, to ensure the protection of human and peoples rights, it has no judiciary powers of its own. It is an arm of the OAU to which it submits reports that do not include recommendations. Despite this shortcoming, the African Commission is playing an increasing role in human rights documentation,

[24] United Nations' Centre for Human Rights, *Human Rights and Elections* (New York and Geneva, United Nations, 1994), p. 6.
[25] A. Eide, 'Realization of social and economic rights and the minimum threshold approach', *Human Rights Law Journal*, 10 (1989), p. 37.

training and education in Africa. The hope is that the African human rights machinery will evolve towards establishing an African human rights court.

Second is the pressure from NGOs in documenting human rights abuses, and exposing the gap between government obligations under international treaties and their actual practice. International NGOs have played a substantial role in monitoring and disclosing information on human rights. Recently there has been a significant increase in the number of African NGOs working on human rights at national, regional and sub-regional levels. One dilemma here is that such activity presupposes the existence of civil rights for such organizations to operate effectively in their own country.

Finally is the role played by the international community in promoting human rights. The World Conference on Human Rights has suggested measures to improve the machinery of the UN in this respect. The problem of the international machinery is that its role is limited to monitoring, discussing, investigating and condemning. Discussions are continuing on how the international community could enforce its decisions on the respect and protection of human rights. It is beyond the scope of this article to discuss all the possible options. However, one of the options linking the respect of human rights to economic aid, known as political conditionality, deserves consideration here.

Democratization, Human Rights and Political Conditionality

Political conditions for aid and economic assistance are not new in international relations, though for most of the time they have been implicit. Respect for human rights as a political condition is rather new. In the USA this can be traced back to the creation of the Sub-Committee on International Organizations and Movements of the House Foreign Affairs Committee in the mid-seventies. The hearings of the Sub-Committee and the further discussions in the House and Congress led to the adoption of the Tom Hakim Amendment to the International Development and Food Assistance Act.[26] According to the amendment, the USA declared the respect of human rights as a condition for American economic aid.[27]

The joint declaration of the European Parliament, the Commission and the Council of Ministers in 1977 was a step towards bringing the human rights issue into the foreign policy of the EEC. In 1986 a second step was taken when the foreign ministers of the European Community decided that respect for human rights was a fundamental principle in co-operation between the EEC and other countries. This was reflected in the Lomé Convention between the EEC and the ACP (African, Caribbean and Pacific) countries, for example in Lomé IV, which required the parties to the Convention to respect human rights.

Political conditionality has now become an issue of foreign policy of most Western developed countries. In the implementation of this policy a number of different pressures can be discerned. One is state interests in the support of

[26] K. Kumado, 'Conditionality: an analysis of the policy of linking development aid to the implementation of human rights standards', *The Review*, 50 (Geneva, The International Commission of Jurists, 1993), pp. 23–30.

[27] The US was criticized as being selective and not genuine in applying the condition on its close allies (Chile, Iran, Sudan, Egypt ... etc.).

regional allies. Another is the trading and investment interests of powerful domestic corporations. A third is the pressure of public opinion responding to widely publicized human rights abuses. Together these result in often inconsistent application of 'conditionality' both between countries and towards the same country over time.

These differing pressures are reflected in two quite different trends in assessing the conditions for effective democracy. One trend wants to link democratization with market economies and to more integration of developing countries' markets in the international economy. This trend links democratization with the IMF/World Bank's structural adjustment and stabilization policies. They rediscovered Barrington Moore's famous dictum, 'no middle class, no democracy'.[28] According to this trend, structural adjustment serves two objectives in pursuing the privatization of public enterprises and the limitation of the role of state in the economy. These are the creation or widening of the local bourgeoisie or middle class and limiting the possibilities of rent-seeking accumulation, corruption and mis-allocation of resources including aid assistance. 'The moving away from statist economic policies and structures', Larry Diamond argues, 'is among the most significant boost to the democratic prospect in Africa'.[29] This trend ignores the other face of the coin, that the implementation of structural adjustment and stabilization policies erodes the legitimacy of the African state, whether authoritarian or democratic. Bjorn Beckman has developed a strong axiom: '(the) political crisis of the African state is also the crisis of SAP'.[30] The simple fact is that opposition to structural adjustment was a driving force towards the recent democratization. The African masses, especially in the urban areas, broke their silence in response to the structural programmes which were imposed by the old two allies: the African authoritarian state and the IMF/World Bank. The incomplete implementation of SAP in some African countries (sometimes even the withdrawal of announced measures), was due to the resistance of the masses (the bread riots so called in Egypt and Morocco). It is hence logical to question the chances of SAP under a democratic regime as well as the future of a democratic regime that attempts adopting SAP.

Within this first tendency the IMF/World Bank are concerned with 'good governance' as a condition which is claimed to lack any *political* significance. The Bank, in a paper presented to the World Conference on Human Rights, asserts that its 'approach to governance focuses on technical criteria connected to efficiency and rationality in the use of national resources'.[31] The Bank makes clear in its paper that its mandate 'excludes explicit consideration of political rights in decisions on assistance activities in borrowing member countries'.[32] How does the Bank interpret 'good governance'? It is 'helping achieve the

[28] D. K. Emmerson, 'Capitalism, democracy and the World Bank: what is to be done?', in Deng, Kostner and Young, *Democratisation and Structural Adjustment in Africa in the 1990s* (African Studies Program, University of Wisconsin-Madison, 1991), pp. 9–12.

[29] Diamond, 'Introduction: roots of failure, seeds of hope', p. 27.

[30] B. Beckman, 'Empowerment or repression? The World Bank and the politics of African adjustment' in P. Gibbon, Y. Bangura and K. Ofsted (eds), *Authoritarianism, Democracy and Adjustment, The Politics of Economic Reform* (Uppsala, Noriska Afrikaninstitutet, 1992), p. 87.

[31] World Conference on Human Rights, *Contribution from the World Bank, The World Bank and the Promotion of Human Rights* (Vienna, United Nations, General Assembly, A/CONF.157/PC?61/ Add.19, 10 June 1993), p. 12.

[32] World Conference on Human Rights, *Contribution from the World Bank*, pp. 12–3.

goals of openness, transparency and accountability'. The Bank's focus on governance

> is limited to those aspects which affect economic development directly, but this extends beyond building the capacity of public sector management. It encourages the formation of the *rules* and *institutions* which provide a predictable and transparent framework for the conduct of business, and promotes *accountability* for economic and financial performance. This includes, at macro level, encouraging audit reforms and strengthening the capability and accountability of ministers and other public entities. At the micro level, it includes encouraging the participation of NGOs and project beneficiaries.[33]

A second trend sees democracy as integrally linked to human rights, and to the democratization, rather than simply the marketization, of civil society and its institutions. This view, shared by most NGOs and human rights activists in both donor and receiving countries, seeks to tie economic aid more closely to the respect for human rights, and to a genuine rather than merely token democratization on the part of the governments receiving aid. This trend has had some success in bringing pressure upon both national and international donors. However, it remains an open question how far a more narrowly economic interpretation of the criteria required for acceptable government will prevail.

Human Rights after Multi-party Elections

Violations of human rights have continued after multi-party elections in most of the countries where these have been held. The situation in Zaire was more disastrous than others. The war in Angola has restarted, endangering the most fundamental human right: the right to life. The Ethiopian experience after the overthrow of the Derg is not satisfactory on several aspects of human rights. This does not only endanger the democratization process in that country, but bears the risk of violent ethnic conflicts. A recent article summarized the human rights situation in Africa:

> More often than not, however, political leaders vowed to respect human rights even as their security forces continued to illegally detain, torture and kill citizens without fear of being brought to justice. Human rights organizations documented killing by the state in Angola, Burundi, Chad, Liberia, Rwanda, Somalia, South Africa and Zaire during 1993. This year, thousands of citizens have been victimized by those same soldiers.[34]

A brief comparison of four countries – Zambia, Kenya, Nigeria and South Africa – will show how patchy the record for human rights has been. During 1993 the elected government of Zambia failed to respond to enquiries on the arbitrary detention of some members of the opposition. On 4 March 1993, the elected President declared a state of emergency. Though the state of emergency was lifted on 25 May, what happened during its period of imposition was a clear violation of human rights. Twenty-six people were detained for different

---

[33] World Conference on Human Rights, *Contribution from the World Bank*, p. 12.
[34] B. J. Kello, 'Human rights, a sorry record', in *Africa Report*, 39.6 (November–December 1994), 59–63, p. 63.

periods before only seven were charged. Some of these detainees were ill-treated during detention.[35] Yet the experience of the state of emergency also revealed one positive aspect of the new democracy in Zambia: the role of an independent judiciary in the democratic system. The detainees were able to contest their detention before the High Court. Even the question of the ill-treatment of the detainees was tackled by the court, which ordered a medical examination to be carried out by doctors appointed by both the government and the detainees. Its positive impact, however, was reduced by the fact that though medical examination proved the ill-treatment, no action was taken against those responsible.[36]

Kenya held its first multi-party elections for 30 years in December 1993. The Kenya African National Party (KANU) continued to rule the country after gaining one hundred of the 188 elected seats. President Moi was returned to office. Kenya is a case where both internal and external forces had acted to initiate the democratization process; but it was the pressure of the external forces (the donors) that compelled President Moi to call for a multi-party election. The Kenyan regime went to the elections in a half-hearted manner, complaining that multi-partyism would rehabilitate tribalism. Many observers accused the Kenyan government of having provoked tribal violence before and after the elections to prove its case.[37] The election itself was not considered by many as free and fair.[38] Following the election all sorts of violations of human rights were reported by human rights organizations and observers. Arbitrary detention and restrictions on the freedom of the press continued in Kenya after the multi-party elections. Human Rights Watch/Africa reported that out of 85 opposition members of the Parliament, 35 were jailed 'at different times for at least short periods'.[39]

A year after the elections, the Catholic Bishops in Kenya expressed their concern in a pastoral letter:

> Only one year after multi-party elections, the hopes of Kenyans have been shattered by the evident derailment of the democratization process. There are visible signs of unwillingness of the government to fully accept the democratization process in Kenya.... There have been calculated moves to silence the voices of democracy, as seen in the arrests, confinement in police cells, and arraignment in courts of protagonists of democracy under flimsy charges. Such acts are aimed at intimidating and defaming the victims, as well as other potential supporters of justice and peace. The continued harassment of a section of the media and the banning of some publications are but some of the incidences of the government's efforts to barricade the corridors of democracy that had begun to open.[40]

---

[35] Human Rights Watch/Africa, *Zambia: Model for Democracy Declares State of Emergency* (1994).

[36] This happened despite the fact that the Zambian Constitution of 1991 prevents ill-treatment of detainees.

[37] Human Rights Watch/Africa, *Kenya: Multipartyism Betrayed in Kenya* (1994), p. 2.

[38] For example, see the Report of the Commonwealth Observer Group, *The Presidential, Parliamentary and Civic Elections in Kenya* (The Commonwealth Secretariat, 1993), p. 40, and the critique of the Kenyan group Mwakenya 'Democratisation in Kenya: should the Left participate or not?', *Review of African Political Economy*, 61 (1994), 475–8.

[39] Human Rights Watch/Africa, *Kenya: Multipartyism Betrayed in Kenya*, p. 22.

[40] Quoted in Human Rights Watch/Africa, *Kenya, Multipartyism Betrayed in Kenya*, p. 1.

The aftermath of the election was mostly characterized by continuing tribal violence that resulted in hundreds of deaths. The opposition parties, both the Catholic and Anglican Churches, and human rights NGOs blame the Kenyan government for initiating, organizing and encouraging the conflict. The government is also accused of exploiting the troubles to declare emergency measures, to restrict the freedom of movement and public meeting and the freedom of the press.

Nigeria presents the extreme case where the result of an election held in June 1993 was rejected by the military government, reversing the democratization process and taking a country into a deep political crisis. The annulled election itself raises many questions about basic civil rights in Nigeria. The first was the military government's decision to limit the number of parties allowed to participate in the election to two. The two parties were in reality formed by the government, and had to reflect in their programme a general national philosophy.[41] This was a clear violation of the right to association. The second was banning 'old politicians' from participation in political life, including forming or participating in the two political parties and hence standing for elections. This was another violation of human rights. The pre-election period witnessed the detention of Nigerians who opposed the military government, 'critical newspapers were shut down, and the courts were routinely barred from questioning military decrees'.[42]

The decision to annul the elections sparked off protests and led to serious violations of human rights. 'During riots in Lagos and other southern cities, soldiers killed more than 150 people', reported Human Rights Watch/Africa.[43] The international community intervened to back the call to respect the result of the presidential election. The US, UK and other Western governments cut off their non-humanitarian aid. General Babangida, the head of the military government, was compelled to resign in August 1993. For three months only the country was nominally under a civilian administration appointed by the military and headed by Ernest Shonekan. In November 1993 the military assumed full power under General Abacha. Since then Nigeria has witnessed the continuous violation of human rights. Paul Adams, the Financial Times correspondent in Lagos, wrote, 'Nigeria is now an absolute military dictatorship'.[44]

The Nigerian experience from 1985, when the military dismantled the Second Republic, is a great set-back to democratization in Africa. This is not only because Nigeria is the country with the biggest population and enormous economic potential, but because it has developed a markedly democratic culture. Since the civil war it has also been able to avoid violent ethnic conflict within its federal system of government. The annulled presidential election results have proved that Nigerians can unite behind a member of an ethnic minority and that Christian Nigerians can vote for a Muslim as their political leader.

---

[41] For an interesting discussion, see Larry Diamond, 'Nigeria: pluralism, statism, and the struggle for democracy', pp. 77–9; and Joseph Okoroji, 'The Nigerian presidential elections' in *Review of African Political Economy*', 58 (November 1993), 123–31.

[42] Human Rights Watch/Africa, *Nigeria: 42. 'The Dawn of a New Dark Age'* (October 1994), p. 3.

[43] Human Rights Watch/Africa, *Nigeria: 'The Dawn of a New Dark Age'*, p. 3.

[44] P. Adams, 'Reign of the generals', *Africa Report*, 39.6 (November–December 1994), p. 27.

The April 1994 elections in South Africa were the result of long negotiations and compromise which involved most of the political actors in the country. The situation of human rights has improved substantially, and a bill of rights is now entrenched in the Constitution. Yet the national transitional government has to resolve some substantial problems if democracy is to be consolidated in South Africa.

Most urgent of these problems is the substantial improvement of the living conditions of the black African majority. This requires the resolution of problems of unemployment, housing and social services, to mention only some. The experience of the post-colonial state in Africa shows that most of its legitimacy crises have been organically related to the failure to meet the expectations of the people. It is true that the main responsibility in solving the economic problem lies with the transitional government and the ANC as the main partner, but the international community must bear its share of that responsibility.

The second problem facing the consolidation of democracy is the peaceful transformation of the state apparatus from one that served an oppressive state to one that serves a democratic one. This is not only a question of replacing some of the white personnel of the civil service, the police, the security and the army with black personnel, and recruiting black Africans to change the relative racial composition of these organs of the state. It is also the building of an efficient, transparent and accountable state machinery. There is a strong link between the transparency and accountability of the different state organs and the respect of human rights, the sovereignty of the rule of law as guarded by an independent judiciary and the equity of the citizens before the law.

The third problem is the tackling of the ethnic plurality of South African Society. The political compromise solution has involved substantial devolution to provincial assemblies and governments. Experience in African countries with plural ethnic composition, however, shows that devolution of political authority without devolution of financial authority and providing enough funds does not solve the problem of power sharing. The even regional allocation of resources and distribution of benefits provide a necessary base for national unity.

Conclusion

This article has discussed the situation of human rights and the process of democratization in Africa. It has argued that the violation of human rights was a common practice before the start of the recent democratization process in Africa. It investigates whether the new developments have led to any substantial improvement in human rights. It questions whether it is possible to establish any democratic society without establishing legislation, institutions and mechanisms that promote and safeguard the respect of human rights according to the standards set by the international instruments. It argues that to sustain the democratization process in Africa, and eventually anywhere, the respect and preservation of human rights must be an organic element in that process. Respect of human rights is a necessary element in the democratization process. It concludes that contemporary events in many African countries, where multi-party elections did take place, have shown that the question of human rights has not been taken seriously. This is likely to lead eventually to the collapse of the democratic process either by halting it at the level of periodical decorative elections that bring the same ruling party to power (the case of Kenya), or its reversal to a new military or civilian dictatorship (the case of Nigeria). There is also the possibility of unstable democracies rising from a conflict between those who want to complete the democratization process and those who want to halt it at a point short of the respect of universal human rights.

A further weakness of the democratization process is that in most African countries there is no class capable of asserting a leadership or hegemonic role within society.[45] Despite the quantitative change in the class structure and the effects of the process of accumulation of capital that has been accompanied by enhancing the role of the local bourgeoisie in national economies, the African bourgeoisie has not been able to generate an ideological and intellectual discourse that would rally the masses under its leadership. The prevailing economic crisis and the harsh austerity measures required by the international financial institutions and donors decrease their chances of reaching compromises on the demands for better living conditions of the masses. This will endanger the stability of the new democracies, especially where there are independent mass organizations. The gap between the state and the institutions of civil society increases and the relations between them become more tense. This again creates a tendency within the state to limit the autonomy of civil society, and to impose restrictions on civil rights. In these circumstances the way to authoritarianism opens up again.

To avoid such a scenario, the democratization process needs patience and tolerance in working compromises, as it needs backing by relaxing the austerity measures and by the provision of more economic assistance. It is not enough to include the respect of human rights and the establishment of multi-party democracy as a new political conditionality in international and bilateral relations. There is a need to support them by economic measures. It is true there is a trend to support the building of political institutions, independent judiciary systems and to train political activists.[46] Larry Diamond has noticed that:

> the US Agency for International Development (AID) has from $5.3 million in 1990 to about $19.3 million in fiscal year 1994 increased its support for democratic governance programs in Africa (election assistance, constitutional drafting, regulatory reform, strengthening legislatures and judiciaries, and fostering local participation and empowerment).[47]

But, as Diamond himself noticed, there is also a need for urgent and substantial economic assistance for the new democracies, for *'suffering must be relieved and economic growth renewed if democracy is to have a chance of making it over the long run'*[48] (italics added).

---

[45] S. A. M. Kaballo (1994), *The Political Economy of Crisis in the Sudan 1973–85* (Ph.D. Thesis, University of Leeds, 1994), ch. 1, pp. 8–12.

[46] L. Diamond, 'Democracy the new wind', *Africa Report* (March/April 1994), p. 52.

[47] Diamond, 'Democracy the new wind', p. 52.

[48] Diamond, 'Democracy the new wind', p. 53.

Regime Security and Human Rights in Southeast Asia

KENNETH CHRISTIE*

This article will examine the Southeast Asian discourse on human rights that has emerged in the 1990s. This discourse is premised on the claims that there exists a 'unique' set of Asian values; and that these justify claims to be 'special' and 'different'. I will make the case that these claims serve as a device for authoritarian regimes in the region to enhance their own, often declining, legitimacy, and protect the security of their particular regime, in a context in which the excuse authoritarian governments employed in the past to justify repression – the need to prevent the spread of communism – has been rendered irrelevant by the end of the Cold War. Despite attempts by many of these regimes to silence and intimidate dissidents and opposition politicians, alternative voices are making democratic inroads as witnessed by declining shares of the popular vote for ruling one-party systems. Democratization in other words is not something simply confined to the former states of the Soviet bloc; it appears to be a global phenomenon and in Southeast Asia many governments are on the defensive. An examination of the claims of these regimes and their defenders to be protecting a distinctive set of Asian values will suggest that, behind the principled assertion of difference, lies a more fundamental concern for their own regime security.[1]

'Western' Versus 'Asian' Discourses

In Southeast Asia calls for the development of a system of human rights based on what are presumed to be uniform 'Asian' values and norms have become fairly frequent. Within the specific regional context, a vigorous debate has developed over the right of Western societies to impose their human rights standards on non-Western nations.[2]

*I am grateful to Dr Denny Roy of the Political Science Department at the National University of Singapore and Dr Stephen Wrage, Visiting Fellow at the National University of Singapore, for their comments on an earlier draft of this paper.

[1] Sometimes the distinction between scholars and regime officials is difficult to tell in Southeast Asia. I use a combination of leaders, officials and academics to make their case. Other scholars not from the region have perhaps made the Third World case much more forcefully. See F. Ajami, *Human Rights and World Order Policies*, World Orders Model Project Working Paper, no. 4 (New York, 1978), cited in S. Hoffmann, *Duties Beyond Borders* (Syracuse, Syracuse University Press, 1981), pp. 172 and 242.

[2] See J. Wanandi, 'Human rights and democracy in the ASEAN nations: the next 25 years', *The Indonesian Quarterly*, XXI (1993), 14–37; B. Kausikan, 'Asia's different standard', *Foreign Policy*, 92 (1993), 24–41; and R. Isberto, 'ASEAN adopts pragmatic view of human rights', *The Jakarta Post*, (28/2/94), p. 4, for claims of 'difference'.

National leaders have become increasingly sensitive to Western accusations of rights violations as their economies have experienced dramatic growth. When the Dutch Government criticized the human rights position in Indonesia after the 1991 Dili incident in East Timor, Indonesia rejected Dutch aid and disbanded the Inter-Governmental Group on Indonesia (IGGI).[3] In June 1993, Myanamar's Foreign Minister U Ohn Gyaw addressed the United Nations conference on human rights stating in opposition to Western ideas about the international policing of human rights that 'there is no unique model of human rights implementation that can be superimposed on a given country'.[4] Ali Alatas, Indonesia's foreign minister was in the forefront of the indignant responses to Western accusations and refutations of Western models. At the United Nations Conference in Vienna in 1993 he argued:

> In a world where domination of the strong over the weak and interference between states are still a painful reality, no country or group of countries should arrogate unto itself the role of judge, jury, and executioner over other countries on this critical and sensitive issue. Any approach to human rights questions which is not motivated by a sincere desire to protect these rights, but by disguised political purposes or, worse, to serve as a pretext to wage a political campaign against another country cannot be justified.[5]

In June 1993, the Voice of Myanamar radio station carried a speech by General Than Shwe, which argued in similar fashion:

> The external forces that bear malice towards us are inciting the people by using human rights and democracy as an excuse. The Western countries' human rights and standards of democracy cannot be the same as our Asian standards. We must choose the human rights standard and the democratic path compatible with the tradition of our country and people.[6]

Thailand's former foreign minister in 1993 also argued that 'because of some weaknesses of our inner constitution, outsiders have taken advantage and try to make Asia a target practice'.[7]

Clearly, Southeast Asian leaders like Lee Kuan Yew, Mahathir and Suharto among others are increasingly prepared to speak out against Western conceptions of human rights and what they see as attempts to interfere with their domestic, internal affairs as their dynamic economies become more and more powerful.[8] Their assertion of different Asian values and standards involves several key issues, including whether human rights are universal or particularistic, whether human rights are Western, and whether human rights should be linked to questions of national development. Each of these issues will be explored in what follows.

[3] See Kausikan, 'Asia's different standard', p. 29.

[4] See 'Protest as Burma addresses rights meet' *Bangkok Post*, (19/6/1993), p. 11.

[5] See *The Straits Times*, (Singapore, 16/6/93), p. 1.

[6] *Straits Times* (Singapore, 16/6/93) p. 4.

[7] Quoted in L. R. Sussman, 'The essential role of human rights', *The World and I*, (July 1993), p. 41.

[8] See M. Richardson, 'East Asia spurns West's cultural model', in the *International Herald Tribune*, (13/7/92), p. 22.

Human Rights: Universalism Versus Relativism

The human rights issue is often politicized into a battle between the West and the developing world. From the latter's point of the view, the West promotes a universal approach, forcing a single conception of human rights – the Western conception – upon the rest of the world. Western theorists, on the other hand, often argue that cultural relativism is an attempt by human rights violators to deflect criticism from their own record.

Relativists offer two critiques of the universalist approach. First, they argue that, despite commonalities, circumstances vary widely enough among individual societies to require differing conceptions of human rights. The specific application of policy is therefore best left to each community to decide for itself. Among the various possible interpretations of rights, none is necessarily better than any other. Indonesia's conception of human rights, based on its own unique experience, is right for Indonesia, Malaysia's is right for Malaysia. The outside world should respect the choices made by individual nation-states.

Secondly, relativists charge the universalists with cultural imperialism. Universalists are considered contemptuous of the principle of non-interference in other peoples' internal affairs and arrogant in their belief that their own conception of rights must apply to everyone. Malaysian Prime Minister Mahathir Mohammed says Western pressure on developing countries over human rights and democratization is intended to cause 'instability, economic decline and poverty. With such a situation, they can threaten and control us'.[9]

The most important and vociferous challenge to the Western creed of universalism has emerged from the highly dynamic growth countries of Southeast Asia, where governments and scholars tend to emphasize the differences between their societies and those in the developed, democratic states. Such states emphasize that countries vary greatly in size, population, standard of living, resource endowments, historical background, culture, ethnic and religious composition and diversity, internal political stability, external security, and so on. Furthermore, human rights themselves involve a complex package of privileges and obligations. Therefore, while all governments should recognize the importance of upholding human rights, each individual country should be allowed to interpret and implement this goal according to its own circumstances.

In response to pressure from the United States, for example, one Filipino observes that America is 'a country that is very rich and stable, and where the government does not have to worry in the same way that most governments have to worry about how their people are going to eat and where they can earn enough for a decent standard of existence'.[10] Accordingly, these Western-inspired concepts and institutions may be appropriate for Europe and North America, but they are alien, unworkable, and perhaps even destructive if introduced into non-Western settings.

---

[9] See 'West has ulterior motives for pushing democracy', *Straits Times*, (Singapore, 31/8/94), p. 14.

[10] See H. G. Guitterez Jr., 'Human rights – an overview' in V. Quisimbumg (ed.), *The New Constitution and Human Rights* (Quezon City, Phillipines, 1979), p. 42.

Communitarianism Versus Individualism

The arguments being made in Southeast Asia often hold that their cultures favour protecting the community at the expense of restricting the freedoms of the individual, while the West takes the opposite approach. James Hsiung argues that 'pressing for one's own interests without regard to the interests of others is seen as no more than the pursuit of individual self-interest, not the pursuit of human rights defined as rights of fellow humans'.[11] Empirically-based assertions are also prominent: the high rates of violent crime, divorce, drug use and homelessness in much of the West, particularly the United States, appear to confirm that the Western model has failed. Over-protection of criminals and deviants has made life miserable for all society. Newspapers in Southeast Asia delight in publishing all the details of the 'decline' of the West, contrasting their thriving, efficient and crime-free states with the decadent, recession-hit, chaotic West.

Singapore's Lee Kuan Yew often speaks of America's narcotics crisis as the epitome of the larger problem of individual versus community rights:

> To protect the community we have passed laws which entitle police, drug enforcement or immigration officers to have the urine of any person who behaves in a suspicious way tested for drugs. If the result is positive, treatment is compulsory. Such a law in the United States will be unconstitutional, because it will be an invasion of privacy of the individual ... So in the United States the community's interests have been sacrificed because of the drug traffickers and drug consumers. Drug related crimes flourish. Schools are infected. There is high delinquency and violence among students, a high dropout rate, poor discipline and teaching, producing students who make poor workers.[12]

To avoid such social deterioration, these writers argue, the rights of the community as a whole must override those of the individual.

The question of imprisonment provides a concrete illustration of the different approaches to community and individual rights. In the US judicial system, the plaintiffs carry the burden of proof, and safeguards against a wrongful conviction are so rigorous that obviously guilty defendants are sometimes acquitted. In Southeast Asia, however, imprisonment without fair, public trials is widespread. An *Asiaweek* editorial defends governments that 'have weighed the risks of jailing the wrong man and concluded that more innocent people are put in danger by letting criminals go for lack of evidence. Critics of preventive detention ought to consider whether the common good should be endangered to protect the civil liberties of a few'.[13]

An intrinsic element of the Western conception is that rights belong to individual human beings, that the struggle for these rights has been in part defined by a struggle against a reluctant state; notions of free speech, free assembly and fair trial have all embodied the idea that the right of the individual against the state has to be protected. Southeast Asian societies,

---

[11] See J. Hsiung, *Human Rights in East Asia: a Cultural Perspective* (New York, Paragon House, 1985), p. 25.
[12] See L. K. Yew, 'Be prepared to intervene directly or don't force pace of change West told', *Straits Times* (Singapore, 21/11/92), p. 31.
[13] See 'The rule of law', *Asiaweek*, (23/3/94), p. 26.

however, are more willing to assert the rights of the group; the group, not the individual, is the starting point in any analysis. From this standpoint, obligations to the community are more important than rights procured from it. This more communitarian conception has been articulated by one of ASEAN's senior statesmen as follows:

> Whether in periods of golden prosperity or in the depths of disorder, Asia has never valued the individual over society. The society has always been more important than the individual. I think that is what has saved Asia from greater misery ... I believe that human-rights standards, as distinct from democracy as a form of government, will become universal. It will not be western standards, because the West is but a minority in this world.[14]

Privileges Versus Entitlements

In the Western tradition, abuse of power by political élites is considered a constant danger. Wise and selfless autocrats are the exception rather than the rule. The history of politics in the Western countries, therefore, has largely concerned the struggle of private citizens to win their freedoms, viewed as natural or God-given rights, from reluctant governments and to preserve these liberties through institutionalization.

Southeast Asian regimes, however, are premised on a completely different view of the relationship between state and society. Here, leaders are traditionally believed to be morally and intellectually superior to the common people. In ancient China, for example, the quality of rulers was supposed to be ensured by the government's civil service examination system, which measured knowledge of classical Confucian writings. Scoring well on the examination would indicate both scholastic skill and familiarity with the codes of virtuous behaviour – appropriate preparation for state officials.

Southeast Asian rulers consequently receive much greater trust than their Western counterparts. People may grumble in private about autocratic leaders but they still defer to them and often vote them back into power or acquiesce in their perpetuity. Compared to Western Europeans and North Americans, East Asians are more likely to accept that individual liberties must be sacrificed for the state to carry out its role of maintaining the security, stability and prosperity of society as a whole. What political rights the people do enjoy are viewed as privileges, gifts from a benevolent leadership, rather than entitlements. This is in line with Confucian ideals regarding government and society.

These differences of political tradition provide convenient ammunition in human rights debates with the West. If the Western understanding of human rights is closely bound up with the West's culture and historical experience, some Asian theorists assert, it cannot serve as an appropriate guide for regions with a vastly different cultural and historical background. Such differences extend to personal behaviour also: 'For an East Asian not to know the rules – that is, to avoid ostentatious confrontation and to observe the need for balancing "freedom of" with "freedoms from" – would be almost incredible'.[15] Many regional commentators assert that 'Asian' and 'Western' values in this

---

[14] See 'The democracy debate – SM', *Straits Times* (Singapore, 17/6/93).
[15] See Hsiung, *Human Rights in East Asia*, p. 25.

respect are fundamentally different. Asians, they typically say, value family obligations, chastity, and hard work, while Westerners are obsessed with their own personal gratification and lack any sense of social responsibility.[16]

Human Rights and Development

Most Southeast Asian states are or have recently been authoritarian rather than democratic, and developing rather than developed. Most regional theorists and politicians therefore argue that their countries should focus on economic progress first, with the expectation that some degree of political liberalization will follow later. Built into this position are the assumptions that economic/social rights are more important than civil/political rights, and that the latter actually hinder economic development.

Southeast Asian societies have formulated two major views when it comes to development. Firstly, development is a collective activity and is primarily supplied by state agencies and other groups in society. Secondly it is an economic and social process perhaps requiring in the short term the infraction of classical civil and political rights. Choice, for instance, might not be so important in employment as in the state directing labour towards certain development projects. The formation of trade unions to protect workers' rights is clearly less important than development goals which in turn might infringe human rights in the process. There is no promise or even proof that, once such development goals have been reached, civil and political rights will be extended to citizens; no social contract is sealed in stone in this process. In the end the fulfilment of collective rights requires the postponement of individual political rights until the perceived level of development is reached in which the latter become less of a comparative luxury. Implicit here is the assumption of a trade-off between basic needs and luxuries, with human rights (in the Western sense) falling into the latter category.[17] Otherwise, there would be no need to leave human rights aside until development was consolidated.

Here we encounter the hotly-debated issue of whether or not authoritarian government is necessary for successful economic and social development. Those who posit this view argue that nation-building requires discipline, austerity, and obedience to measures that may be unpopular in the short run but will yield great dividends in the future. In such circumstances, effectively a national emergency, governments cannot ensure the successful prosecution of their policies without limiting civil liberties such as the freedoms of speech and of the press, the right of accused criminals to a fair trial, freedom from physical abuse by the police, and so on. As a society becomes wealthier, more orderly and more educated, civil and political privileges will naturally increase. But if the basic goals of development are not achieved, all subsequent aspirations,

---

[16] Denny Roy argues succinctly that this challenge to the West begins 'much like the West's traditional Orientalist scholarship, with the premise that Asia and the West are fundamentally different. But this time Asia turns the tables by making the West its Other, contrasting favourable "Asian" traits such as industriousness, filial piety, selflessness, and chastity, with caricatures of negative "Western" culture'. See D. Roy, 'Singapore, China and the "soft authoritarian" challenge', *Asian Survey*, XXXIV (1994) 232–3.

[17] See J. Donnelly, 'Human rights and development: complementary or competing concerns' in G. W. Shepherd Jr. and V. P. Nanda (eds), *Human Rights and Third World Development* (Westport, Greenwood, 1985), pp. 27–8.

including human rights, are doomed. It is therefore unfair for the West whose sense of human rights developed within its political and historical context to demand that poor, politically unstable underdeveloped countries immediately guarantee as broad a range of individual freedoms as exists in the developed world. The problem with this is the uncertainty of when a society becomes developed enough to embrace human rights; at what stage does it determine that human rights are not expedient and are elevated to a different plane in terms of priority?

In contrast to this sequential approach to human rights, others argue for concurrency: human rights, particularly civil liberties, do not threaten economic and social development, and therefore can and should be implemented immediately even by Third World countries. These theorists question the logic of the argument that civil liberties undermine nation-building. Allowing fair, constructive political debate of major policy issues, protecting citizens from torture by state authorities and from imprisonment without a fair trial, and permitting freedom of worship are not incompatible with economic development. Indeed, preservation of these rights is likely to increase a government's legitimacy and encourage hard work and sacrifice for national goals. In this light, Western-style human rights are seen as a benefit, even a necessity, for the poor, not a luxury of the rich. As empirical support for this argument, proponents could point out many cases in which restrictions on civil liberties coincided with economic stagnation rather than economic progress – the Philippines under Ferdinand Marcos, India during Indira Gandhi's 'emergency', and the Soviet Union and Eastern Europe under communist rule.

Critiquing the Debate on Human Rights

How convincing should we judge the argument against universal human rights based on a theory of 'Asian distinctiveness'? Central to this argument is a rejection of the individualist tendency of 'Western' human rights and democracy, and the claim that it will undermine the social cohesion deriving from a more collectivist tradition. Warnings such as those of the Singapore government in 1990 about the Western 'vice of individualism' are common-place.[18]

However, we could question whether it is the human rights agenda that constitutes the chief source of individualist challenge, rather than social changes taking place in the societies themselves. Most societies in Southeast Asia have been significantly modernized and this has led to an increasing role for the individual and in turn the development of the individual's relationship to the state. Certainly in some countries (the United States and Western Europe), the process of modernization has been implemented far earlier and more rapidly than in many countries in the developing world, but still the consequences of industrialization and modernization inevitably leads to greater emphasis on the individual. Traditions are eroded by these processes as

---

[18] See T. L. Tan, *The Singapore Press: Freedom Responsibility and Credibility* (Singapore, Times Academic, IPS Occasional Paper No. 3, 1990), p. 5. Ironically, one aspect of popular culture in Singapore, Kiasuism (which means 'scared to lose' in Hokkien), is obsessively selfish and far more individualistic than anything the West could produce.

individuals become divided by class, status, occupation, sex, religion and education, among other factors. Many Southeast Asian societies are already feeling the impact of these processes as they rapidly industrialize; increasing divorce, crime and drug rates are the symptoms of such change. This was and is the case in the West and there is no reason to believe that Eastern cultures in all their variety will be immune to the problems of industrialization and modernization. Self-centred individualism is rapidly becoming the norm in East and Southeast Asia as governments move to reinvent and reassert their different versions of Asian values upon their own populations and these versions are not necessarily uniform.

It is not the individualistic tendency of Western human rights that undermines traditional, family-oriented societies in Southeast Asia but the processes of industrialization and urbanization which in turn produces an increasing individualization of society.[19] One party regimes have themselves acknowledged the trends towards individual behaviour; in a Government White Paper released in 1991, the People's Action party of Singapore stated that 'traditional Asian ideas of morality, duty and society which have sustained and guided us in the past are giving way to a more Westernized, individualistic and self-centred outlook on life'.[20] However, when Lee Kuan Yew, Mahathir and Suharto cite the moral disintegration and decay in Western societies as a result of too much liberal allowance for individual rights and democracy, they choose to ignore the evidence that individualism is the consequence not of democracy and human rights, but of industrialization, increasing literacy rates and other changes at the societal level. The contrast between societies that are characterized by individualism, selfishness and materialism and those that display community and family values is difficult to maintain except in rhetorical terms.[21]

The claim therefore that a Western inspired individualism will undermine traditional communitarian values, overlooks the irreversible social changes that are already undermining them. A similar objection can be made to the claim that a rights-based democracy is inconsistent with the drive for economic development, which is after all their societies' primary economic and social goal.[22] Again this argument is misleading. Recent research has reasserted the ideas of modernization theory that socio-economic development itself is one of the most important factors in democratization; countries in East Asia (such as Taiwan and South Korea) and Latin America were all prompted to turn towards increasing democracy by high levels of economic growth in the 1980s. So the case can be made for the correlation being the opposite of Southeast Asian claims. It is not individualism and democracy which will undermine economic growth; it is economic growth which will undermine authoritarianism and lead

[19] A useful overview of this can be found in R. E. Howard and J. Donnelly, 'Introduction' in Donnelly and Howard (eds), *International Handbook of Human Rights* (New York, Greenwood, 1987), p. 15.

[20] See the White Paper, *Shared Values* (Singapore, Singapore National Printers, 1991), p. 1.

[21] See J. Clammer, 'The establishment of a national ideology' in G. Rodan (ed.), *Singapore Changes Guard* (New York, Longman Cheshire, 1993), p. 40.

[22] In 1992, Lee Kuan Yew, the Senior Minister of Singapore stated in a lecture in the Philippines that he did not believe that 'democracy necessarily leads to development. I believe that what a country needs to develop is discipline more than democracy. The exuberance of democracy leads to indiscipline and disorderly conduct which are inimical to development'. See the *Economist*, (27/8/94), p. 15.

to democracy and increasing respect for human rights.[23] Several societies in the east Asian region that have adopted forms of democracy and increased respect for individual human rights such as Japan, South Korea, Taiwan and more recently the Philippines have in fact experienced as high rates of economic growth and development as the south east Asian states which have decried so called Western individualism, such as Singapore, Malaysia and Indonesia. These countries are on the defensive with the wave of democratization that has developed in the 1980s; of the thirty-one countries that experienced democratization or became more liberalized between 1974 and 1989, twenty-seven were in the middle income range. Countries that were previously classified as non-democratic, once they progress to middle income status appear to proceed through a 'transition' stage in which pressures for democratization, greater pluralism and human rights gain more credibility. It would be hard to attribute the reluctance of Southeast Asian states to embrace more openness to differences of 'culture' and 'Asian values' given the gradual democratization of other equally Asian societies like Taiwan and South Korea. Once socioeconomic development replaces economic development as an indicator, the correlation with democracy strongly increases.[24]

Questions concerning the correlation between democracy and economic growth are far from being definitive, but more and more research is supportive of the view that democracy underpins economic freedoms and this in turn promotes growth. Empirically, the world's richest societies, (Western Europe, the USA and Japan) are fundamentally democratic and many of the underdeveloped countries are not. Moreover, democracy appears more conducive to long term economic growth than dictatorship. Security of property (so important to individuals in the middle classes) goes hand in hand with regard for individual rights; even benevolent dictatorships cannot provide the same security democracy offers.[25]

In the light of the evidence that pressures towards individualism and democracy are societally generated, we need to look more closely at the historical and political context in which the distinctiveness of 'Asian values' is being asserted. On the one hand it represents a measure of self-confidence at the acknowledged success of the Asian economic model. With the relative decline of once-overwhelming American economic and military strength, and the impressive recent growth posted by Japan, China and the East Asian newly-industrializing countries, many Asians have concluded that the West is in decline, and their own region will be the next centre of global power. In this perspective, the debate on human rights and their prioritization involves some well-directed criticism of Western failures to protect not only socio-economic

---

[23] In fact, Samuel Huntington argues that the change to democracy is most prominent in the middle income countries; 'in poor countries democratization is unlikely, in rich countries it has already occurred. In between there is a political transition zone; countries in that particular economic stratum are most likely to transit to democracy and most countries that transit to democracy will be in that stratum'. See S. P. Huntington, *The Third Wave: Democratization in the Late Twentieth Century* (London, University of Oklahoma Press, 1991), pp. 60–3. This is based on the three classifications of countries into low, middle and high income countries by the World Bank.

[24] See United Nations, *Human Development Report* (New York, Oxford University Press, 1992), 3, 12–24.

[25] See M. Olson, 'Dictatorship, democracy and development' in the *American Political Science Review*, 87 (1993), 572–3.

rights but some civil rights as well, as this typical extract from *Asiaweek* exemplifies;

> Singapore opposition parties do not get equal time on television, but disadvantaged minorities do not riot, loot and burn. Malaysia detains dissidents without trial, but children are not gunned down at school. Taiwan does not allow free speech advocating communism, but its inner-city youth do not dissipate their energies on drugs. In South Korea one can be arrested just for publicly harbouring affection for Kim Il Sung but may walk the streets without fear of muggers.[26]

On the other hand, the assertion of Asian distinctiveness and communitarian values represents a thoroughly defensive response to criticism of their own political record on human rights. The attack on the individualism of human rights not only represents an attempt to contain societal changes; it also serves as a legitimation for repression by authoritarian regimes which are under challenge from internal opposition. That such regimes have much to be defensive about can be seen from an examination of their own record in the treatment of political opposition.

Human Rights and Political Opposition

In many states in the region a wide ranging set of emergency laws and provisions designed to bolster internal regime stability, can be utilized to provide 'security'. These are also significantly ingrained in constitutional provisions and ideological formulas. As an ideology and rhetorical formula for instance, the Indonesian programme of Pancasila has in fact been seen as supportive of the idea of human rights; its 'open' character however has allowed it to remain open to interpretation and widespread abuse. In terms of Pers Pancasila for instance the ideology limits press freedom and in Demokrasi Pancasila the number of political parties has been reduced and decoupled from their constituents. As one writer argues 'the right to *organize* appears, in reality, to be the right *to be organized*'.[27]

In August 1994 for instance, the International Confederation of Free Trade Unions (ICFTU) argued for the release of detained independent trade unionists in Indonesia. In effect it was a protest at the arrest of Muchtar Pakpahan, the leader of 'Sejahtera Buruh Serikat Indonesia' (SBSI), an independent trade union group. This group of 125,000 members had been campaigning for months to double the minimum wage to 7000 rupiahs (US $3.3 dollars a day) and to improve working conditions; the group was officially banned by the Indonesian government in June 1994.[28]

Moreover the government tends to interpret Pancasila in relation to the integralistic staatsidee which sees the state as the embodiment of the entire

---

[26] See 'The common good' *Asiaweek*, (9/2/94), p. 19.
[27] See T. M. Lubis, *In Search of Human Rights: Legal-Political Dilemmas of Indonesia's New Order 1966-1990*, (Jakarta, PT Gramedia Pustaka Utama, 1993), p. 295.
[28] See B. Mantiri, 'Labour-Indonesia: ICFTU presses Jakarta to release Union leader', (Interpress News Agency, 16/8/94); and 'Labour-Indonesia: Jakarta told to stop jailing trade unionists'. (Interpress News Agency, 18/8/94).

people;[29] the idea that individuals owe certain duties to the family and the state is clearly emphasized. As the state exists to protect the rights of the people, therefore human rights do not require a guarantee for individuals who themselves form the state. Duties are stressed as more important than rights against the state, again a reference to the notion that rights are privileges and not entitlements.

The notion of democracy in Indonesia relies on its interpretation; it is defined as *musyawarah* and *mufakat* which means consultation and consensus, words widely used in ASEAN circles. Deferential values are more important than directness, and open criticism is strictly off limits. In June 1994, the government banned three top magazines; *Tempo*, *Editor* and *Detik*. In the case of *Tempo*, the authorities argued that they had violated laws relating to national stability. This included recent coverage of divisions between the Indonesian cabinet and the military, while the others were closed down reputedly from 'administrative' concerns.[30] The Jakarta government has also taken strong action against cases of reputed defamation.[31]

Malaysia has experienced fairly stable and peaceful conditions of internal order in the 1980s and 1990s, despite the government's constant heightened sensitivity to potential security threats. The Internal Security Act, for instance, is still in use despite the end of the threat of communist insurgency. There has been a state of emergency in operation since the widespread riots in 1969 despite the fact that normal government operations were back in 1971. These emergency powers became a major issue during the 1983–4 constitutional crisis and, by early 1984 the government had used these powers as well as other types of security legislation such as the Internal Security Act (the ISA), to stop any kind of activity that in the view of the government was a threat to national security and public order.

The Federal government in Kuala Lumpur has large powers to curtail personal liberty and impose restrictions on most things that Western democracies take for granted, including freedom of speech, assembly and association and religion as well as others. The most important basis for action is however threats to national security; recently a religious sect in Malaysia, Al-Arquam, was banned on these very grounds.

In terms of freedom from arbitrary arrest, detention or forcing people to leave the country (exile), there are three laws which allow the authorities to hold suspects without recourse to judicial review or a formal charge process. These are the 1960 Internal Security Act (the ISA), the emergency Ordinance of 1969 (Public Order and Prevention of Crime) and the Dangerous Drugs Act (1985). Long term detention is still in use over perceived threats to national security. In the middle of July 1993 it was reported that there were 1,947 people in Malaysia being detained without trial, most of whom were being held under

---

[29] One could argue that to see the state 'as the embodiment of the entire people' is to adopt a central concept of Fascism.

[30] See 'Indonesian Government bans three top magazines', *Straits Times* (Singapore, 22/6/94) p. 1.

[31] In January 1994, 21 students were awaiting trial on charges of 'defamation' against Suharto. One of them Nuku Soelaiman, who handed out stickers claiming Suharto was to blame for Indonesia's problems, was sentenced to four years in prison. See 'Human rights activist brought to trial on defamation charges', *Jakarta Post* (6/1/94), p. 2; and 'Human rights activist Nuku gets four year prison term', *Jakarta Post* (25/2/94), p. 1.

the Dangerous Drugs Act. The state of emergency (Article 150 of the constitution) has been amended six times since the 1960s but it is immune to any legal procedure; a 1981 amendment, for instance, made Article 150 a non-justiciable issue, which cannot be challenged by the courts.[32]

The ISA was passed when an active Communist insurgency threatened national security at the beginning of the 1960s. These measures allow the authorities to detain people who are seen as a threat to security of the country for up to 60 days. This, it is claimed, is to prevent internal subversion, despite the fact that this threat had totally disappeared at the end of the 1980s, even according to official statements. The ISA is also used against passport and identity card forgers. In July 1993, 37 of these were being held in detention.

In April 1994, Malaysia expelled a Filipino news correspondent based in Kuala Lumpur on the grounds that she wrote an article that was deemed a threat to national security. Leah Palma Makabenta was given 48 hours to leave Malaysia after her work permit was cancelled on the 1st of April.[33]

The Malaysian government has also used the ISA to prevent alleged 'secessionist' plots against the federal government. In 1990 and 1991, the authorities detained seven Malaysians from the East Malaysian state of Sabah, including the brother of the chief minister. In 1993 all of the detainees had been released but with restrictions on their movement. Political liberalization is not on the agenda; Mahathir continually derides disorder and the erosion of values in the West to promote his personal and party interests. 'Let us not be slaves to democracy' he says 'if by practising certain aspects of democracy we run the risk of causing chaos in our party and country, we have to choose our party and country above democracy'.[34] Here, quite explicitly, national interests are used as a pretext for individual regime interests and the limitation of democratic rights.

Despite phenomenal economic growth in the Southeast Asian region, many one-party dominant regimes are losing their previous support and seeing their legitimacy erode. In Singapore the government still engages in large scale social control to stem the tide of democratization. The decline in its share of the popular vote has become a worrying preoccupation of the one-party regime over the last decade. In 1980, the PAP managed a very respectable 75.5% of the popular vote; in 1984 this decreased to 62.9% and in 1988 and 1991, 61.8% and 61% respectively, indicating a substantial electoral decline over this period. After the last election in 1991, the new Prime Minister of Singapore, Goh Chock Tong, indicated his unhappiness and discontent with the result. He stated that 'life cannot go on as it did before. Certain things have to change now'.[35] Singapore's Prime Minister in 1988, Lee Kuan Yew, had been equally unhappy with the decline and apparent liberalism of the Singaporean electorate

[32] See L. K. Siang, 'Human rights – an overview', *Human Rights in Malaysia* (Petaling Jaya, Human Rights Committee, 1986).

[33] See 'Malaysia expels correspondent for "security" reasons' in the *Jakarta Post*, (5/4/94), p. 11.

[34] See 'Mahathir cautions against being slaves of democracy', *Business Times* (Singapore, 31/5/93), p. 1.

[35] See *The Sunday Times*, (Singapore, 1/9/94) for this speech. Figures and explanations for the electoral decline can be found in G. Rodan, 'Preserving the one-party state in contemporary Singapore' in K. Hewison *et al.* (eds), *Southeast Asia in the 1990s: Authoritarianism. Democracy and Capitalism* (St. Leonards, Allen and Unwin, 1993), pp. 75–109, and G. Rodan, 'The growth of Singapore's middle class and its political significance' in G. Rodan (ed.), *Singapore Changes Guard* (New York Longman Cheshire, 1993), pp. 52–72.

when he said 'nobody has the right to subvert me'.[36] This seems very much the despair of an élite at the prospect of losing its popular support.

In Singapore the dominance of the People's Action Party (PAP) is criticized by opposition leaders who seek alternative and more democratic rule. An enormous effort is made to maintain political stability and some would argue the authoritarian one party system, through various methods. In 1988, the regime accused an American diplomat, E. Mason Hendrickson, of pushing local lawyers to stand for office against PAP candidates; the Deputy Prime Minister at the time Goh Chock Tong said that such activity threatened to 'break up the cohesion of our society ... [and that] thirty years of bonding and nation building would come to naught' as a result.[37] Another commentator notes the 'exemplary punishment' the regime reserves for those who question its authority and pose a political challenge: 'Mr Jeyeratnam, a leading opponent of the PAP has been bankrupted for criticizing Lee's autocratic style; former attorney General Francis Seow was forced into exile after running as an opposition candidate in 1988. More recently, university lecturer Chee Soon Juan was dismissed from his post for the alleged misuse of $250 worth of research funds'.[38] The recent case of the reaction to Dr Lingle's critical article on Singapore in the *International Herald Tribune* exemplifies the limitations on freedom of expression.[39]

What we find in many countries of the region, then, is a widespread restriction on the rights of opposition and dissent, which is justified in the name of social cohesion and the preservation of traditional values. The very fact that such dissent has to be suppressed, however, itself calls into question the degree of social agreement on these same values.

Consensus on Asian Values?

The fact that there is no consensus on collective 'Asian' values or 'Asian' versions of human rights is underscored by the various dissenting under-currents in Southeast Asia. Common to the dissenters is an appeal for civil and political rights as universal rights, and the insistence on their being given equal status with economic and social ones. Thus, for example, the 1993 Bangkok NGO Declaration of Human Rights, endorsed by over 100 regional non-governmental organizations, asserts that 'one set of rights cannot be used to bargain for another' (i.e. economic and political rights are equally important). This is a common refrain.

Some regional dissidents have accused East Asian regimes of using socio-economic rights as an excuse to repress political opposition. Vitit

---

[36] See 'The appeal of Singapore's style' in the *Economist* (5/11/1988), p. 35.

[37] See G. C. Tong, 'Why we had no choice but to react', *Straits Times* (Singapore, 1/6/88), p. 14.

[38] See J. M. David, 'Don't count on me Singapore', *National Review* (16/5/94), pp. 59–61.

[39] The article was entitled 'The smoke over parts of Asia obscures some profound concerns', in the *International Herald Tribune* (7/10/94), which was framed as a rebuttal to an article by Kishore Mahbubani, a permanent Secretary in Singapores Foreign Ministry entitled, 'You may not like it, Europe, but this Asian medicine could help,' in the *International Herald Tribune*, (1–2/10/94). Apparently, the authorities took exception to Lingle's statement that regimes in the region relied on 'a compliant judiciary to bankrupt opposition politicians'. Despite no charges being filed at the time police confiscated materials and documents from the lecturer who shortly thereafter resigned his position. Also see, 'Singapore's philosophers' in the *Asian Wall Street Journal*, (19/10/94). Lingle was subsequently charged with 'contempt of court'.

Muntarbhorn, law professor at Chulalongkorn University in Bangkok, argues that many ASEAN governments restrict political and civil rights, not to promote prosperity, but 'to perpetuate the longevity of the regime in power'.[40] Similarly, Malaysian political activist Abdul Razak Ahmad complains, 'The leaders of the nation often called for a "strong" government to fight its enemies and like all repressive governments of all political hues and complexions what the government in power really demands and wishes for is a compliant and obedient populace'.[41] Even as severe a critic of the West's human rights campaign as Chandra Muzaffar laments that 'southern élites deprive their people of their basic human rights ... The arbitrary exercise of unlimited power which is not checked by strict adherence to the principles of accountability must lead inevitably to the suppression of the masses'.[42] Such criticisms suggest many Southeast Asians believe unlimited state power to restrict civil liberties can be detrimental to the very quality of life such control is supposed to protect.

The special claims that currently emanate from Southeast Asian states on the basis of a different value structure thus appear politically contrived. From a universalist point of view the argument is problematic. First, it is in a sense, self-destructive. By answering charges of human rights violations with the claim of cultural relativism, the claim might be made that these governments are effectively arguing that Asians have a relatively high tolerance of or requirement for torture and other cruel punishments – ironically, the same kind of argument that allegedly racist Western Orientalists have often made in the past.

Second, this argument is too often employed as a refuge for some of the most heavily documented human rights abusers. Burma, run by a military junta that brooks no political dissent and has kept Nobel laureate Aung San Suu Kyi under house arrest, is explicitly cynical when it stands on the principle that 'Asian countries with their own norms and standards of human rights, should not be dictated [to] by a group of other countries who are far distant geographically, politically, economically and socially'.[43] Perhaps the last word on cultural relativism and human rights can be left to Chinese physicist and human rights dissident, Fang Lizhe, in a reference to China:

> Recent propaganda to the effect that ' China has its own standards for human rights' bears an uncanny similarity to pronouncements made by our 18th century rulers when they declared that 'China has its own astronomy'. The feudal aristocracy of 200 years ago opposed the notion of an astronomy based on science. They refused to acknowledge the universal applicability of modern astronomy, or even that it might be of some use in formulating the Chinese calendar. The reason they opposed modern astronomy was that the laws of astronomy, which pertain everywhere, made it quite clear that the 'divine right to rule' claimed by these people was a fiction. By the same token the principles of human rights, which also

[40] See V. Muntarbhorn, 'Repression and oppression still prevalent in ASEAN', *The Nation* (Bangkok, 15/5/94), p. A4.

[41] See A. Razak Ahmad in L. K. Siang *et al.*, *Human Rights in Malaysia*, p. 33.

[42] See C. Muzaffar, *Human Rights and the New World Order* (Penang, Malaysia, Just World Trust, 1993), pp. 30–1.

[43] See the *Far Eastern Economic Review*, (17/6/93), p. 5.

pertain everywhere, make it clear that the 'right to rule' claimed by some today is baseless. This is why rulers from every era, with their special privileges, have opposed the equality inherent in such universal ideas.[44]

Conclusion

Recently there has been widespread criticism in East and Southeast Asia concerning the alleged imposition of Western values, mainly in the form of 'meddling' in the issue of human rights. These societies maintain they are unique and reserve the right to apply their own standards and judgements on such questions. The difficulty of reaching agreement on specific rights is understandable in a region such as East Asia, which includes states as diverse as Myanmar and Japan. Of the non-communist East Asian countries, only Japan, South Korea and the Philippines are signatories of both the International Covenant on Civil and Political Rights and the International Covenant on Economic, Social and Cultural Rights.

The notion that there is a consensus on Asian values, democracy and human rights has emerged more strongly and directly form Southeast Asian regimes than any others. These are increasingly insecure governments which are ripe for democratization, and feel the winds of global change. The principles of situational uniqueness and cultural difference are deployed as a pretext to insulate them from the forces of political and social change. The argument here is not that their human rights records are all disgraceful in comparison to other parts of the world; if we were to compare some of these regimes with ones in Latin America and Africa they would appear positively benign. However, they are increasingly resorting to strong rhetoric and claims of 'difference' that illustrate the urgency with which their political élites seek to maintain and preserve their neo-authoritarian forms of government. The lack of real regional institutions to support and promote human rights in the way that other regions have, illustrates the antipathy towards such notions.

At the international human rights conference in Vienna in June of 1993, little was resolved between the various groups, and members of ASEAN were at the forefront of demands that economic development must take precedence over other kinds of rights. This is despite the fact that some of these countries have higher economic growth rates than any other part of the globe at present. Despite the end of the Cold War and the accompanying political and social changes, Southeast Asia remains apparently immune to changed global concerns over human rights. And it appears unlikely that we will see the emergence of an extracommunal and cosmopolitan notion of such principles from the region in the near future.

---

[44] F. Lizhe, 'Human rights in China'. This speech was reprinted in D. Ravitch and A. Thermstrom, *The Democracy Reader* (New York, Harper Collins, 1992), pp. 276–8.

Index